The

Groovy

Gospel

Part 1 of The Blistering Bible series

davehopwood.com

Available in paperback and on Kindle also by Dave Hopwood:

Some Children's Adventures (non-religious)

Last of the Superheroes (Danny Garret 1)

White Knuckle Time (Danny Garret 2)

The Seven Wonders (Danny Garret 3)

Lucy Housestairs and the Assassins

120 Interactive Bible Stories for All Ages:

Telling Tales

31 Parables Retold for Adults:

Top Stories

The Groovy Gospel

By
Dave Hopwood

with cartoons by
Tim Wakeling

1. Awesome Ancestors

Did you know Jesus was related to Walt Disney, Simon Cowell, Henry VIII, Margaret Thatcher, Alfred the Great, Jessie J, James Bond, Cleopatra, Harry Potter and Clark Kent?

Actually, he wasn't!

But it'd be funny if he was.

He was related to quite a few important people in his history and that's where his story begins, with a huge great list of his relatives from the past.

Early on in the story about Jesus there's a list which is a bit like that programme *Who d'you think you are?* Where famous people find out about their families in the past, but I guess in olde language that might have been *Whom Dost Thou Thinkest Thou Art*. Olde language is funny because it makes things sound more religious somehow, but actually God doesn't mind what language you use.

This brings us to our first multiple choice quiz. There are plenty of these in this book.

What language do you think Jesus spoke?

1. English
2. Elvish
3. Scottish
4. Aramaic

Answer: 3. Only kidding – it's 4.

I wrote it small to stop any cheating!

Jesus spoke the ordinary street language of his day. His Bible was written in an older special language called Hebrew, and it was what we now call the Old Testament. Much later on, Bibles in England would be translated into Latin, then into old English, which had lots of 'thous' and 'thys'.

D'you know what thou and thy are?

1. They're a hip-hop double act
2. They're a first century Ant and Dec
3. It's olde English for you and your
4. It's olde English for fish and chips

Answer: 3

Old language isn't better or worse; it isn't more holy than ordinary language. And when Jesus taught his disciples to pray what we now call *The Lord's Prayer,* he taught it to them in the ordinary everyday language they spoke, Aramaic.

Hebrew was more 'religious', but Jesus wasn't interested in that. He wanted people to understand about God.

He also told lots of funny stories about life and God that people would remember and pass on to others. Like those jokes people pass round on Facebook and by email.

This book follows the same line of thinking. I hope Jesus would like this book. By the way, if Facebook had been around in Jesus' time what d'you think it would have been called?

1. Facescroll
2. Ye Olde Booke of the Face
3. LeggBook
4. Big Toe Parchment

Answer: 1. (That's what I think, anyway!)

Books hadn't been invented. Instead things were written down on big scrolls of parchment. If Facescroll had been around back then, I'm sure Jesus would have had his own Facescroll page so he could communicate with lots of people.

Let's carry on.

Why do all these people in Jesus' Whom Dost Thou Thinkest Thou Art list matter?

1. They make the Bible longer.
2. To test whether you can pronounce them all.
3. It's like a family photo album.
4. They're not names, they're anagrams.

Answer: 3

Jesus was related to some important people. We may not have heard of them, but the people living back then certainly had. And it showed them that Jesus came from a long line of men and women who were part of

God's big plan. God's big jigsaw. Jesus was the next part of that jigsaw, the next part of the plan. And a very important, very special part.

Jesus was related to people with names like Boaz, Salmon, Nahshon, Amminadab, Admin, Arni, Methuselah, Lego, Aldi, Wagamama and Ikea.

Actually, I added the last four.

Methuselah is interesting because he lived longer than anyone else. How long d'you think he lived?

1. 969 years
2. 269 years
3. 9,069 years
4. A million and 69 years

Answer: 1

Methuselah was Noah's grandfather. He died the year the flood came. His name may well mean something like 'when he is dead it shall be sent'. So it seems that while he was alive the flood would not come, he was a walking-talking message to everyone. Something was coming and people should take note.

Perhaps that's why he lived for so long, because God did not want to send the flood. He wanted people to listen up and change their ways, so there would be no need for the flood.

There are 4 women mentioned in the list of Jesus' relatives. They are called Tamar, Rahab, Ruth and Bathsheba. This is amazing because women weren't often mentioned in lists like this. Only the men were seen as important. But we'll come back to that.

All these women have interesting and surprising stories, especially Ruth. She was a poor homeless refugee, and had to go out begging for food. Yet God turned her life around – she married a kind man who helped her and her mother-in-law, and her son became the grandfather of the famous King David.

Plus she was the great, great, great, great etc. (28 greats, in fact) grandmother of Jesus.

Bathsheba became the wife of David, but after they first met, what happened?

1. They went bowling
2. They went ice-skating
3. They went on *Strictly Come Dancing*
4. David killed her first husband

Answer: 4

Which is a bit shocking really.

If you were going to plan a right royal family for Jesus you would not have picked some of these people for relatives. But that's life. And Jesus did not want to be protected from the ups and downs and difficulties of things. He came from an ordinary, quite poor family, learnt his dad's trade, and experienced ordinary life.

How long d'you think he lived that normal life for?

1. Till he was 21
2. Till he was 30
3. Till he was 33
4. Till he was 969

Answer: 3

For most of his life Jesus was one of the regular guys. It was only in his last 3 years that he gave up his job and started to live a very different life.

But we're racing ahead here. Let's back up a little and go right back to the beginning. And let me wish you a very Happy Christmas.

You can check out these stories in the Bible here:
Matthew ch 1 vv 1-17
Matthew ch 6 vv 7-14
Genesis ch 5 vv 21-25
Ruth chs 1-4
2 Samuel ch 11

2. Cracking Christmas

Jesus didn't have an easy start and neither did his mum and dad. They weren't married when his mum, Mary, got pregnant. Which was very unusual back then. It was a very unusual story really. For a start: who do you think told Mary she was having a baby?

1. A midwife
2. An angel
3. A bus driver
4. A king

Answer: 2

Mary had no boyfriend, partner or husband when this happened. She did have a fiancée though, called Joseph. They lived in a village called Nazareth and they were going to get married. It was going to be a big village celebration. But the people in her village were shocked to find out she was going to have a baby. So it all got messy.

In the end an angel had to tell Joseph not to panic or dump her. The angel appeared to him in a…

1. Dustbin
2. Dream
3. Duffel coat
4. Dracula costume

Answer: 2

Joseph saw the angel, who told him not to worry, to marry Mary and look after her baby, because it was a miracle baby. It was not going to be easy but Joseph did what the angel said and they got together.

Not long after this Joseph had to travel to Bethlehem because the Romans, who were running the country, wanted to make a list of everyone. He took Mary with him, even though she was pregnant and it was a long journey. He probably took her with him because he was worried about leaving her alone in Nazareth.

How far d'you think they had to travel from Nazareth to Bethlehem?

1.   7 miles
2.   17 miles
3.   70 miles
4.   77 miles

Answer: 3

Most people think that Jesus was born in a stable in Bethlehem, because there was no room at any of the inns or hotels. But it's probably not true. The word in the story for 'inn' also means 'spare room'. And Joseph probably had relatives in Bethlehem who would have let them stay. Plus he was descended from a famous king – King David – so people would have heard about him. There was no spare room for Mary and Joseph so she had the baby in the bit where the animals were kept.

Rich people might have had big barns or stables for their animals but not average people. Where do you think they kept their animals?

1. In the bathtub
2. In the kitchen
3. In the downstairs loo
4. In the bedroom

Answer: 4

Normal houses had two rooms – one was a family room, used for both living and sleeping for the family. The other was used for a guest bedroom.

The animals would have been kept at one end of the main family room, where the ground sloped down and there were holes cut in the floor. What do you think they were used for?

1. Weeing in
2. Holding soup
3. Storing hot porridge
4. Hay for the animals

Answer: 4

These feeding bowls were called mangers and Jesus was placed in one of these when he was born. So although it wasn't a stable as the Christmas cards often show, it was a room with animals and straw and cow poo.

It didn't smell great!

Who came to visit the baby while he was there?

1. Shadrack Meshack and Abednego
2. Sheryl Cole
3. Shepherds
4. Kings

Answer: 3

A bunch of shepherds came which was amazing because everybody joked about shepherds as being scruffy, messy losers. They were always dirty and smelly from the sheep. But it seemed as if God didn't mind that at all – he sent a posse of angels to sing them a rap about the new baby, and the story went something like this:

While shepherds watched their flocks one night
All seated on the ground,
The Angel of the Lord came down
And bright light shone around.

'Fear not!' the angel said, for they were
Scared out of their minds.
'I've got good news: it's looking good
For you and all mankind.'

'For you in Bethlehem today
A king has just popped out;
A Saviour who is Christ the Lord,
Get down and check it out!'

'You'll find a little baby there
In a stable made of wood,
He'll be lying there on some animal hay
And the place won't smell too good!'

And when the angel stopped his rap
A million more turned up –
All looking cool and singing strong,
And praising God above.

Then all them shepherds leapt on up
And cruised into the town
Went round in circles trying to find out
What was going down.

They saw this stable lit up bright
Just like a Christmas tree.
They all rushed over, crept inside,
And dropped on bended knee.

The parents of the baby there -
They looked surprised and stressed.
The shepherds grinned, the baby stared,
The sheep were not impressed.

They worshipped him, then took right off –
Went dancing out the gate.
Then had to tell their waiting wives
Just why they'd come home late.

All glory be to God on high
And to the earth be peace.
Goodwill henceforth from heaven to men
Begin and never cease.

Later some wise men arrived. They're sometimes called Kings, and children often wear paper crowns in school plays. But they weren't kings; they were guys who studied the stars and had expected a new king to be born for a quite a while. What gifts did they bring?

1. Gold, frankincense and myrrh
2. Gollum, Frankenstein and Muppet
3. A Man United football kit
4. Some book tokens and a set of X-Box games

Answer: 1

Gold was a sign that Jesus was a king, frankincense was the kind of stuff you set fire to as a religious offering to God, and myrrh is something they put on a dead body to embalm it. So not exactly the sort of thing you'd expect to find in your Christmas stocking. But they showed the kind of life Jesus was going to have.

You can check out these
stories in the Bible here:
Matthew chs 1-2
Luke ch 2 vv 1-20

3. The Name's Son-of-Joseph, Jesus Son-of-Joseph

We don't know a whole lot about Jesus as a boy. He probably got up to all the usual fun and games. And would have been taught in his village. His mum and dad would have grown their own vegetables like cucumbers, onions, leeks and beans. His dad was a ...

1. Builder
2. Sky TV salesman
3. Window cleaner
4. Carpenter

Answer: 1 and a bit of 4

He's known as a carpenter, but he was really a builder sometimes doing things with wood. As Jesus grew up he learnt his dad's job and helped him out. His mum would not have had a job; she had plenty to do bringing up the family. Jesus had brothers and sisters. How many brothers and sisters do you think he had?

1. 1 of each
2. 2 of each
3. 3 brothers, 3 sisters
4. 4 brothers, 2 sisters

Answer: 4

We know of 4 brothers: Jacob, Joseph, Judah and Simon; there may have been more. And we know he had at least 2 sisters, but there may have been more. Mark's story tells us that he had sisters, but not how many. I wonder whether they argued about anything...

We know that Jesus went to the temple in Jerusalem when he was 12, which to him would have been like going to Disneyland or Wembley. It was an exciting place to visit, full of wonder and new experiences.

He got into trouble there because his mum and dad lost track of him. In the end they found him talking with lots of religious teachers, and they were amazed at what he knew. I sometimes wonder whether his mum and dad then grounded him for the next 18 years, which is why we next jump ahead to when he's 30!

One thing we do know: he wasn't called Jesus Christ. That's a Greek version of his name (thanks to top conqueror Alexander the Great – more about him later). Know what Christ really means?

1. Son of God
2. Messiah
3. Carpenter
4. It's short for Christopher

Answer: 2

He would actually have been known as Jesus son of Joseph, or Yeshua Ben Yehosef. Or Yeshu for short. How popular do you think Yeshu was as a name for boys back then?

1. Really popular
2. Not popular at all
3. He was the only one
4. His mum and dad made it up

Answer: 1

It was the sixth most popular name to call your son. At the moment the sixth most popular name in the UK is Liam. So Jesus is like that. A boy's name that lots of people like. Why did they like it? Cause Yeshu is the same name as Joshua, and Joshua was a big hero from the past that everybody loved.

I'd like to tell you about him but maybe I'll wait until I do the next book.

Ever heard of Ian Fleming? You've probably seen some of his work, because he wrote about…

1. Harry Potter
2. Charlie Bucket
3. Twilight
4. James Bond

Answer: 4

When Ian Fleming was looking for a name for his new superspy he wanted a really boring sounding one, and he came across a book written by a man called James Bond. So Ian Fleming thought – I'll have that name, it sounds ordinary, it doesn't sound like a superspy at all. Nowadays it sounds exactly like a superspy!

That's what has happened with the name of Jesus. Originally it was just like Liam. A regular boy's name. Now it has special meaning. Now people have ideas in their head when you mention the name of Jesus.

> You can check out these stories in the Bible here:
> Mark ch 6 v 3
> Luke ch 2 vv 41-52

4. The Bearded Baptist

Jesus had a cousin called John. Some people probably called him The Weirdo with the Beardo.

He wore camel's hair clothes with a belt around his waist, and ate strange food, and he started baptising people in a nearby river.

FIRST BAPTIST MINISTER

(SOME PEOPLE THOUGHT HE WAS A BIT, WELL, ODD.)

What did John eat?

1. Marmite and wasp sandwiches
2. Locusts with honey
3. Snake and kidney pie
4. Burger King Whoppers

Answer: 2

Why do you think John wore hairy clothes and a belt?

1. To impersonate someone else
2. To be cool
3. To keep cool
4. To start a new trend

Answer: 1

He dressed a bit like an old prophet called Elijah, who was hairy and wore a belt. (Hopefully he wore other things too!) Elijah was a man of God and John wanted people to know that he was too. He gave people a chance to think about changing, to start getting ready for a new start. John told people a new leader was coming, someone who would change things forever.

John didn't know his cousin would be the person he was waiting for. Lots of people didn't realise Jesus was important.

This is what John said in an interview:

'I'd been baptising lots of people, getting them ready for the new leader who was coming. When I saw my cousin I suddenly realised – it's him! He's the new leader, the new Prime Minister! You could have knocked me over with a sneeze. Amazing! We used to play as kids.'

What did Jesus ask John to do when they met?

1. Bow before him
2. Wash his feet
3. Lend him some money
4. Baptise him in the river

Answer: 4

You can check out these stories in the Bible here:
Matthew ch 3
John ch 1 vv 1-34

5. Chuckling Charlie

Charlie Chaplain once entered a lookalike competition to see if people could recognise him. Where do you think he came in the competition?

1. First
2. Second
3. Third
4. Last

Answer: 3

If Jesus entered a lookalike competition I wonder where he might come?

If I was judging it, he'd probably come about 12th. For one thing he was a lot shorter than we might expect. He's often portrayed as tall, good looking, with blue eyes. OOPS! No way. The average person in his country was about 5 feet or 1 metre 52 cm tall. And they didn't have blue eyes. He may have been good looking, but he didn't need to be.

What actor might you like to see playing him? Someone like Will Smith? Or *Twilight* actor Robert Pattinson? Or someone younger like *Harry Potter* actor Daniel Radcliffe? Or maybe someone funnier like Rupert Grint (Ron Weasley) or Jack Black or Adam Sandler?

Children and teenagers loved hanging round with Jesus, and he probably made them laugh with his funny stories. We'll come to his stories later on, but he didn't walk around looking really serious or dull. He went to parties, had favourite food, and laughed, chatted and argued with people. Just like us.

He often got told off for not looking religious enough. He seemed to enjoy life too much!

What do you think the seriously religious people said when they saw him go to Matthew the tax collector's house for a party?

1. Save some sausage rolls for us
2. Are you dancing Gangnam Style?
3. Why does Jesus eat with that scum?!
4. Like your outfit

Answer: 3

Matthew threw a big party when he joined Jesus' group of friends. He celebrated the start of his life with Jesus by throwing a great celebration and inviting all his mates.

6. Blessed Are the Cheese-makers

Somebody once told a funny story about Jesus. Or rather, about the people listening to him. There was a crowd of people listening to Jesus as he was talking on a hillside. Jesus said to everyone, 'Blessed are the peacemakers.' But some of the people couldn't hear and thought he said, 'Blessed are the cheese-makers!'

So I wondered what else they might have misheard? How about…

Blessed are the prawns… (the poor)
Blessed are the geeks… (the meek)
Blessed are those who know Percy (show mercy)
Blessed are the custard tarts (the pure in heart)

But what did Jesus mean when he said all this?

The poor, the meek and humble, the peacemakers, those who show mercy and kindness, those who have pure or good hearts – these people really matter to God, and when Jesus said they are blessed he meant that God was on their side. Even if their lives were hard, he was with them in their troubles.

People thought that when they had problems God had abandoned them, but Jesus was telling them he had not. And not only was he telling them, Jesus came to show people that too. He spent lots of time with the poor, the kind and the peacemakers. And Jesus himself was like that – he wasn't rich, he loved peace, he was kind and humble with a pure heart. He encouraged all he met to be kind, humble peacemakers too.

Jesus finished his talk with a funny story about two builders. One of them built a house on good solid foundations, the other built on... what?

1. Soup
2. A swamp
3. Cheesecake
4. Sand

Answer: 4

THINGS THAT ARE BLESSED

THINGS THAT ARE NOT SUCH A GOOD IDEA

When there was a big storm that night, guess which house fell down?

1. The house on the sand
2. Both
3. Neither
4. The White House

Answer: 1

He said that listening to his advice and doing something about it was like building a house on solid rock. But ignoring what he said was like building something on sand. Or a swamp. Or a blueberry cheesecake. Any building built on anything that soft (no matter how delicious) would just collapse. Splat.

He told a comedy story about a man building his house on top of a squelchy pile of swampy sand. Even though he could see another guy building on a good solid piece of rock, the man still went ahead and built his house on soggy sand. Then a storm came along. Crash! Awkward...

> You can check out these
> stories in the Bible here:
> Matthew ch 5 vv 1-12
> Luke ch 6 vv 20-26
> Matthew ch 9 vv 9-13
> Luke 18 vv 15-17

7. The Great Israeli Disciple Challenge

Jesus went around healing some sick people, telling stories about God and showing the best way to live a caring kind of life. Then after a while he chose twelve guys to be his closest friends. We asked a few of them how they felt about that.

Peter: Great! Bring it on! Walking on water? I can do that too! And fighting Roman bad guys? I've got a sword. I can't wait.

Thomas: Er... Not sure I'm up to the job. I doubt erm... what was the question again?

Judas: How do I feel? Confident. I got plenty of ideas what Jesus should do. And he should do them quick.

John: I think we're gonna be really good mates.

Matthew: I dunno. I'm not sure he'll like me when he gets to know me. My mates are not very religious. We all go to lots of parties and dance a lot. Hope that's okay with him.

James: There's this village near us full of horrible people. Samaritans they're called. Yuk! I want Jesus to nuke them and wipe them out. He's a pretty powerful guy so he should be able to do that. That'd be cool.

That was six of Jesus' twelve close friends, or disciples. What were the other six disciples called?

1. Sleepy, Grumpy, Dopey, Snoozy, Lazy & Silly
2. Zain, Harry, Niall, Louis, Liam & Simon
3. Laa-laa, Dipsy, Po, Tinky Winky, Snork & Drooper
4. Andrew, Philip, Bartholomew, Simon, Thaddeaus & James

Answer: 4

Peter and Andrew were brothers; James and John too. These four were fishermen. Peter was originally called Simon, but Jesus gave him a new name – Peter – which meant Stony or Rocky. Jesus may have been the first to use this word as a name. When JM Barrie wrote Peter Pan he made up the name Wendy and we've used it ever since. Might be the same with Jesus and the name Peter.

Peter, James and John were his closest buddies, and having changed Simon's name to Peter, he gave a kind of nickname to the other two.

D'you know what he called them?

1. The Blue Eyed Boys
2. The Brat Pack
3. Union J
4. The Thunder Boys

Answer: 4

He called them 'sons of thunder' – can you guess why?

1. They were full of hot air
2. They made a big noise
3. Their dad was called Thunder
4. He couldn't remember their real names

Answer: 2

It's probably because they had big mouths and spoke their minds. They said what they thought. Like thunder clapping across the sky. One day James asked Jesus to kill a load of people he didn't like in a Samaritan village. They probably got it from their mum – she was outspoken too. She told Jesus to make James and John his right hand men.

Peter, James and John were Jesus' closest friends, he sometimes took just these three along with him.

Apart from Matthew, who was a tax collector, we don't know what jobs the other disciples did before they met Jesus. But we do know what they did after they met Jesus. They went all over the place telling people about him.

There are lots of stories and legends about what they did, but who do you think travelled the furthest?

1. Peter
2. Thomas
3. Matthew
4. John

Answer: 2

It's reckoned that Thomas went all the way from Israel to India. He's only ever remembered as doubting Thomas – but he was just being honest. He didn't hide what he thought. He spoke it out. And in the end he went further than any of the other disciples to tell people about his friend Jesus. But I'm jumping ahead. It's not the end yet. Nowhere near. Let's get on to some stonking stories.

> You can check out these stories in the Bible here:
> Matthew ch 10 vv 1-4
> Mark ch 3 vv 13-19
> Matthew ch 16 vv 13-20
> Luke ch 8 vv 51-55
> John ch 14 vv 5-7
> John ch 20 vv 24-29

8. Stonking Stories

Nowadays when people read stories from the Bible they quite often put on very serious voices. But when Jesus told his stories he would have moved about, surprised people and made them laugh. Jesus was a rabbi (a Jewish religious teacher) and rabbis told lots of stories to help people think about life and God.

'Imagine a man who had a huge wooden tent peg sticking out of his eye,' Jesus said one day, 'telling someone else to worry about a tiny speck of dust in their eye.' That would be a bit like a woman who had a huge smear of bird poo on her face telling someone off for having a tiny crumb of cake at the corner of their mouth. That would be stoopid, wouldn't it?

He told a story about a woman who ripped her house to pieces with a JCB digger in order to find a 10p coin she had lost. The woman searched everywhere to find her lost coin because it was important to her. When she found it she threw a big party. Jesus said that the angels in heaven throw a big celebration when one person turns to God.

Sometimes Jesus told stories about men, sometimes about women, because he wanted everyone to be interested in what he was teaching. He also got children involved in his stories too. One day when his friends were arguing about which one of them was the coolest and the best, he got a little child, probably a little girl, to stand next to him, and he told his friends to do what?

1. Give her some pocket money
2. Make her laugh
3. Buy her an ice cream
4. Act like her

Answer: 4

Jesus said that children are really important and can show us so much about God. He said that adults need to be more humble and trusting like children if they want to get to know God better. Children also speak their mind and say what they think – adults need to be more honest like that too sometimes.

Jesus had women disciples as well as men, even though that was kind of breaking the law. Men and women were treated differently back then and only men were supposed to be disciples of rabbis like Jesus. But Jesus wasn't bothered about that; he cared about men **and** women.

So women went with him on his special missions, they provided money to buy food and stuff, and a close friend of his called Mary (there were lots of people called Mary back then) got into trouble with her sister

Martha for hanging around with the other disciples, listening to Jesus.

How many Marys do we know about who knew Jesus?

1. Two
2. Three
3. Four
4. Five thousand

Answer: 3

We know of at least four. Mary his mother; Mary Magdalene who Jesus helped and cured, who then became his good friend. Mary who had a sister called Martha and a brother called Lazarus. These two sisters were really good mates with Jesus and he often went to their house to get some time out. They lived in a place called Bethany, which means House of the Poor, so they probably did a lot of work helping homeless, poor and sick people. They were good guys.

And Mary who was married to someone called Clopas. She may have been a relative of Jesus, possibly his aunt. It's funny to think of Jesus having relatives, but of course he did. Fishermen James and John may have been his cousins. And another man called James was his brother who became... what?

1. A church chief
2. A police chief
3. A fire chief
4. A handkerchief

Answer: 1

Jesus' brother James was the leader of the church in Jerusalem. He was a pretty important guy when the church first began a couple of thousand years ago. He probably didn't wear a dog collar but you could say he was the first vicar.

You can check out these stories in the Bible here:
Matthew ch 7 vv 1-5
Luke ch 15 vv 8-10
Matthew ch 18 vv 1-6
Luke ch 10 vv 38-42
Luke ch 8 vv 1-3
John ch 19 v 25

9. Leaping Lazarus

Recently, a man came back from the dead after eight years. He had disappeared and been legally declared dead by a judge. However, he returned home after eight years away and created a problem. He was supposed to be dead!

Jesus had a habit of bringing people back from the dead. Have a look at this story, about his close friends, two sisters Mary and Martha, and their brother Lazarus.

Mary and Martha were really different, though they were sisters. Do you know why?

1. Mary was blonde and Martha was a redhead
2. Mary was into *TOWIE*; Martha liked *X Factor*
3. Martha supported Arsenal
4. Mary was quiet and Martha was noisy

Answer: 4

Mary got into trouble for sitting quietly listening to Jesus in a room full of men. In those days women were supposed to leave the men on their own, and go off to make the food for everyone, and Martha was good at that. She was often busy working and she told her sister off.

When their brother got sick they sent a message to Jesus, asking him to come and help. They believed Jesus could make Lazarus better. It was really urgent but Jesus didn't go to help them straight away. He waited before he went. D'you know why?

1. He had other plans
2. He was busy on Facescroll
3. He was playing *Angry Birds*
4. He was out shopping

Answer: 1

It was dangerous for Jesus to go to the area where Lazarus lived, because some people there wanted to kill him, but that wasn't the reason he stayed away for a while. He decided to wait so that he could bring Lazarus back from the dead so that many people would know about God and his power over death.

When Jesus got there, he asked them to open Lazarus's tomb. What was Martha worried they would find?

1. A hedgehog
2. A big stink
3. Lazarus had dug a tunnel and escaped
4. A hobbit

Answer: 2

Lazarus had been dead four days and it would have smelt very bad in there. His sister Martha was worried about this. But Jesus was not bothered. He told them to open the tomb and there was no smell – because Lazarus was alive!

What happened next?

1. Some people were angry
2. Some people were amazed
3. Some people trusted in Jesus
4. Some people told other people

Answer: 1,2,3 & 4

There were all kinds of reactions. The frightening thing was that some of the religious leaders made a plan to kill Jesus and Lazarus. Which was a bit strange as Lazarus had only just got back from being dead. They wanted to kill Jesus because lots of people started to believe in him after he brought Lazarus back to life again.

You can check out these stories in the Bible here:
John ch 11

10. A Lotta Losers

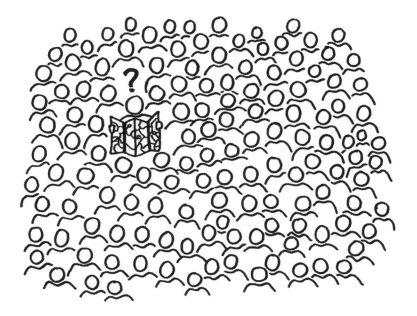

One day Jesus told three parables in a row, and they were all about the same thing. Was it...

1. Getting lost
2. Getting rich
3. Getting hip
4. Getting to sleep

Answer: 1

A farmer had lots of sheep and he lost one. There was nothing special about that sheep – except that he got lost. The farmer took a big risk, left his other sheep to look after themselves and went looking for the lost one. When he got back, what happened?

1. The other sheep had all run off
2. The other sheep were doing handstands
3. The other sheep were crying
4. They all had a big party

Answer: 4

The farmer threw a big party to celebrate with all his friends. The lost sheep was like us. The good shepherd, Jesus, cares about us. We don't have to earn that or be good at anything. He just cares about us.

In the next parable a woman lost…

1. Her marbles
2. Her coin
3. Her WiFi signal
4. Her iPod

Answer: 2

She lost a coin and like the farmer with his sheep she looked high and low for it. I mentioned this parable earlier. When she finds it she invites her friends and neighbours round for a big party. Yay! The lost coin is found. Nowadays it might be the lost iPod. Or the lost car keys. Or the lost TV remote. Or the lost mobile phone. Someone might lose one of these, hunt high and low, and then when they find it they would…

1. Tweet all their followers about it
2. Facebook all their friends about it
3. Text all their mates
4. Run down the street singing the latest One Direction song

Answer: all of the above! They'd be so happy!

You can check out these stories in the Bible here: Luke ch 15

11. Humongous Hairs

Have you any idea how many hairs are on the average person's head?

1. 1 hundred thousand
2. 5 hundred thousand
3. 1 million
4. 10 million

Answer: 1

This is only an average of course, but Jesus said something interesting about this. He was talking about how well God knows people, and used hairs as an example. Who can count how many hairs any one of us has? No one really. No one that is except God. He does know. Jesus said God knows us that well. Because he designed us and he's really interested in us.

Jesus also talked about birds on the same day. Did he say...

1. Bird pie is really tasty
2. Bird's Eye make great fish fingers
3. Little birds are cute
4. Little birds die

Answer: 4

He did say they die, but he also said that God knows about that too. Jesus said that God sees all that happens in nature. And though God cares about the birds we are much more valuable to God than a whole sky full of birds.

Jesus spoke about flowers too. What do you think he said?

1. They don't have jobs
2. They do have jobs
3. They have cool outfits
4. They are great in a vase

Answer: 1 & 3

He said that the flowers don't work all day and night for a better car or a bigger house, yet they look fantastic. Jesus said they don't worry or sweat a lot about life. And if God cares about flowers that are here today and gone tomorrow, he certainly cares about people.

You can check out these
stories in the Bible here:
Luke ch 12 vv 22-31
Matthew ch 10 vv 29-31

12. Kalamitous Kids

One day some families brought lots of children to see Jesus, but Jesus' friends got all uppity about it and tried to get rid of them. What did Jesus do?

1. Agreed with his friends
2. Took a collection from everyone
3. Ignored them all
4. Had a go at his friends

Answer: 4

Jesus told his friends to stop shooing the children away. He wanted to see them and spend time with them. Then he told his disciples that God's kingdom belonged to the children. Which must have been a shock because they probably thought that the big religious leaders were in charge of God's kingdom.

On another day Jesus said that if you have a child, and they ask for a fish finger sandwich you wouldn't give them...

1. Snake surprise
2. Cockroaches in a bun
3. Marmite on toast
4. KFC

Answer: 1

He said that if your child asks for some nice fish you would not give them a snake instead. That would be mad. Also he said that if they asked for an egg you would not give them...

1. A trampoline
2. A puppy
3. A scorpion
4. A stick insect

Answer: 3

He said a parent would not give their child a dangerous scorpion. Parents may not be perfect but they know how to give good things to their children. Then he said that God is a very good parent indeed.

And he knows how to give good things to his children too.

So, whether they are adults or children, when people are kind to each other, that's a bit like a picture of God. It's like being a living YouTube clip for anyone who happens to be watching.

You can check out these
stories in the Bible here:
Luke ch 11 vv 11-13

13. Mysterious Messiahs

At the time when Jesus was walking around, people in his town were waiting for someone they called the Messiah. It didn't mean someone who was the son of God, it just meant a hero who would be their new leader. Someone who was brave and clever. Like James Bond, or Indiana Jones or Tintin.

So they sometimes asked Jesus if he was the one they were waiting for, if he was the Messiah. He didn't like answering this question. The problem was... well, what was the problem?

1. They had the wrong ideas about the Messiah
2. Jesus wasn't the Messiah
3. They didn't need a Messiah
4. Jesus lived next door to the Messiah

Answer: 1

They had the wrong ideas. They thought the Messiah would fight the bad guys for them and solve all their problems. Their country had been invaded by the Romans and they wanted the Messiah to...

1. Pull faces at the Romans
2. Make up some new jokes about the Romans
3. Throw eggs at the Romans
4. Kill the Romans

Answer: 4

They wanted a Messiah who would lead an army that would fight and kill the Romans. Then the people in Israel would be free again. Jesus was not going to do that – he was a peacemaker, not a violent man.

He did tell one person that he was the Messiah though. A woman he met one day at a well. When Jesus and his friends were travelling they needed to get water from wells that were around. They were no taps in their houses and running water in the way we have now. So they carried... what?

1. Waterproof bags
2. Collapsible buckets
3. Long hosepipes
4. Big water pistols

Answer: 2

They had collapsible leather buckets which they could use to get water out of wells in the ground. One day, as they came to a well, Jesus let his friends go off to buy some food. He let them go with the bucket they carried. Soon a woman came to the well and Jesus needed a drink. What did he do?

1. Grab her bucket and get a drink
2. Offer her some money for a drink
3. Go to the nearest Starbucks
4. Ask her for a bit of help

Answer: 4

Jesus asked the woman if she could get him some water. This was shocking because the woman was...

1. A Samaritan
2. A smartie-pants
3. A smooth operator
4. A superstar

Answer: 4

Jesus was a Jew and the woman was a Samaritan. Jews and Samaritans would not share drinks or food. Jews and Samaritans hated each other because they both claimed to be the true people of God. The Samaritans had been Israelites in the past, but had married people who were not from Israel. The Jews did not like this at all, and felt that the Samaritans had 'sold out' and were no longer true Israelites.

This argument had lasted a long time and the two sides hated each other. But Jesus was different. He did not hate Samaritans, and when he met this woman he decided to start a conversation and see where it went. What did they talk about?

1. Husbands
2. Hot dogs
3. Hoovers
4. Hats

Answer: 1

Jesus talked to her about the men in her life. She had been married five times but all the men had left her. She needed to be with a man because in those days a woman needed a man to earn money while she had a family and look after the home. Jesus knew that she had been dumped by five men and the more they talked the more he could see she was a deep-thinking woman.

In the end he said told her she was talking to the Messiah. She then ran back to her village and said, 'Come and see a man who…' what?

1. Can juggle
2. Drinks lots of water
3. Doesn't hate Samaritans
4. Told me everything I've ever done

Answer: 4

Other people in her village probably gossiped about this woman, because she'd had five husbands. It was the women's job to collect the water each day and the other women went to the well to get water together, but she went alone. This was most likely to avoid their gossip about her. Suddenly she burst back into the village shouting about a man who knew all about her – and yet didn't hate her. He liked her. He accepted her. He even understood her. This must have been a surprise for everyone because they all came back to the well to see…

1. Whether Jesus could juggle
2. Whether there was any water left
3. Whether he could tell them everything they'd ever done
4. Who this Jesus was

Answer: 4, but maybe 3 too

They invited Jesus to stay with them in their village which means they must have liked him. Samaritans would never normally have invited a Jew for a sleepover.

You can check out these
stories in the Bible here:
Luke ch 7 vv 18-23
John ch 6 vv 14-15
Luke 23 vv 35-43
John ch 4 vv 1-42

14. Incredible Impressions

What do Alistair McGowan, Jon Culshaw, Jim Carrey, Robin Williams, Ronni Ancona, Lenny Henry, Rob Brydon, Steve Coogan, Francine Lewis and Jesus have in common?

Yes! Impressions. They all do impressions. Not many people realise that Jesus did impressions, but he did. Not so much the funny voices and facial expressions which Francine Lewis was so good at on the 2013 *Britain's Got Talent* show, but he certainly copied lots of other people, and he wanted those watching to see that he was doing that. Why?

1. He enjoyed doing impressions
2. He had no GCSEs
3. He wanted to be famous
4. He could do anything

Answer: 2

Normally a leader like Jesus would have been trained up at a proper school but he had not done that. Jesus had been a builder like his dad. So he had no qualifications as a leader. So to help people see that he was like their old heroes, Jesus did the kind of things the old heroes did. He impersonated them, the way his cousin John impersonated Elijah. Here's just a short list of the people he copied and what they did.

Moses   controlled water when he made the Red Sea open up for the people to walk through. He fed people with miraculous food from heaven, called Manna. He gave the people instructions on a hillside. We call these the Ten Commandments.

Jonah   disappeared into the depths for 3 days when he got on a ship and the sailors threw him overboard in a storm.

Elijah   miraculously raised a boy from the dead. And instead of dying he was taken up to heaven.

Elisha   miraculously raised a boy from the dead.

The people would know these stories really well and have been taught them as children. So when Jesus did things that were similar to these great heroes, people would have noticed that.

Jesus controlled water like Moses when he calmed a storm. He also gave instructions with his sermon on the mount and fed thousands of people with miracle food when he multiplied five loaves and two fish.

Jesus went into the depths of death for 3 days when he died, and even told people he would do this just like Jonah had done. And like Elijah and Elisha he raised people from the dead. When he left earth he rose up to heaven like Elijah had done. All these things would have reminded the people of their old heroes and made them think that Jesus was a new hero sent by God.

You can check out these stories in the Bible here:
Exodus ch 14 vv 15-22
Exodus ch 16
Exodus ch 20 vv 1-17
Jonah ch 1 vv 15-17
1 Kings ch 17 vv 17-24
2 King ch 4 vv 25-37
2 Kings ch 2 vv 9-12

You can check out these stories in the Bible here:
Mark ch 4 vv 35-41
Matthew ch 14 vv 13-21
Matthew chs 5-7
Matthew ch 12 vv 39-41
Mark 5 ch 21-43
Acts ch 1 vv 6-11

15. It's All Greek to Me

Alexander the Great was a clever dude and prime fighter. He came from Macedonia and spoke Greek. He'd been all over the place conquering countries and getting other people to speak Greek.

One day some people from another country came to meet Jesus. And they spoke Greek because Alex the Great had dropped by. When Jesus heard they were looking for him he said… what exactly?

1. 'Great! I'm famous!'
2. 'This shows it's soon time to die.'
3. 'I love Greeks.'
4. 'I'm busy right now updating my Facescroll status.'

Answer: 2

When Jesus heard that people were really taking note of him, he knew that it would soon be time to do the most important thing. Die.

That sounds strange to us. He described it like this: when a seed falls to the ground it dies and produces lots more fruit. Jesus would soon die and as a result lots more people would be coming to get to know him. Like many people today. These days there are how many Christians in the world?

1. One million
2. One thousand
3. One Direction
4. One billion

Answer: 4

Which is amazing when you think that at first Jesus only had a small group of friends in a little place called Galilee in Israel. That small group of friends sitting round a camp fire listening to Jesus telling stories has grown and grown and grown. Nowadays there are Christians in every bit of the world.

Why were Christians first called Christians?

1. It was a joke
2. It was a codename
3. Their group leader was called Christian
4. It's a secret

Answer: 1

It was in a place called Antioch and the local people made up a name which mixed together the word for slave and Messiah – the Messiah's slaves. We might not like to think of ourselves as slaves, and in fact Jesus said that he wanted to call us his friends, rather than slaves or servants.

Back then the people in Antioch were having a laugh at the followers of Jesus, who were then called "Followers of the Way". It's never been easy to be a Christian; people sometimes don't understand it, and so they laugh about it. But it's always been like that.

Jesus said to follow him is a bit like when you build a tower. It's not easy, it takes time, and you have to work hard. So he said this: 'Think about it first, decide if you want to do it.'

What do the following people have in common?

1. JK Rowling
2. Walt Disney
3. Steven Spielberg
4. The Beatles
5. Abraham Lincoln
6. Oprah Winfrey
7. Michael Jordan

They all had to keep going in order to make it. At first they were rejected and told to give up. Jesus was rejected lots of times by the people he was trying to help.

You can check out these
stories in the Bible here:
John ch 12 vv 20-29
Acts ch 11 v 25
Luke 14 vv 28-29

16. Dastardly Death?

A film director called Woody Allen once said, 'It's not that I'm afraid to die, I just don't want to be there when it happens!'

In a comedy sketch by Monty Python, a greedy man eats a meal so big that he explodes. It's a funny, cartoon kind of thing. He just goes on eating and eating and eating till it makes him go bang. You could say his greed kills him. Like the rich man in Jesus' story who just kept getting more and more and just storing it away until he died.

There's a song on YouTube called *Dumb Ways to Die,* all about the silly things you can do which will kill you. Which of these do you think are mentioned in the song?

1. Poke a grizzly bear
2. Use your private parts to catch piranha fish
3. Eat a really old pie
4. Take your helmet off in space

Answer: all of them

It's a funny song about avoiding all those things which will be bad for you, especially playing around trains and railway tracks. They want people to stay alive.

Jesus was afraid to die. When those Greeks came looking for him, he quietly said to his friends, 'I'm worried about what will happen. Shall I pray that I won't have to go through with this terrible thing? Shall I ask God for another way out?' Then he thought for a minute and said, 'No! This is why I've come. My death will be difficult and sad, but it will be the way for lots of people to start new lives. Lots of people being helped. And this will bring lots of praise to God.'

Jesus' death was not like anyone else's. It's a kind of difficult mystery. Sherlock Holmes couldn't crack the case. It's really deep. When Aslan was killed by the White Witch in Narnia he came back to life. He said the White Witch did not know that 'when a willing victim who had committed no treachery was killed in a traitor's stead, the table would crack and Death itself would start working backwards.'

Like Aslan, Jesus' death was not going to be the end of him. It was really difficult for him but he died to help us.

You can check out these
stories in the Bible here:
Luke ch 12 vv 13-21
Luke ch v 52
Isaiah ch 53 vv 1-12
Hebrews ch 10 vv 19-22
1 Peter ch 3 v 18

THIS IS WHERE THE PLOT
REALLY THICKENS...

17. Fabriffic Fish and Facescroll

Jesus wasn't really on Facescroll, but if he had been he'd have started with a few friends, then added loads more as he got more and more popular. Then lots of them would have unfriended him. Then he would have lost pretty much all of them when he got arrested. But let's not jump ahead.

He was really popular when he fed thousands of people. Some people think he fed 5,000 people, but it was probably way more because it was only 5,000 men, and most of them would have come with their families too. So maybe up to 20,000! That's a lot of Facescroll friends.

What happened was that Jesus was telling stories and talking with them, and they all forgot about the time. Suddenly Jesus realised they were hungry and so he got his close friends round and told them to feed everyone.

His friends laughed. Like how could they do that? But one of his friends, Andrew, got chatting to a little boy who had what?

1. Bread and fish
2. A pot noodle
3. Some sushi
4. Fish and chips

Answer: 1

The boy had five small loaves and two small fish.

He gave them to Jesus, though he may have been worried about losing his lunch. Jesus said a prayer, split up the food and did what?

1. Ate it himself
2. Got out Jamie Oliver's cook book
3. Gave it to his friends to give out
4. Turned it into enough for everyone

Answer: 3 & 4

The food became enough for everyone – but only when Jesus gave it to his friends to give out. Jesus liked getting his friends to do things with him.

His friends must have been well embarrassed because they had big hands and only tiny bits of food, but they got people to sit down in groups and started to hand out what they had.

Incredibly everyone had loads to eat! The food multiplied. They even collected up lots of leftovers. A bit like when you eat croissants and there seem to be more crumbs on the table than the croissants you ate.

What was great about the meal was that everyone ate together. Rich and poor, clever and not-so-clever. Musical people, sporting people, quiet people, noisy people. Famous and not-so-famous. Those who loved Marmite and those who hated it. This was like a Facescroll picture of God's best way. Everyone invited to a big party by Jesus, eating and being together in peace.

The next day though things turned nasty. Do you know why?

1. No special diets
2. No ketchup
3. No fries
4. No seconds

Answer: 4

Everyone came back to Jesus the next day wanting more food. But Jesus wouldn't do it – he wouldn't just make magic bread for them to eat every day. He wanted them to follow him, not just come for his catering. He wanted to get to know them. But the people were annoyed. They'd probably bought some of their friends and family members along and they wanted to impress them with Jesus' *Great Israeli Bakeoff*. But Jesus wasn't into that.

The day before he fed them because he cared about them being hungry. Now they had only come back for a quick foody miracle, a bit of a magic show – not to spend time with him.

So what happened when Jesus tried to talk to them instead of making lunch?

1. They started eating the grass instead
2. They listened to him
3. They put their fingers in their ears
4. They argued

Answer: certainly not 1, and definitely 4. But it may have been 2 and 3 too

There was a big old argument about Moses and the way he fed everyone with magic food from heaven. It was called Manna, which means 'What is it?' or maybe 'Whatsit.' So when people said to Moses, 'What is it?' he said, 'Yea, that's right. What is it.' And that might have gone on for a long time.

But Jesus called himself the bread from heaven and he wanted the people to receive him, not just the free food. In the end most people left him that day. They unfriended him.

You can check out these
stories in the Bible here:
Mark ch 6 vv 30-44
John ch 6 v 22-69

18. You're Gonna Need a Bigger Boat!

How many times do you think Jesus fed people with fish?

1. Once
2. Twice
3. Three times
4. Four times

Answer: 4

He fed four thousand people one day and then later on five thousand people. But he also fed his friends with two massive catches of fish. The first time it happened, Peter and Andrew had been out fishing all night and they had caught nothing. Not even a fish finger.

They were both tired, but Jesus asked them if he could borrow their boat to talk to people. He got Peter to row out into the water so everyone could hear him. It was a good way for lots of people to be able to hear and see Jesus.

Then, after Peter had heard all Jesus' stories, Jesus said to him…

1. Do you pray a lot?
2. Are you a Christian?
3. Why not throw your fishing net over there?
4. Do you come here often?

Answer: 3

Peter was a fisherman and thought he knew lots about fishing. He expected to know more than Jesus who was a rabbi. But Jesus told Peter to throw his net into the water at a certain place and bingo! Peter caught a huge amount of fish. A massive catch. It was like winning the lottery for Peter and his family and friends. This meant that Peter could give up fishing for a while and spend time with Jesus.

Later on, after Jesus had risen from the dead, it happened again. Jesus was on the beach, doing what?

1. Cooking breakfast
2. Getting ready to surf
3. Catching crabs
4. Sunbathing

Answer: 1

Peter and his friends had been out all night and caught nothing, but Jesus called to them and told them to try one more time. They did and yet again - bingo! It was like winning the lottery all over again. Jesus cooked them breakfast and then asked Peter to start a new job, as a leader. Peter could do this because Jesus had just provided loads of fish to feed his family for a while. Result!

You can check out these
stories in the Bible here:
Mark ch 8 vv 1-10
Luke ch 5 v 1-11
John ch 21 vv 1-14
John 21 vv 15-17

19. Sea Shenanigans

What unusual mode of transport did Jesus use to cross the Sea of Galilee?

1. Water skis
2. Jet skis
3. Surf board
4. Hover board
5. None of the above

Answer: 5

He walked of course. But that's as impressive as all the others put together. When did you last see anyone walking on water?

The big question is why?

1. He was showing off
2. He'd forgotten his snorkel
3. He was taking a short cut
4. He was showing his friends he could control the waves

Answer: 4

Moses had controlled water and made the Red Sea open up so all the Israelites could walk through. Jesus wanted to show his friends he was similar to their big hero Moses. He could control water too.

Mind you Jesus didn't do this sort of thing very often. He spent most of his time walking on the roads and paths like ordinary people. He preferred to do that so he could meet folks and hear their stories and tell them some tales about the kingdom of God.

One night Jesus and his friends were in a boat and a storm quickly started. It can do that where they lived. They were really frightened and thought they might all soon be fish food. What did Jesus do?

1. Sleep through it all
2. Put up an umbrella
3. Make a speedboat for them
4. Tell the storm off

Answer: 4

He was asleep but they woke him up and he shouted at the storm to be quiet – and it was!

At the beginning of John's story about Jesus, John describes Jesus as the Word – through him God spoke and made everything. We're told that God made everything through Jesus, and here he was showing his friends that he had incredible power over the world. He could make it do anything. But he didn't do it often.

Once, when they needed to pay their taxes, he told his friend Peter to get a coin out of... where?

1. A giant's armpit
2. A soldier's ear
3. A sheep's nose
4. A fish's mouth

Answer: 4

Jesus could have done this a lot, but he didn't. He worked as a builder for much of his life. Later, when he was travelling a lot, lots of friends gave him money to help him pay his bills. He didn't go around making magic money all the time, even though he could.

You can check out these
stories in the Bible here:
Mark ch 6 vv 45-52
Matthew ch 8 vv 23-27
John ch 1 vv 1-5
Matthew ch 17 vv 24-27
Luke ch 8 vv 1-3

20. I'm A Tax Collector - Get Me Outa Here...

If Zacchaeus had been a celebrity he'd have been a short one like Lady Gaga, Christina Aguilera, Tom Cruise or Daniel Radcliffe. Actually he'd have been shorter than all of them. Probably somewhere around four feet eight or 1 metre 42 cm. A whole 30 cm shorter than another short Zac – Zac Efron.

Zac (not Zac Efron) lived in a town called Jericho and nobody liked him because he was a tax collector. Why do you think they didn't like him?

1. Because he wore terrible clothes
2. Because he smelt like dead piranha fish
3. Because he talked like a chipmunk
4. Because he stole money from them

Answer: 4

He sent his men round collecting lots of money from people for the Roman taxes. But he demanded way too much money, a bit like the Sheriff of Nottingham in the tale of Robin Hood. He took more money than he should have done to make himself rich. And people needed a kind of Robin Hood to rescue them. Then one day Jesus arrived.

Everyone went out to meet Jesus because he was a famous celebrity. He'd never been on the X Factor or Strictly Come Dancing but people had been talking about him a lot. The local folk did what they always did for famous people – they organised a party for him and a place to stay. That's what they did for celebrities who visited their town. But oh-oh … Jesus arrived and – epic FAIL! He didn't want to stay; he kept on moving through the town and out the other side.

And that's when he saw Zac. Where was he?

1. Up a tree
2. Up a chimney
3. Up the junction
4. Up at the North Pole

Answer: 1

He was up a tree. And that's when Jesus changed his mind. Zac looked pretty stupid because men like him didn't normally climb trees. It would be a bit like the Queen jumping out of a helicopter with James Bond at the Olympics. It looked daft. So everyone shouted insults at Zac and told him he looked stupid while they had the chance.

But not Jesus; he said, 'Hey – how about I come back to yours for a party? And maybe I could stay the night?'

Zac nearly fell out of his tree, but he took Jesus to his home and they had a meal and a chat.

I grew up singing a song about Jesus going to Zac's house for tea and I wondered what sort? PG Tips? But no – it was way more than a cuppa. It was a huge party.

Everybody else was well miffed because Jesus had scuppered their plans. But what they didn't realise was this. Jesus was helping the whole town. How was he doing this?

1. Zac was going to give up watching *EastEnders*
2. Zac was giving away his old pants
3. Zac was giving away free money
4. Zac was giving up smoking

Answer: 3

When Zac met Jesus he started to change. And he decided to stop taking loads of money off people in their taxes, and even to give some back! So the whole town just got better.

You can check out these stories in the Bible here: Luke ch 19 vv 1-10

21. Now I Don't See You, Now I Do

There was once a blind beggar called Bartimaeus (or we'll call him Bart for short). He lived in a town called Jericho and made his living by begging for money. And people were very happy to pay him. Why?

1. Everyone had loadsamoney
2. It got rid of their loose change
3. They only gave him Monopoly money
4. It was their way of giving to God

Answer: 4

This might sound odd but, when Jesus was around, everyone expected to give money away as part of their worship to God. It was just like praying prayers, or singing hymns and worship songs: you gave money away because God wanted you to. Their Bible told them that God loved to see people giving things away to help others.

So when people gave money to Bart, what do you think he did?

1. Threw it down the drain
2. Swallowed it
3. Did a magic trick with it
4. Shouted at the people passing by

Answer: 4

Imagine if you bought a copy of *The Big Issue* and the seller then shouted it out to everyone, yelling about how you're a fantastic person! What would you do?

1. Run like mad
2. Take a bow
3. Buy another five copies
4. Hide in a drain

Answer – it's up to you really. Though buying another five copies to give away might not be bad!

When you gave money to someone like Bart back when Jesus was around, the person begging would shout it out to all those passing by, and tell everyone what a great person you were, and how much you loved God. Imagine that…

Then one day Jesus came to Jericho and Bart heard about it he shouted out to Jesus, asking for his help.

What do you think everyone else did?

1. Told Bart not to be so bonkers
2. Told Jesus to give Bart some money
3. Told Bart to shut up
4. Told Bart to speak up

Answer: 3, and maybe a bit of 1 too

Everyone else told Bart to 'shut it', but not Jesus. He was always interested in people like Bart, and he asked him a really important question. He asked Bart what he wanted.

Now Bart didn't have any qualifications or exams. He'd never been trained in anything or been to school. Begging was his way of making money. If Jesus fixed his eyes and made him better, he'd have to start all over again. It wouldn't be easy.

What did Bart say to Jesus?

1. Can I have some change for a burger?
2. Is this the way to Amarillo?
3. I want to see
4. Can I have a new baseball cap

Answer: 3

Bart was ready for Jesus' question. He wanted to start again. And so he said to Jesus, 'I want to see.' And Jesus cured his eyes. A miracle!

You can check out these stories in the Bible here: Mark ch 10 vv 46-52

22. Nick in the Night

Another man came to see Jesus really late one night. He was called Nicodemus. Jesus told him that becoming a Christian is like…

1. Being born again
2. Being bored again
3. Being in bed again
4. Being bopped on the head again

Answer: 1

He told Nicodemus it was like starting your life all over again. Not as a little baby, but with everything a little bit new. And many things changed. Not necessarily feeling different, but wanting to be different. Like coming to a crossroads and choosing to take a new road.

This was a big thing for Nicodemus because he thought he had everything sorted out, yet here was Jesus telling him start again.

What else did Jesus talk about with Nicodemus?

1.   A snake on a pole
2.   A vulture in a pie
3.   A tiger in a tank
4.   A dog on a tightrope

Answer: 1

In the Old Testament there's a story about Moses making a snake out of bronze and lifting it up on a big pole. Some people had been bitten by desert snakes and when they looked up to the snake on the pole, what do you think happened?

1. They got better
2. They got worse
3. They got measles
4. They got famous

Answer: 1

When the people looked at the snake on the pole, God cured them of the snake bites. It wasn't the snake on the pole that cured them; it was doing what God asked them to do.

Jesus said that one day soon Nicodemus would see him lifted up, not on a pole like the snake, but on a cross made of wood. When anyone looked to Jesus on that cross they would find a whole new life. They could start again. Like the people in the desert starting again after their snake bites. And then Jesus said something to Nicodemus that has become a famous saying. He said that God loved the universe so much that he…

1. Sent a policeman to arrest all the bad people
2. Sent a teacher to tell everyone off
3. Sent a referee to give bad people red cards
4. Sent his son to rescue people and help them

Answer: 4

Jesus said that he had come to give people real life, full life, eternal life, God's life. Not always an easy life, or a life full of fame and riches. But a different kind of life.

A life with Jesus at the centre. And it started by believing in him.

Nicodemus went away and had a good long think about this. And later on, after Jesus had been killed and lifted up on that cross, he risked his life to do something. He came to the authorities and asked if he could look after Jesus' body. So it seems as if Nicodemus did make a whole new start.

You can check out these
stories in the Bible here:
John ch 3 vv 1-21
Numbers ch 21 vv 4-9

23. Ker-ching! Peter's Penny Droppeth

The first part of the Bible is called the Old Testament and it has lots of stuff in it that happened before Jesus was born. The New Testament is the second part of the Bible – a bit like a sequel to the Old Testament – and it begins with the story of Jesus told by four different people.

D'you know what they were called?

1. John, Paul, George and Ringo
2. Matthew, Mark, Luke and John
3. Alvin, Theodore, Simon and the Chipettes
4. Shaggy, Scooby, Daphne & Velma

Answer: 2

But back to the Old Testament for a minute. It's all about a bunch of folks called the nation of Israel, or the Israelites, who were asked by God to show and tell all the other countries in the world what God is like and to invite them to know him and worship him. But poor old Israel kept messing up, so after a while a new idea seemed to be coming from God: instead of Israel showing the world what God was like, God himself would come and do it.

One man who got this message was called Daniel, who by the way nearly got eaten by…

1. Llamas
2. Leeches
3. Lions
4. Ladies

Answer: 3

He was thrown in a den of lions by the king's men because he worshipped God. But God looked after him and made the lions vegetarians, or vegans, or on a diet, or just plain not hungry. And Daniel survived and became a hero.

One day Daniel saw a vision of someone he called the Son of Man. This person would one day be king of the world and would rule over everyone in a really good way. The best kind of King. This Son of Man wanted to help people and to stop the bad guys messing up everything.

So by the time Jesus was born, everyone had heard about Daniel's story of this strange Son of Man and everyone was asking – who is he? When's he going to come? We want him now! And a lot of people might say that today too. Bring on the person who can sort out the mess in the world.

Jesus, of course, knew this story too. So one day he got his friends together for a chat and he asked them what the word on the street was – who did people think this strange Son of Man might be?

They had a few guesses… which of these d'you reckon they said?

1. David Cameron
2. John the Baptist
3. Bill Gates
4. Lady Gaga

Answer: 2

There were lots of ideas but some thought that Jesus' cousin John the Baptist might be this son of man who would make everything good. So then Jesus asked them another question. He said, 'So who do you think I am then?'

Now, Peter wasn't always the sharpest hook on the fishing rod, but now he began to think. Jesus had asked two questions. Who was the Son of Man? And who was Jesus? Tick, tick, tick… you could hear the wheels of Peter's brain whirring round for a moment, then he said, 'You! You're the Son of Man! You're the one we're waiting for – you're the Messiah sent from God!'

He put the two questions together and made the same answer. The Son of Man, Daniel's king of the world, was Jesus and Jesus was the Son of Man.

Why d'you think Jesus asked these two questions like this?

1. He liked quizzes
2. He wanted Peter to work it out
3. He got confused
4. It was in his crossword puzzle

Answer: 2

Jesus didn't like telling people about himself out loud; he always wanted them to think for themselves and work it out. Jesus wanted to people to think for themselves, to look at the clues and the signs and make up their own minds.

This is the same today. It's the same with this book. It's full of thoughts and questions about Jesus. But in the end it's up to you to think and work things out for yourself. Decide what you think about Jesus and what you want to do.

You can check out these
stories in the Bible here:
Isaiah ch 49 vv 5-6
Daniel ch 6
Daniel ch 7 vv 13-14
Matthew ch 16 vv 13-20

24. Catastrophic Cliff-edges

Some Cliffs get famous. Like Cliff Richard. Other cliffs get walked all over. Like the White Cliffs of Dover. And some cliffs are dangerous. Like the one that Jesus nearly fell off.

Why d'you think Jesus nearly fell off a cliff?

1. He was out walking a dog
2. He was abseiling in a storm
3. He was peeping over the edge
4. He was attacked

Answer: 4

Although Jesus was really powerful, he never used his power to fight others. But other people used their power to fight him. Nazareth was his home town, the place where he grew up and used to work as a builder.

One day he was back there and he went to the synagogue, where they were holding a kind of service. Because he was getting quite famous they invited him to do their Bible reading. But Jesus read the wrong bit! He read an old, old reading about... what exactly?

1. Batman vs Superman
2. The Lion, the Witch and the Wardrobe
3. The Hunger Games
4. A Shocking Hero

Answer: 4

He read them a reading written by a dude called Isaiah, and it said that God had sent him to bust people out of prisons, to stand up for the poor, to help those being hurt by others and to make the blind see.

It wasn't what people expected. They'd seen Jesus as a wee lad, running around, messing about with the other boys, looking scruffy. And while they were thinking about all this he said something which really upset them. What did he say?

1. He told stories about God helping foreigners
2. He told jokes about their town
3. He told them they needed to shape up
4. He told them to get into One Direction

Answer: 1

He told a couple of stories about who God helped people in Old Testament times, but the people weren't from Israel. This got everyone really annoyed, because they thought that God belonged to them, and only wanted to help them. So they grabbed Jesus, pushed him to a cliff edge and tried to throw him off. How did he escape?

1. He zapped them all so they couldn't see
2. He made lightning strike them dead
3. He said, 'Look, a squirrel!' and then ran off
4. We don't know

Answer: 4

We don't really know how he did it; he just somehow slipped out of their hands and quietly escaped through the crowd. Maybe they were all arguing about what to do and got distracted; maybe it was some kind of miracle. Either way, Jesus quietly escaped, no fuss or bother. But it must have shaken him up, and maybe showed him what it was going to be like in the future. People would get angry with him, and want him dead.

You can check out these
stories in the Bible here:
Luke ch 4 vv 16-30
2 King ch 5 vv 1-19
1 Kings ch 17 vv 8-24

25. Suffering Samaritans

When someone asked Jesus how to get eternal life, Jesus asked the man what he thought. The man knew all about religious things and he knew that Moses had given everyone God's guide to a good life a long time ago. So he told Jesus some of this. What did he say?

1. Live long and prosper
2. May the force be with you
3. Prepare for awesomeness
4. Love God and care about people

Answer: 4

Jesus said, 'Well done – do that and you'll live.'

However, Jesus knew that the man was trying to test Jesus, seeing if he would say anything that his enemies could use in evidence against him. And Jesus also knew that the man could not simply love God and care about people all the time. It was too hard. Jesus understood that we all make mistakes, and it's not easy to keep doing the right thing.

The man wanted to make Jesus' answer a bit easier, so he asked Jesus exactly how many people he had to love. He wanted a ball park figure, as they say. Ten people? Twenty people? What did Jesus say?

1. He told a joke
2. He told a horror story
3. He didn't answer
4. He did a mime

Answer: sort of 1, 2 and 3

Jesus didn't tell the man how many people the guy should care about; instead he told the man and everyone else listening a story that was funny and shocking. It was about a man that no one liked who was a hero and helped a man just like them. This hero was a Samaritan and I think we've already cleared up what they thought of Samaritans. But Jesus made him the hero – the Samaritan rescued a Jew just like them, a man who had been attacked and was dying. The Samaritan risked his life to do what?

1. Take him Pizza Hut
2. Take him to a Travel Inn
3. Take him to the cinema
4. Take him dancing

Answer: 2

He took him to a place like a travel inn and paid for the man to stay there for a few days while he got better from the attack. Jesus told this story and then asked who the kind neighbour in the story was.

The man did not want to say that the Samaritan was a neighbour, so he just said, 'The one who helped the man.' This was the point of the story really: to be a person who helps others. Whether we like them or not. According to Jesus a neighbour is not just someone we like; a neighbour is someone we help.

There was something else in the story. Two other people walked past the man who had been attacked but did not help him. They didn't act like neighbours. The man had asked Jesus the question, 'Who is my neighbour?' Jesus didn't really answer that question. Instead he said,

1. 'Go and be a neighbour.'
2. 'Everyone is your neighbour.'
3. 'Neighbours is a TV programme.'
4. 'A neighbour lives next door.'

Answer: 1

You can check out these
stories in the Bible here:
Luke ch 10 vv 25-37

26. Funeral Blues

Nowadays if you don't have a job you can go and get help from the government. Back in Jesus' day the Roman government would have stuck their tongues out at you. They didn't really care. When a woman lost her husband she had to look to her son to work and get money for her. But what could she do when her only son died?

One day Jesus came to a place called…

1. Nazareth
2. Nain
3. Newcastle
4. Neverland

Answer: 2

The first thing he saw was a funeral. Men were carrying the coffin of a widow's son. Jesus saw her crying and it broke his heart, so he said to her, 'Don't cry.'

Then what did Jesus do?

1. Clapped his hands over the coffin
2. Zapped the coffin
3. Stared at the coffin
4. Stuck his fingers on the coffin

Answer: 4

Jesus walked up and touched the coffin and then...

1. Nothing happened
2. The coffin stopped moving
3. The coffin burst open
4. The man inside sat up

Answer: 2

The men stopped moving, everyone stopped moving. It was a very tense moment. No one knew what might happen next. The street fell quiet.

Then Jesus said,

1. 'Get up.'
2. 'Get down.'
3. 'Get away.'
4. 'Get over it.'

Answer: 1

Jesus told the dead young man to get up. And he did!
Jesus had ruined another funeral. The widow was over
the moon. Not only did she have her son back, but now
she would be all right again. She would not have to beg
or become homeless. Without her husband and her son
she had no hope. Jesus brought her son and her hope
back to life.

You can check out these
stories in the Bible here:
Luke ch 7 vv 11-17

27. Tumultuous Transfiguration

Not long after Jesus had asked his friends who they thought he was, he took a few of them for a climb. Where did they go?

1. Up the Eiffel Tower
2. Up a skyscraper
3. Up a mountain
4. Up the Empire State Building

Answer: 3

He went up a mountain with Peter, James and John. And while they were up there, something amazing happened. Jesus started to pray and he began to look very different. He was bright and shiny. What did his friends do?

1. They went for a burger
2. They fell asleep
3. They played football
4. They clapped their hands

Answer: 2

Whilst Jesus started to look very different, his disciples fell asleep and missed what was happening. Then two more people appeared from nowhere. Who were they?

1. Health and safety inspectors
2. The Queen and Prince Philip
3. His mum and dad
4. Moses and Elijah

Answer: 4

When the disciples woke up they noticed a couple of things. First that Jesus was lit up as if a thousand floodlights were shining on him. Secondly that he was no longer alone. Moses and Elijah had somehow time travelled out of the Old Testament and were standing there chatting to Jesus.

What did Peter do?

1. Scream and run round with his shoes on his head
2. Faint
3. Start a football match
4. Start talking madly

Answer: 4

He offered to build them shelters on the mountain. He was probably so amazed and blown away by what was happening that he wanted to stay up there forever.

Why bother going back down the mountain? Life down there was hard and dull. This was epic! Like being in an incredible big screen movie. What stopped him doing the building work?

1. He couldn't find a hammer
2. James and John rugby tackled him
3. Everything went foggy
4. Peter hit his thumb with a sledgehammer

Answer: 3

A cloud came down and no one could see a thing. They did hear something though. A voice boomed at them from the cloud. It said...

1. 'Peter – grow up.'
2. 'Moses – you must be really old by now.'
3. 'Boo!'
4. 'Jesus is my chosen one: listen carefully to him.'

Answer: 4

When the cloud went away again Moses and Elijah had gone. Jesus led Peter and James and John back down the mountain. And then they got another shock.

1. Moses and Elijah jumped out on them
2. Everyone was waiting for them with a tough challenge
3. The others were really angry to have missed out
4. It had been snowing

Answer: 2

After the incredible time up the mountain Jesus and his friends were met by a crowd begging for help. They had a boy who was ill and some of Jesus' friends had tried to help but failed. It was all going wrong.

What did Jesus do?

1. Ran back up the mountain again
2. Got Moses and Elijah to sort it out
3. Lost his temper
4. Helped the sick boy

Answer: 3 & 4

Jesus was frustrated at first, perhaps because it was a shock after the encouragement of being up that mountain and hearing God's voice. Then he healed the sick boy and made him well again. It was a classic example of having a great time and then suddenly being hit by a difficult problem.

You can check out these stories in the Bible here: Mark ch 9 vv 2-10

28. Fearful Farmyard Fires

As the time came close to Jesus dying, he was walking into Jerusalem when he stopped and shook his head. And he started to talk about a kind of bird. Which one?

1. Eagles
2. Seagulls
3. Ducks
4. Chickens

Answer: 4

He was sad for Jerusalem and the people who lived there. He said that he had often wanted to hug them close to himself, a bit like the way a mother hen pulls her chicks near and they hide under her wings for safety.

Sometimes, in the farmyard where chickens lived, there could be a fire. If the chicks hid under the wings of their mothers they would be saved from the fire. The wings would protect them, but sadly the mother would die. Jesus was probably thinking about this when he talked about gathering people under his wings. He was going to die, so that other people could be protected and live.

You can check out these stories in the Bible here: Matthew ch 23 vv 37-39

29. Horrendous Hacking and Potty Plucking

What did Jesus say we should cut off if it causes us to do things that are wrong?

1. Our hand
2. Our finger nail
3. Our big toe
4. Our fringe

Answer: 1. Ouch!

And what should we do with our eyes if they get us into trouble?

1. Wear sunglasses
2. Wear eye shadow
3. Pluck them out
4. Play marbles with them

Answer: 3. Ugh!

Mind you – Jesus was using what we might call picture language. Cartoons. Another word for this is 'metaphor' – when you say something that has a deeper meaning. Jesus didn't really mean us to cut off our hands and rip out our eyes. Not at all. Because just hacking off your right hand won't stop you getting into trouble or causing trouble for others. And having no eyes wouldn't stop you either. Blind people and one armed people can get into trouble like anyone else can.

ALFIE WAS ARMLESS BUT HE DEFINITELY WASN'T HARMLESS.

So what did he really mean?

1. Buy a nice pair of mittens
2. Find a way to avoid the danger
3. Chop other people's hands off instead
4. Walk round with your eyes shut

Answer: 2

If you know that watching something will make you be angry or mean to your family, then don't watch it. If you know that sticking your hand in a fire will burn you, then don't do it. Keep away from or get rid of the things that will cause the problems. Cut them out of your life. If you know that daydreaming about having loads of things will just make you greedy, then do your best not to do it.

But don't do any hacking off or plucking out of bits of you or anybody else. That's never a good idea. And Jesus knew that. He cured people who had bad arms and eyes – he didn't make them worse!

You can check out these
stories in the Bible here:
Matthew ch 5 vv 29-30

30. Fearsome Farmers Fight Back Furiously

Once there was a farm. And there some men who needed a job. The owner hired some of these men to look after his farm and work there for him. But the men got an idea – they decided to take over the farm and make it their own. When it was time for the harvest, the owner sent three servants to see what was happening. What did the men do?

1. Hide behind the sofa
2. Beat them up
3. Throw rotten fruit at them
4. Kill them

Answer: 2, 3 & 4

They beat up one of the servants, threw stones (and maybe rotten fruit) at the second and then killed the third one. This was getting serious. The owner heard what had happened to his servants and so he paced up and down in his lounge and had a think. What did he decide to do?

1. Hide behind the sofa
2. Beat them up
3. Throw rotten fruit at them
4. Send someone else

Answer: 4

He decided to give the men another chance. He took a very big risk and sent his son along. Hopefully they would listen to the son. What happened?

1. They hid behind the sofa
2. They beat him up
3. They threw rotten fruit at him
4. They killed him

Answer: 4

The men at the farm thought that if they killed the owner's son they would be able to own the farm, because the owner would have no one else to give the farm to. So they grabbed the son, took him outside the farm, beat him up and killed him. This was getting very serious now. So what did the owner do now?

1. Hide behind the sofa
2. Beat them up
3. Throw rotten fruit at them
4. Kill them

Answer: 4

The owner called up the chief of his army and sent his soldiers to kill the men in the farm. It was a terrible end. They all got slaughtered. It was the opposite of those chicks who hid underneath the mother's wings. They weren't protected; they died.

Who was the story about?

1. The world
2. Jesus
3. People
4. Farmers

Answer: 1,2,3 & 4

The farm was like the world, and the farmers in the story were the people who wanted to say the world belonged to them and not to God, the owner. God sent his servants along – some of those people like Moses and Elijah and others in the Old Testament – and often the people hurt and killed them. So God took a big risk and sent his son along. Surely people would listen to him. What happened?

1. Some people listened
2. It ended badly
3. The son died
4. There was a surprise at the end

Answer: 1,2,3 & 4 (again)

Jesus was telling people what was going to happen to him. And that's where we're going next.

You can check out these
stories in the Bible here:
Mark ch 12 vv 1-9

31. Mad Man or Good God

Jesus had a problem. Imagine if someone came up to you and told you they were God. You'd probably think they were a bit mad. You might laugh at them. You might feel sorry for them. You might get annoyed if they kept on telling you. Which is why Jesus didn't do it that way. He spent three years telling stories, helping people, challenging what was wrong and pointing people to God. But he hardly ever told anyone that he was God. And you can understand why. Instead he left them clues and signposts. In John's story about Jesus he said that the first clue was... what?

1. Jesus made lots of wine
2. Jesus made lots of friends
3. Jesus made lots of enemies
4. Jesus made lots of noise

Answer: 1

When Jesus went to a wedding, and the wine ran out, he turned 180 gallons of water into the best kind of wine. Not just cheap plonk. John said that this was the first sign that Jesus was not ordinary. From there Jesus left a trail of clues for people to follow, like a detective mystery. Not so much a Whodunnit; more like a Who-is-he?

You can check out these
stories in the Bible here:
John ch 2 vv 1-12
John 4 vv 46-54

32. Good Guys and Bad Boys

Sometimes the bad guys don't like the good guys and so they tell everyone that the good guys are really the bad guys and that the bad guys are really the good guys. Got it?

Well, that's what some people were saying about Jesus. That he was a bad guy. Lots of people loved him, especially the poor people, and those he had been helping. But the rich and powerful people were worried. So they said he was a baddie.

Jesus had two kinds of enemies:

1. The religious leaders (called the Sadducees) who made lots of money out of charging people to go to their big temple in Jerusalem.

2. The Romans who had invaded the country (they had invaded lots of countries) and did not like anyone causing trouble.

The religious leaders were worried about Jesus because he had lots and lots of followers, and they thought that Jesus would make his followers into an army to fight the Romans. If he did this, the Romans would not only kill Jesus and his friends, they would kill lots of other people too, and pull down their special place – the temple. So the religious leaders wanted Jesus to be killed. But to do this, they needed the Romans.

So they went to a man called Pontius… what?

1. Partridge
2. Pumpkin
3. Pipkin
4. Pilate

Answer: 4

They asked him if he would kill Jesus for them. Pontius Pilate didn't want to. His wife had recently had a…

1. Dream
2. Doughnut
3. Baby
4. Haircut

Answer: 1

She had a dream that he shouldn't get involved with this man Jesus. But in the end the religious leaders persuaded him. And Jesus was condemned to death. Even though, like Aslan in Narnia, he was guilty of no treachery. But I'm jumping ahead again. We'll come back to all this later.

You can check out these stories in the Bible here:
John ch 10 vv 22-42
Matthew ch 27 vv 11-19

33. Anyone for Sliced Ear?

Jesus' friends had a secret wish. A hidden hope. They wanted Jesus to get an army together and fight the bad guys. The Romans. They were hoping that this would happen at the big Passover Festival in Jerusalem, when loads of people had come to visit. Jesus was getting more and more popular, and it would be easy for him to hold a big outdoor festival, speak to everyone and tell them to come with him to fight the Romans. Other people had done it, so why not Jesus? Why not indeed?

1. Jesus was a man of peace
2. Jesus was a friend of the Romans
3. Jesus was too busy
4. Jesus was distracted

Answer: 1, 2, 3 & 4

Jesus had already shown his friends that he was a not a man of violence – remember – he told them blessed are the cheese-makers, or rather the peacemakers. Jesus was the ultimate peacemaker. Jesus had helped some of the Romans he had met, and he was called the friend of sinners, the friend of those who make mistakes and those who get things wrong – that includes everyone really.

Jesus had another plan anyway, and strangely this involved a friend of his who had got confused.

Who was this friend?

1. Zacchaeus
2. Judas
3. Mary
4. Peter

Answer: 2

Judas, like all the other friends, was hoping for a revolution. He believed Jesus was the man to start it. However, he was getting bored and fed up. Jesus was taking his time, and he was helping Romans instead of fighting them. Something had to be done. Judas decided to make a plan to help Jesus start the revolution. What was it?

1. To make Jesus angry
2. To buy Jesus a sword
3. To get Jesus arrested
4. To buy Jesus a uniform

Answer: 3

Judas figured that if the bad guys came to arrest Jesus then there would have to be a fight, and a fight meant the start of the revolution. Jesus had been quite careful, hiding out with friends, and only appearing in public places when there were lots of people around, so Judas needed to fix it so that he could help the bad guys come to arrest Jesus in a dark quiet place. So he went to the bad guys and made a plan. What did he get paid for doing this?

1. A bag of gold
2. A bag of sweets
3. A bag of silver
4. A bag of sprouts

Answer: 3

Judas got paid 30 pieces of silver, which incidentally was the price for selling a slave. So this was a bit like Jesus getting sold as a slave. Judas made a plan with the Sadducees, who ran the temple and wanted to get rid of Jesus. He would bring them to Jesus late at night, when he was with his friends in garden.

Jesus had a big celebration meal with his friends. We now call that his last supper, but they were celebrating the Passover festival. A painter called Leonardo Da Vinci painted a picture of it, but the painting isn't quite right. Why?

1. They were eating bacon sandwiches
2. They were all sitting on one side of the table
3. There weren't enough people
4. They forgot to smile for the picture

Answer: 2 & 3

Jesus would have been celebrating with lots of his friends, not just the twelve men. And they would have sat all around the table.

During the meal Judas ran off to set up his plan, and afterwards Jesus took his friends for a late night walk into a valley where there was a big walled garden called Gethsemane. They stopped to rest there. Jesus prayed. What did the disciples do?

1. Play Scrabble
2. Play five-a-side football
3. Pick flowers
4. Have a snooze

Answer: 4

The disciples fell asleep yet again! Do you remember they did the same thing when Jesus took them up a mountain to meet Moses and Elijah? They're always falling asleep at crucial moments. Last time they woke up to see Jesus talking with Mo and Eli. This time they woke up to see Judas hanging out with all the wrong people. He'd brought a bunch of soldiers and priests to get Jesus. Awkward...

However, that night Judas wasn't the only one who wanted a fight. One of the other disciples had brought a sword with them.

Who was it?

1. Mary
2. Martha
3. James
4. Peter

Answer: 4

The big fisherman was ready (once he'd stopped napping) when the bad guys came with Judas, and in the darkness he lashed out with his sword and cut off the first thing he could find. An ear.

What happened next?

1. Peter cut off an arm too
2. He got covered in blood
3. Everyone started cutting off ears
4. Jesus turned back time

Answer: 4, though 2 may be true as well

In effect Jesus reversed time. He picked up the ear and placed it back on the injured man's head. As if it had not been cut off. What was the injured man's name?

1. Maximus Decimus Meridius
2. Methuselah
3. Michaelmas
4. Malchus

Answer: 4

Jesus fixed his ear immediately by putting it back on and curing the wound. And that was that. The fight was over. What did Peter do?

1. Stuck his tongue out
2. Pulled out another sword
3. Cried like a baby
4. Stamped his feet

Answer: 3

Peter broke down and cried. But not at first. First he watched in horror as Jesus was taken away. Judas and Peter were both amazed. Jesus would not fight! This couldn't be happening. He had fed thousands of people, turned water into wine, walked on water and calmed massive thunder storms. Why could he not fight off a few soldiers?

Because it was not his plan.

All of Jesus' friends then did what?

1. Ran away
2. Chased after Jesus and the bad guys
3. Had a prayer meeting
4. Put out the news on Facescroll

Answer: 1

Everyone ran away. Except Peter and Judas; they followed Jesus to see what would happen. This was easy for Judas because the bad guys knew he was helping them. But Peter got into trouble. Three times people stopped to ask if he was friends with Jesus. What did Peter say?

1. 'Can I phone a friend?'
2. 'You're having a laugh.'
3. 'I can't remember.'
4. 'Let's ask the audience.'

Answer: 2

Peter said that he did not know Jesus at all. Never seen him before. Oh dear. That's when he started to cry. Peter realised he had given up on his closest friend. He fell to his knees in the dark and cried. It was no surprise though.

Why not?

1. It was all part of the plan
2. Peter was always making mistakes
3. Peter was a coward
4. Jesus had told him this would happen

Answer: 4

Jesus had told Peter earlier that day that he would pretend he did not know him. But he also said something else, something Peter should have remembered. Something that would have helped him. What was it?

1. Always look on the bright side of life
2. It'll be all right in the end, so if it's not all right, it's not the end
3. Be cool
4. Afterwards, help your mates

Answer: 4

Jesus had told Peter this. 'You will be tested. But I've prayed for you and afterwards I want you to strengthen your friends.'

In other words, Peter may have blown it by denying he knew his friend, but it wouldn't be the end. Afterwards, Jesus had a new plan for Peter.

But for now it's over to a man I mentioned earlier – a man called Pilate, Pontius Pilate.

You can check out these
stories in the Bible here:
Mark ch 14 vv 10-11
Mark ch 14 vv 43-50
John 18 vv 12-17
Luke ch 21 vv 31-34
Luke ch 22 vv 54-62

34. Frightful Fit Up

It was a horrible night for Jesus. The worst kind. And in some ways you could say it was the worst night in the history of the world. Terrible. Yet it was also the best. That's weird, isn't it?

When Jesus got arrested by those soldiers in the garden, he was taken to a powerful man called Annas, who asked him tough questions. Then he was taken to Annas's son-in-law, Caiaphas, who was a powerful priest. He asked Jesus more questions. Then Jesus was thrown in a prison cell for a while, before being taken out and beaten up. Then he was taken to a big meeting of lots of religious leaders who asked him more questions. This was like being in court. The religious leaders had already decided their verdict though. This was not a fair trial. They wanted Jesus dead. And to do that, they needed the help of the Romans. Why?

1. The Romans owned all the crosses
2. The Romans said that they were the only ones who could execute people
3. The Romans liked Jesus
4. The Romans were good at killing

Answer: 2 (although 4 is true as well)

The Romans were very good at killing people. They had worked out the best ways to do it, which is why they had a massive world empire that lasted about a thousand years. But that's another story. The main reason the religious leaders needed the Romans was to kill Jesus for them. The Jews were not allowed to do it.

So they sent Jesus to Pontius Pilate. Who was he?

1. An airline pilate
2. A fighter pilate
3. The Roman Emperor
4. The head honcho round those parts

Answer: 4

He was in charge of that bit of the world. He didn't live in Jerusalem, but whenever there was a big festival like Passover, he came to visit, to remind everyone that he was in charge. So the religious leaders took Jesus to Pilate. Pilate didn't want to get involved really. You may remember his wife had had that dream, warning him about this man Jesus. But Caiaphas and Annas and the others persuaded him. How did they do that?

1. They offered him free chocolate
2. They said he was their hero
3. They said they'd tell on him
4. They said he was a big baby

Answer: 3

They threatened to tell the Roman Emperor if Pilate refused to kill Jesus. They told him that Jesus was causing trouble, and was going to start a revolution. The Romans did not like people starting revolutions, so things looked bad. But Pilate decided to send Jesus to someone else. The other big leader in that part of the world – the Jewish king – Herod. So they dragged Jesus to see him. What did Herod say?

1. 'Pleased to meet you!'
2. 'What's your name again?'
3. 'Are you after my job?'
4. 'Do a quick miracle, go on!'

Answer: 1 & 4

Herod had heard about Jesus and was desperate to meet him. He had also heard about Jesus' miracles and wanted to see one for himself. However, Jesus said nothing. Not one word, and Herod was disappointed. So he got his men to dress Jesus up. What clothes did he give him?

1. A technicolour dreamcoat
2. A camel's hair onesie
3. A duffel coat
4. Bright shining clothes

Answer: 4

Bright shining clothes, probably white.

Then Herod sent Jesus back to Pilate, all dressed up, and he was most likely sending Pilate a message with these clothes. He was saying, 'Jesus looks innocent enough to me. Here he is for you, dressed up white and bright.'

Pilate was...

1. Pleased
2. Jealous
3. Dazzled
4. Asking to borrow the clothes

Answer: 1

Pilate was pleased because he thought Jesus was innocent and so did Herod. But the religious leaders were still calling for death. So in the end Pilate offered them a way out. He brought out another criminal, Barabbas. What does the name Barabbas mean?

1. Big strong rebel
2. Substitute
3. The father's son
4. The mother's daughter

Answer: 3

Barabbas's name means 'the son of the father', which is interesting because Jesus was the son of God the father. Pilate said that the people could choose which man to set free. Barabbas was a big rebel, a man of war who wanted to kill the Romans. Jesus was another kind of rebel, a man of peace who wanted to help the Romans. And everyone else. Pilate offered to kill one of them, and asked which one he should release.

I guess we all know the answer by now. The religious leaders told everyone to shout for Barabbas. Barabbas was then freed and Jesus was taken away to die. It was a horrible fit up. A complete set up. And yet God used it. It looked as if everything had gone wrong, and yet this was the plan God used to change everything.

Jesus was nailed to a cross, the punishment for rebels and slave, between two others and there he died. How many things did he say before he died?

1. One
2. Three
3. Five
4. Seven

Answer: 4

Here's a list.

1. He asked God to forgive everyone for what they had done.
2. He asked for a drink.
3. He asked his friend John to look after his mother for him.
4. He told one of the men dying beside him that he would be in paradise with Jesus that very day.
5. He cried out in terrible anguish – asking God why he had forsaken him.
6. He told everyone that his death finished something.
7. He committed himself into God's hands.

After six hours he was dead. They took him down from the cross and Nicodemus helped put him in a tomb he owned.

The End

Or is it?

1. Yes
2. No
3. Maybe
4. Keep reading

Answer: You choose

You can check out these
stories in the Bible here:
John ch 18
Luke ch 23
John ch 19
Matthew ch 27 vv 45-66

35. Shambolic Shocking Surprises

Question: where was everyone?

The day we now call Easter Sunday was full of shocks. To start with Jesus may have got a shock when he walked out of that tomb early on Easter Sunday morning. Because there was no one there. There were no decorations, no band playing, no party food, no fireworks.

And yet he'd told his friends again and again that he was coming back. He'd told them that the Romans would kill him, but that three days later they would see him alive again.

So where were they all?

1. Asleep
2. Hiding
3. In a hole in the ground
4. Gone to *Specsavers*

Answer: possibly 1, 2 & 3, but definitely not 4

They were all scared. They were shocked that Jesus had been killed, they thought he would fight back or do a miracle to escape. They were now scared that the Romans would come looking for all Jesus' friends and kill them too. So they were nowhere to be seen.

Or were they? Actually there were a few people there. All of them were women. In some countries where it is dangerous to move about the men stay inside so they cannot be attacked or killed. But often the women can move around safely because the bad guys don't think they will cause any trouble.

So a group of women who had been friends of Jesus went to the tomb to see his body. It had only been left temporarily in Nicodemus's tomb. The women wanted to make sure it was ready to be buried properly.

But it wasn't there!

What do David Copperfield, Penn and Teller, Paul Daniels, Derren Brown and Jesus have in common?

They all did famous disappearing tricks.

The people who killed Jesus put guards on his tomb to stop anyone stealing the body.

But the guards fell asleep and then there was… what?

1. A mini earthquake which made them run like mad
2. A flash mob routine which made them join in
3. An ice cream van which made them buy 99s
4. A fire drill which made them run to the nearest exit

Answer: 1

The ground shook and the guards ran away scared. The earthquake cracked open the cave where Jesus' body was being stored and when the group of women arrived and looked in the tomb, what did they see?

1. An angel
2. A couple of angels
3. Some shepherds and three wise men
4. Casper the friendly ghost

Answer: 1 & 2

There was a lot of confusion and running about that morning – why wouldn't there be: a body was missing! In the TV series *Fawlty Towers* there was chaos and confusion when they unexpectedly found a body in a bed. This is the other way round – they were supposed to find a body and couldn't! So there was chaos and confusion and the stories afterwards from those who were there are all a bit mixed up.

Some say there was an angel in the tomb, some say there were two. What they all agree on is this: there was no Jesus. He was absolutely and totally not lying there stone cold dead in the tomb. He had gone. And there was no Casper the friendly ghost either. No ghosts at all. And the shepherds and the wise men may have made a big fuss at his Christmas birth, but it was only his close friends who caught his death-smashing Easter moment.

So… had someone stolen the body? The woman ran back to the rest of the gang and told the men. Peter and John, Jesus' closest mates, came running back to the tomb. They had forgotten the danger now. They wanted to find out what was happening. Who got there first?

1. Peter
2. John
3. Usain Bolt
4. Casper the friendly ghost

Answer: 2

He may not have been able to run quite as fast as Mr Bolt but John was younger and he sped ahead.

However, he didn't go in. He may have been faster because he was younger, but he may have been more nervous too. It was Peter, the big blunderer, who pushed past him and went straight in. They needn't have worried. All they found was an empty pile of cloth – grave wrappings – no Jesus. Peter was confused. John started to put two and two together and work out the mystery.

Mary was left alone by the tomb after all the fuss had died down. What happened next?

1. She saw a gardener
2. She fell asleep
3. Some grave robbers made her jump
4. Jesus crept up on her

Answer: 1, 3 & 4

She looked in the tomb and saw two angels who asked her why she was crying so much. She asked them if they were grave robbers. And if so could they give her the body back. Then she saw the gardener and she asked him if he knew where the body was. The gardener said her name and suddenly she knew.

Massive shock! Her eyes burst wide and her mouth fell open. She started crying and laughing at the same time and she ran to hug him. It was Jesus. He was back. It was the best feel-good ending of them all. The feel-good ending to feel-good-end all the feel-good-endings in the history of the world.

The rest of his friends took a while to find out. Maybe they should have all gone to *Specsavers*; then they would have been ready to see what Mary and lots of other people have been finding out ever since, Jesus wasn't dead. Against all the odds he was alive.

You can check out these stories in the Bible here:
Matthew ch 28 vv 1-15
Mark ch 16 vv 1-14
Luke ch 24 vv 1-12
John ch 20 vv 1-31

36. Astronomical Ascension

Just when everything looked amazing, fabtastic, wackawonderfabulous and hunky dory – it all fell apart again. Why?

1. Jesus told them he was leaving
2. Jesus went back to being a builder
3. His friends started playing *Angry Birds* on their new iParchments
4. They all entered *Nazareth's Got Talent*

Answer: 1

Just when they were over the moon about having him back, Jesus told them he was going over the moon back to his father. Actually, he wasn't really flying up in the sky – but back into another dimension. God's dimension. So how did he go?

1. On a hovercraft
2. On a skateboard
3. He flew
4. He cartwheeled

Answer: 3

He took his friends for a walk to a place called the Mount of Olives. There he said a few goodbye words about them travelling throughout the world and then just sort of flew up into the air. But not by flapping his arms, or getting on a plane. Instead he gently rose up and melted from one dimension to another. A cloud came down and he disappeared into it.

It was a bit like the way Elijah went up to heaven in Old Testament days, and when Elijah went he gave his power to Elisha, the man he left behind. So it would have reminded the guys of that. It was another sign that Jesus was from God. But why did he go?

1. He was bored
2. He wanted a holiday
3. He wanted to leave someone else in charge
4. He was scared of the Romans

Answer: 3

He needed to go away so that his friends would start doing what he had done. While he was around they might keep asking him to do everything. By going he made it possible for them to have his power.

It was as if Jesus went away to turn on the electricity so that everyone could use it. He told his friends that if he went away they'd be able to do even more than he had done.

What did the disciples do?

1. Made loads of plans
2. Stood around looking silly
3. Got confused
4. Tried to flap their arms and fly after him

Answer: 2

They weren't sure what to do next, so two angels had to show up and tell them to go back to Jerusalem and wait for Jesus to turn on the power. They still wanted Jesus to come back and make everything okay, but the angels told them to get busy doing nothing for a while. So they did.

You can check out these
stories in the Bible here:
Matthew ch 28 vv 16-20
Mark ch 16 vv 19-20
Luke ch 24 vv 50-53
Acts ch 1 vv 6-11
2 Kings ch 2 vv 11-12

37. Powerful Pentecost

The rest of the story begins with the day we now call The Day of Pentecost. Jesus turned on the power and his friends, those ordinary, scared people, started to change the world.

You can read the story in...

1. The Book of Acts
2. The Book of Beadle the Bard
3. The Dangerous Book for Boys
4. The Big Book of Bedtime Stories

Answer: 1

The stories of the first Christians and their ups and downs are told in the book of Acts in the New Testament. I might do a sequel one day, a book like this all about their adventures. Watch this space, as they say...

In the meantime, here's a potted version of what happened next. The story of the day when the church began, the Day of Pentecost:

Now not long ago down Jerusalem way
A bunch of folks from the town got together to pray.
Well they prayed all night and they prayed all day
And they waited on the Lord to see what He would say.

Then all of a sudden, as a matter of fact,
The Holy Spirit came down and they all got zapped!
And they all jumped up, started praising the Lord
In languages they never even heard before.

Well! They had a praise meeting and the ground it shook
And it weren't like nothing in the new common worship book.
And Peter got up and he hit 'em fast
With a 3 point sermon like a shotgun blast.

And the apostles translated every single phrase
Into 9,327 different languages...
And the people couldn't cope when they heard it all
So they all come forward for an altar call.

"You'd better be baptised," they heard Peter say.
So 3,000 people took a bath that day.
And once again the Holy Spirit came down
But it was all in good taste and theologically sound.

And there were healings and miracles, it all happened so fast
And the people wondered if it could ever last.
But the Holy Spirit – he gave 'em a shove -
Pushed 'em out round the world to share God's love.

You can check out these
stories in the Bible here:
Acts ch 2

38. Messiah's Thirteen - Can You Name 'em?

Earlier in this book, in the chapter called *The Great Israeli Discipleship Challenge*, I wrote about Jesus' friends. The gang he gathered together to go with him on his adventures. The dudes who went from fishing and taxes and revolutionary gangs and jobs about which we know absolutely nothing, to changing the world.

Well, here's a final chapter about those guys. And ultimately there weren't twelve - there were thirteen.

Why was that?

1. Jesus miscounted
2. One of the disciples pulled a sickie
3. Thirteen is a Saviour's dozen
4. An extra snuck in with a false beard on

Answer: 2

It was more than a sickie actually. Judas killed himself after getting Jesus arrested. He wasn't likely to be going on any more adventures with the rest of the gang. So the others prayed about it, made a short list of two, and put the names in a hat. And the winner was... well, let's see.

Can you remember all the names of Jesus' friends, also known as the disciples? And looking at this list can you guess which one's which?

1. The Shouty One
2. The Go-between One
3. The Doubty One
4. The Naughty One
5. The Well-liked One
6. The Clumsy One
7. Not The Shouty One
8. The Money-grabbing One
9. The Friendly One
10. The One We Know Nothing About
11. The Fighty One
12. Not The Naughty One
13. The Replacement One

Answers (check out Matthew 12, Acts 1):

1. **The Shouty One**. James, nicknamed a 'Son of Thunder' presumably 'cause he was 'a bit loud'. (Mark ch 3 v 17 & Matthew ch 10 v 2)

2. **The Go-between One**. Andrew, only the guy who brought (drum roll) Peter (fanfare) to Jesus. Oh and he only kicked off the biggest miracle in history, the one

with five thousand munchers and all the leftovers. He brought the kid with five loaves to Jesus. Often remembered as Peter's brother. Maybe just a tad frustrating for a sibling? A little overlooked perhaps? (John ch 1 vv 35-43 & John ch 6 vv 8-9 & Matthew ch 10 v 2)

3. **The Doubty One**, a.k.a. 'The Twin'. Thomas, went down in history as the only one who ever doubted. Yeah, right. Don't know who his twin was though. Terry, maybe? (John ch 20 vv 24-28 & Matthew ch 10 v 3)

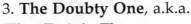

4. **The Naughty One**. Judas Iscariot, of course. (Mark ch 14 vv 10-11 & John ch 12 vv 4-6 & Matthew ch 10 v 4)

5. **The Well-liked One**. John. The disciple who was really close to Jesus, according to... er... John. (John ch 13 v 23 & John ch 1 vv 1-10 & Matthew ch 10 v 2)

6. **The Clumsy One**. Peter, of course. Previously known as Simon. Always making bloopers and putting his foot in it. Couldn't even walk on water, for goodness sake. Tried to do surgery on a servant in a garden. (Matthew ch 14 vv 22-32 & Matthew ch 26 vv 69-75 & John ch 18 vv 10-11 & Matthew ch 10 v 2)

7. **Not The Shouty One**. James, another James. a.k.a. the son of Alphaeus. As was Matthew (Levi) maybe they were brothers? (Mark ch 2 v 14 & Mark ch 3 v 18 & Matthew ch 10 v 2)

8. **The Money-grabbing One**. Matthew (Levi). The one with the most to lose. He had a good job making lots of money for himself and the Romans. He couldn't go back to work if the following Jesus went pear-shaped. It was all right for them fishermen – they could just jump back in the boat again, if things didn't work out. Which is exactly what they did. But Matthew couldn't do that. When you jump ship from working with the Romans they don't welcome you back with a hug and a caramel smoothie. It's worth noting that the rest of the gang didn't trust him to look after the money. They

gave it to a much more reliable disciple – Judas. Ah… bit of a snag there… (Mark ch 2 v 14, Matthew ch 9 vv 9-13, John ch 12 vv 4-6 & Matthew ch 10 v 3)

9. **The Friendly One**. Philip. Brought his mate
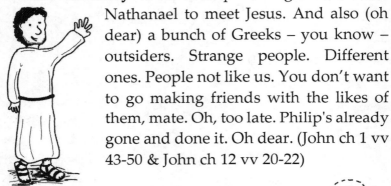
Nathanael to meet Jesus. And also (oh dear) a bunch of Greeks – you know – outsiders. Strange people. Different ones. People not like us. You don't want to go making friends with the likes of them, mate. Oh, too late. Philip's already gone and done it. Oh dear. (John ch 1 vv 43-50 & John ch 12 vv 20-22)

10. **The One We Know Nothing About**, Bartholomew. A.k.a. Nathaniel, maybe. He was the one who was, er… alive. Yup. And a man. Unless that was a false beard he was wearing. (John ch 1 vv 43-50 & Matthew ch 10 v 3 & Acts ch 1 v 13)

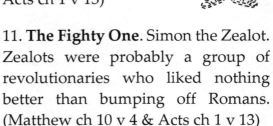

11. **The Fighty One**. Simon the Zealot. Zealots were probably a group of revolutionaries who liked nothing better than bumping off Romans. (Matthew ch 10 v 4 & Acts ch 1 v 13)

12. **Not The Naughty One**. Judas, son of James. Ooh! Unfortunate name. Not the Judas who ended up killing himself. This one was also known as Thaddaeus. Perhaps not a bad idea to have an alternate name in this case. (Matthew ch 10 v 3 & Luke ch 6 v 16 & Acts ch 1 v 13)

13. **The Replacement One**. The one who stepped into Judas's shoes. Hard act to follow? Er… no not really. He got picked on that old quiz show – *Have You Got the Discipleship Factor?* 'So please welcome your hosts Peter, James and John. (lots of applause and overblown music) And please welcome our two finalists – Barsabbas and Matthias. Only one of these great men can go through… which one will it be? Will it be Barsabbas or Matthias? Matthias or Barsabbas? Barsabbas or Matthias? Matthias or Barsabbas?

(Prolonged tense music plays, both look nervous, judges confer, the phone lines close, then Peter holds up the card with the result on it.)

This year's winner of *Have You Got the Discipleship Factor* is…. (long, long, long, long, long, long, long, long, long, long, long………….. pause………) Matthias!

Congratulations! Barsabbas - sorry mate. Maybe next year? You just have to wait for another disciple to er... oh... let's not go there... never mind.' Mind you, even though Matthias got picked we don't hear anything else about him. (Acts ch 1 vv 12-26)

39. Messiah's Thirteen II: Dubious Deaths

There's an amazing thing about Jesus' friends: they separated and went all over the place, and every one of them was willing to die for the Messiah they met all those years ago in a little-known place going by the name of Galilee. And as a result, as I mentioned earlier, there are now...

1. One thousand Christians
2. One million Christians
3. One billion Christians
4. One trillion Christians

Answer: 3

A few friends of Jesus has now become millions and millions.

So, now you know the names of those first thirteen disciples, and you know my descriptions, would you like to know what happened to them? Warning – it's not nice. These guys really gave everything for Jesus. So feel free to close the book now. And if you are doing that, thanks for reading this book, and this is...

The End

However, if you would like to know more, then here's another quiz. Can you put a name to these deaths? They happened to the different disciples.

Caution – if you are still reading you might need a cushion to hide behind.

1. Killed by a sword
2. Crucified upside-down
3. Died of old age on an island somewhere
4. Skinned alive
5. Crucified diagonally
6. Crucified upside-down with his mate Bartholomew, but while he was on it he preached a sermon
7. Possibly beheaded
8. Unknown; possibly burned, stoned or beheaded
9. Stoned and stabbed with a lance
10. Definitely beheaded
11. Sawn in half
12. Died of old age in Rome
13. Hung himself

See what I mean. A bit shocking, eh?

Answers (these are according to legend and Wikipedia so it must be absolutely and totally true…):

1. **Killed by a sword**. James. Possibly by Herod in

Jerusalem. Although one story claims he was clubbed to death in Egypt. And there are pictures to prove it! Not photos though, just painted ones.

2. **Crucified upside-down**. Peter. That Roman nutter Emperor Nero took revenge for the fire-starters in Rome by killing lots of Christians. Peter was one of them. If Nero

wanted to catch the real perpetrator, he should have looked in the mirror. He was most likely the real fire-starter.

3. **Died of old age on an island somewhere**. John,

probably on Patmos, after seeing the big screen bit of the Bible, a.k.a. Revelation. Worth noting that the one book in the Bible entitled 'Revelation' is the one we can't understand. Maybe some pictures could have helped? Cartoons and a bit of video?

4. **Skinned alive** then crucified. Bartholomew. In  Albania after converting the King of Armenia. The king's brother was well-miffed. WELL-miffed. As you can tell from the outcome.

5. **Crucified diagonally**. Andrew. In Greece. Legend has it he requested to be crucified in an X-shape, because he didn't see himself as good enough to  die in the same way Jesus did. I reckon Andrew was a humble guy, often in his big brother's shadow.

6. **Crucified upside-down with his mate**  **Bartholomew, but while he was on it he preached a sermon**. Philip - and his sermon was good enough to get Bartholomew set free from the cross beside him. Now that's what I call preaching.

7. **Possibly beheaded**. Matthew. Probably. He went a long way, whatever. Converted Ethiopians, Macedonians, Persians and Parthians. Busy man. He is now the  patron saint of bankers – which rather misses the point because... well... not to put too fine a point on it, didn't he give all that up? Awkward.

8. **Unknown; possibly burned, stoned or beheaded**. Judas a.k.a. Thaddaeus. When he was in Syria with his mate Simon the Zealot. Spreading the gospel, not on holiday.

9. **Stoned and stabbed with a lance**. Thomas. In India.  Which just goes to show that you can be the biggest doubter in history and still go half way round the world converting people.

10. **Beheaded**. James son of Alphaeus. Herod Agrippa ordered it in Jerusalem. Both Jameses are said to have been topped by this bad guy.

11. **Sawn in half**. Simon the Zealot. Actually - there are  lots of theories about him. Sawn in half in Persia. Killed in a Jewish uprising by the Romans (because as a Zealot he was a revolutionary). Crucified in Samaria. And even... came to Glastonbury and got bumped off in the UK in Lincolnshire. Probably depends which first century newspaper you read.

12. **Hung himself**. Judas Iscariot (the naughty one).  Also fell in a field and split open. Depends which way you read the story. Maybe hung himself and then his body fell, bounced against a rock, flew up a little, spun in the air, got shaken up and burst on impact. A sticky end either way.

13. **Died of old age in Rome**. Matthias. Or crucified in Georgia. Or stoned and beheaded in Jerusalem. There are different stories. I know which one I'd choose.

40. Wonderful Women

But what about those other disciples – the women you have been reading about? They are just as important of course. We know that lots of women had been friends of Jesus – Salome, Susanna, Joanna, Mary and Martha, and plenty of others. Some of them got into trouble for being disciples but it didn't stop them.

So, what happened to them after Jesus left?

1. They gave up
2. They disguised themselves as men and put on false beards
3. They went on *The Great Israeli Bake Off*
4. No idea

Answer: 4

We don't really know, but we do know this. Jesus had treated women just like men, even though he wasn't supposed to in his day. Women were seen as what we call second-class citizens by the men. They could not vote in an election, for example. Men were seen as much more important.

But Jesus taught the women the same things that he taught the men, and he took them out on his missions. No other rabbis did that. Plus – and this is the BK Whopper, the Big Mac, the Double Whammy – when

Jesus rose from the dead he appeared to the women first, not the men. TO THE WOMEN!

Why was this so daft?

1. The women might scream and faint
2. The women were not trusted to tell the truth
3. The women might forget
4. The women might give up and go on *The Great Israeli Bake Off*

Answer: 2

Women could not stand up in court and give evidence. So why bother appearing to them, when they couldn't be trusted to tell the truth about this amazing thing? Because Jesus didn't see it like that. He trusted them and asked them to spread the news, just like the men.

Women went on to be really important in the church, and after Jesus left them to carry on the work they did very radical things. For example: baby girls were often left abandoned by their parents, as people wanted their children to be boys not girls. Boys were seen as more important.

So what did the friends of Jesus do when they saw these abandoned babies?

1. Ignored the babies
2. Felt sorry for them
3. Collected money for them
4. Became their mums and dads

Answer: 4

The friends of Jesus went round rescuing these baby girls and giving them a home. They then looked after them as their own children. Which is why there were a lot of females in the first churches.

We may not know precisely what happened to Salome, Joanna, Susanna, Mary, Martha and the others, but you can bet they went on to do really important great and small things for Jesus. In the Bible we hear the stories of some other women though. Like Tabitha. What do you think she did?

1. She made ice cream
2. She made clothes
3. She made mistakes
4. She made Prime Minister

Answer: 2

Not only did Tabitha make clothes, but she gave them away. She helped people who were poorer than her.

Just like Mary and Martha had been doing in Bethany, in their House of the Poor. Damaris, Rhoda, Lois and Eunice are just a few of the other women who were among the first Christians, working hard, praying, caring and helping others.

I think that's enough from me now. I hope you have enjoyed this book. I read other books to learn about the stories and get ideas. So here's a list of them.

Books I read that have helped me to write this one:

Whatever Happened to the Ark of the Covenant?
The Wrong Messiah
Kingdom of Fools
All by Nick Page

Jesus Through Middle Eastern Eyes
By Kenneth Bailey

The New Testament For Everyone series
By Tom Wright

That's about it for now. Thanks very much for reading The *Groovy* Gospel.

Dave

Made in the USA
Charleston, SC
23 August 2015

THE
CENTRE
OF MY
EVERYTHING

ALLAYNE L.
WEBSTER

RANDOM HOUSE AUSTRALIA

The author gratefully acknowledges the support of Arts SA in the writing of this book.

A Random House book
Published by Penguin Random House Australia Pty Ltd
Level 3, 100 Pacific Highway, North Sydney NSW 2060
www.penguin.com.au

Penguin
Random House
Australia

First published by Random House Australia in 2018

National Library of Australia
Cataloguing-in-Publication entry

Creator: Webster, Allayne L., author
Title: The centre of my everything/Allayne L. Webster
ISBN: 978 0 14378 333 6 (pbk)
Target audience: For young adults
Subjects: Interpersonal relations – Juvenile fiction
           Families – Juvenile fiction
           Social problems – Juvenile fiction
           Young adult fiction

Cover images: boy Alex Shahmiri/Moment Select/Getty Images;
background Luba V Nel/Shutterstock.com
Cover design by Marina Messiha © Penguin Random House Australia Pty Ltd
Typeset by Midland Typesetters, Australia
Printed in Australia by Griffin Press, an accredited ISO AS/NZS 14001:2004
Environmental Management System printer

Penguin Random House Australia uses papers that are natural, renewable and
recyclable products and made from wood grown in sustainable forests. The
logging and manufacturing processes are expected to conform to the environmental
regulations of the country of origin.

For Peter, my beloved stepfather

I'll hesitate, procrastinate and think about the past.
I'll irritate and suffocate my feelings in a glass.
And I'll keep on chasing shadows, till the dying light of day.
With serenity and God's grace, I'll make it through the day.

– Bec Willis, 'Alcohol and Loneliness'

Corey

My head's gunna explode. I drank Jäger bombs all night. Lost count after ten. That stuff stitches you up good.

Flashes of Craig Carter's eighteenth spin in my head. Clinking bottles. Thrashing tunes. Schoolgirls dancing barefoot on the kitchen bench. Cammo Gibson playing snooker with jocks on his head. Singing vintage INXS into beer-bottle microphones. Spitting out someone's sucked-dry olive pip. A pig, head and all, rotating on an electric spit. Raspberry vodka shots. Craig wearing his mum's nightdress with two strategically positioned rockmelons. Kylie Martin crying hysterically because she'd swallowed a cigarette butt that was floating in her wineglass.

Our usual caper.

My form is probably slipping a bit, but that's what you get after five days on the turps. I got back to town Saturday morning after a footy coaching clinic in Melbourne. Bunch of players from all over the region went, and me and Hamish Johnson were the only Mildura lads to get a guernsey.

As it was, Hamish only scraped in by the skin of his nuts. The stupid idiot thought it'd be a fine idea to take a leak on the oval in front of the CWA ladies, didn't he? Eighty-nine-year-old Mrs Marshall copped an eyeful and practically had a coronary. Coach Robson barrelled Hamish something fierce for that little number, reckoned he'd ban him from the end-of-year footy trip. I had to step in and spin some BS about Hamish having a UTI. Lucky for Hamish, Coach ate it up and told him he could go on the condition he kept it in his pants.

On a footy trip? *As if.*

So the coaching clinic turned out awesome. Full on, but. Those Blanchetown boys gave us a run for our money on *and* off the field – mob of first-class pissheads. I could barely keep up. It's no wonder, after a week like that, we found it hard to pull up sweet for Craig's eighteenth. But we made it, and last night was worth it. *So* worth it.

Things started out all right, like they always do. Hamish was in there, having a crack at Mildura's princess pair: Tara Ramsey and Amy McGovern. He was shooting out of his league, but you have to give him points for trying.

Me? I tried my luck with Keita Sanders. Keita's usually up for it, but last night she pulled the plug for no reason. After the footy trip, I was hanging for some, so what she did was pretty savage, especially after I'd fixed her up with a whole night's worth of grog. I lost the plot. Rammed a pool cue into the table, smashed a perfectly good bottle of whisky. And that's when the fun *really* started. Blokes started swinging and it was on. I reckon we'd been brawling for about five minutes before Craig's old man rocked up, did his trolley and turned a garden hose on the crowd.

Me and Hames didn't stick around. We took my car and laid rubber on the highway – some of my finest circle work too – then hit the cemetery and, well, let's just say we rearranged the furniture. Actually, I don't remember much about that last stop. I do know we gave the council mob something to moan about.

Geez, I need a whiz.

The open bathroom window dangles off the tracking and a mini mountain of black moths pile on the ledge. I take my time, tender bits resting against the cool porcelain bowl. Out in the kitchen, cutlery chimes against china, metal chair legs scrape against slate. Kettle boils, fridge door slams, bottles rattle. A pocket radio dribbles rusty country talkback.

The phone rings and I hear the old man go spare.

'Hey, woman! Ya getting that or what?'

''Cos I've got fifty pairs of hands, haven't I?'

'Flamin' heck!' *Clank. Rustle. Clank.* 'Williams' residence. Oh, g'day, Daryl. How are ya, mate?'

For the next few minutes, all I hear is the old man repeatedly gasping, 'No joke. Is that a fact?'

When he hangs up, the old girl is quicker than flies to a carcass. 'What was that about?'

'*That* was Daryl Sanders.'

Keita's dad. *Shit.* Was he ringing to give me a serve?

'Daryl reckons the cemetery got trashed. He saw the coppers picking over headstones this morning.'

Great. It was worse than I'd thought. I have to buzz Hamish.

'Which cemetery?'

'Not the Murray Pines one, the other one. What's it called?'

'Dunno. You're the one telling the story.'

'Nichols Point Cemetery.'

'Yeah? How bad?'

'Bit of damage to the older plots, a few headstones smashed up. Some of the graves are a bit unstable due to all that recent flooding. Council mob reckon a few stiffies are floating back up for a second coming. I guess it made it a lot easier for the buggers. One grave got broken into.'

'Broken into?'

'They took bones.'

I close my eyes and see Hamish's shadowy outline tossing lumps of dirt and concrete. The pair of us laughing like maniacs. A blackened cavity in the ground. Chiselled white bones glowing in the moonlight.

'*Whose* bones?'

'Do I look like the CSI to you, woman?'

There's a pause. She's probably giving him one of her death stares.

'They know who did it?'

'Had to be outta-towners.'

'Catch 'em?'

'Nah. They're long gone. Left a trail of evidence up Sturt Highway. Skiddies all over the road, the mongrels.'

Heart hammering, I head back to my room. I'm too slow. The old man spies me as I slip past the door.

'Ya suffering, eh, boy?'

'Nah, I'm right . . .'

4

'Yer can't handle it, can ya?' He guffaws, his ample belly bouncing in time with his balding head. 'Yer nothin' but a bloody Cadbury.'

'Steady on,' the old girl cautions. 'Corey doesn't need any encouragement.'

Mum says I'm already a chip off the block at the tender age of eighteen. More like a shaving, says the old man.

'Hurry up and have a shower, Corey. There's stuff your dad needs help with.'

'Oi!' the old man yells. 'If you keep this up, you might even get a patch on ol' Sparksy.'

Old Man Sparks is the town drunk. No one has a patch on him. *No one.* Sparksy spends his days at the pub, holding up the bar. Legend has it, the day he doesn't turn up, the place will fall down.

'I think I'm a fair way off being like Sparksy.'

'Hurry up and get in the shower. We've got the yard to sort out.'

'Where's Felicity? Can't she help?'

The old man's voice jumps an octave. 'Your sister's doing her homework. Year Twelve this year, yer know that. Not that you bloody passed, you lousy no-good dropout.'

'But I've got things I have to –'

'Pull yer finger out! It's eleven o'clock! Other blokes have done a day's work by now and, meanwhile, you're Sleepin' Bloody Beauty!'

I know better than to argue. The last argument we had scored me a shiner. In fact, the last thirty arguments I had scored me something – bloody nose, cork thigh, tinnitus. The old man isn't selective. 'Yeah, all right, give me a minute.'

'*Hurry the fuck up!*'

I close my bedroom door. I kneel on the carpet by my bed and lift the faded blue valance, searching for my phone. Shoving aside soiled jocks, crushed ciggie packets, takeaway containers and empty beer bottles, I find it – screen cracked, a glob of dried gravy stuck to the back. I dial Hamish. I keep dialling until he picks up.

'Geez, Corey . . .' comes Hamish's groggy voice. 'What time is it?'

'The cops know about the cemetery . . . Hamish?'

'Yeah, I heard ya.'

'Where'd you put it?'

'The bag?'

'No, I mean the bowl of bloody goldfish. Of course I mean the bag!'

'Yeah, righto. Settle down. It's under my bed.'

I imagine a set of skeletal teeth smiling up at him. Hollow eyes staring him down. A mottled grey leg bone poised to kick him in the pants. 'Good, 'cos we've gotta take the body back.' *Damn.* 'I mean, we gotta take the bones back.'

'What's the hurry?'

Hamish is thicker than a plank of two-by-four. 'What part of "the cops know" don't you understand?'

'Yeah, but I thought we'd have some fun first. Freak Cammo and the boys.'

And right there – that's Hamish in a nutshell. The cops are crawling all over it and his first instinct is *still* to take it to the limit. If we tell the lads, we're screwed – it'll be all over town. We may as well rock up to the Mildura police station and sign up for council dunny scrubbing.

'We're not telling the boys, Hamish. You can't say a word to anyone.'

'Why not?'

''Cos I'm not getting busted over this! You got that?'

I don't bother telling him my conscience is biting me big time. It might've been funny last night, stealing those bones, but now I'm feeling pretty low about it. What if we dug up a kid? Or a cancer victim? Someone's grandma? My gramps is buried in that cemetery. The idea of disturbing that old coot *is* disturbing.

Hamish laughs. 'Stop stressing, you pussy. We'll sort it out.'

'Look, Hamish, you can't say anything about it, right? Not to anyone.'

The dial tone echoes in my ear. Seconds later he snaps a selfie with overlaid text: *Boner.* There he is: shaggy hair, scruffy three-day growth, grinning at me smug-as. He's holding one of the bones – a long one – to his groin.

Nothing like recording the evidence. Or overcompensating on size.

Hamish Johnson might be pure dynamite on the footy field and wicked good value for a night out, but he's also a bit of a knobhead. Everyone knows you can screw around when you're tanked, but you've gotta know when to stop. There are limits. There's the stuff you do that makes you a legend and the stuff you do that makes you a dickhead.

With Hamish, I regularly feel like I'm straying into dickhead territory.

I grab my boxers and a pair of jeans and head for the shower. The warm water is gold and I'm in no hurry even with the old girl bashing on the door, yelling about the water bill. I consider rubbing one out, but I'm scat and can't even raise a semi.

I scrub and scrub, but as much as I try, I can't wash away what happened last night. Rest in peace, they say. Well, I can't rest – not until all the pieces are back where they should be.

Tara

Squabbling birds fight in the cedar tree outside the kitchen window.

I twist my head under the tap and gulp metallic-tasting water with three ibuprofen. This time they stay down – just. My head spins. I feel like I'm going to spew again. I should've shoved two fingers down my throat as soon as I got home.

I hoist myself onto the marble bench and let the cool stone soothe my bare legs. Thank God Mum's not here to see this. She'd be giving me hell. Deadset, she'd think it was the funniest thing ever. Mum reckons she was exactly the same at my age: partying every weekend, bringing home boys, skipping school, slagging off nerds like that annoying Abo chick Margo Bonney. Difference is, or so Mum says, she knew how to handle it.

I doubt that. She can't even handle it now.

There's no way Mum will find out about last night. She's out of town, camping somewhere up in the Flinders Ranges with her new boyfriend, Trevor. (Forty-eight-year-old women should not have *boyfriends*.) Last time she called, the answering machine got it; I was at school. *Mobile coverage issues, Tara. I'm sorry I forgot to recharge. I lost my phone for a whole day and then I found it in the esky – would you believe that? Of all the places!*

Convenient. And almost believable.

I gulp more water and ignore the nausea swimming in my stomach. Hungover or not, Craig's eighteenth was the bomb. Best party in ages. I laugh out loud when I think of Hamish asking me if we could go somewhere a bit more private – in his dreams! As if I'd ever! And Cammo, total desperado, trying to see up my skirt. That guy is such a sleaze. And then there was Corey. Good old Corey. I wonder how he's feeling after he cut sick at Keita and rammed a pool cue into Craig's dad's table. I bet he woke up to a case of regret-its. Perhaps an even worse case than mine. Or Amy's.

Amy.

She drove us home *smashed*. On her Ls. We'd swerved all over the road because she was trying to get the radio back to FM. At some point we stopped to pee behind a power pole. Amy forgot to pull the handbrake, so the Kombi started rolling and we had to run after it and jump in action-hero style. After that, she turned off the headlights. I'm not even sure what time we stumbled in the door. I've had, like, two hours' sleep.

I ease myself off the bench and head back to bed. If there's one thing I've learned, it's that sleeping off a hangover is the only thing that works.

'Tara! Come quick!' Amy hisses, stopping me in my tracks. She's wearing a white tank top and two-sizes-too-small fluoro green undies. (Hello, bikini wax!) Her black hair is matted with pink glitter. 'Quick, Tara! I mean it!'

I follow her to the living room. 'Amy, if you've chucked on my mum's rug again, I'm not cleaning –'

She points at the couch. 'Who. Is. That.'

My heart pulls up short. A total random is sprawled there, near naked. His hairy legs hug a throw cushion.

Amy looks at me. 'You didn't, *you know* . . .?'

I cock an eyebrow.

'Well, I didn't!' She pauses, rethinking. 'At least, I'm pretty sure I didn't.'

Random Guy is sleeping, one hand buried inside his boxer shorts. Somewhere in the fog, it crosses my mind he could belong to Mum. She's brought home the odd takeaway after a big night out. But this guy looks too young – even for her.

'What do we do?' Amy whispers.

'Call the police.'

'Are you forgetting the police is *my dad*?'

'Breaking and entering is kind of his thing.'

'And how will we explain the Kombi?'

The Kombi.

I go to the window and prise open the blinds. There it is, with one side of my driveway's iron gate stuck to the fender, flowerbed flattened, sandstone mailbox horizontal underneath. 'I'll text Corey. Or Hamish. They'll know who this guy is. They know everyone.'

Amy tips her head sideways, levelling hers with the intruder's. 'Maybe we should panic a bit more. What if he's a mass murderer?'

'Mass murderers don't wear Bugs Bunny boxers.'

Amy goes to the kitchen and grabs a serrated knife. 'I'm not taking any chances.'

I carefully finger the pile of clothes beside him. 'Maybe he has some ID.'

Random Guy stirs. He sits up, leaning on one arm, rubbing a lazy hand over his scrunched-up face. His dark eyes gaze around the room until he focuses on the two of us standing in front of him like some kind of welcoming party. Only then do I remember I'm wearing floral undies the size of Western Australia and my hot-pink bra.

He scratches his neck, half smiling. Then he sees Amy and the knife, and lurches to his feet. He reaches for his jeans, struggling to balance as he shoves in one leg, then the other. 'I'm guessing Zac doesn't live here, then?' He slips into a yellow rainbow-emblazoned T-shirt and grabs his sneakers, clutching them to his chest. He backs across the room, eyes glued on Amy and the knife. Resting against the door, he tugs on his shoes. 'Thanks for the place to crash and, um, sorry.'

The door slams behind him.

I look at the couch, unsure if I dreamt it. Amy plucks a red phone from between the cushions. 'It's dead,' she reports, swiping at the smudged screen.

The doorbell goes off.

Amy thrusts the phone into my hand. 'It's your house.'

I open the door. Couch-crasher slouches against the wall, a hand running through his thick, brown curls. There's a tattoo of a woman's face on his upper arm with a name scrawled beneath but I can't read it. I pass him the phone.

'Cheers.' He points at the Kombi. I see it clearly now: iron bars of our front gate attached to it, like it's some sort of medieval battering ram. 'Had a big one, huh?'

'I'm not the one who slept on a stranger's couch.'

His eyes rake over me. 'I didn't pick a bad house for it.'

I can't help but smirk.

He puts out his hand. 'Justin.'

I don't take it – I can't remember exactly *which* hand was buried in his boxer shorts. 'Tara.'

The intensity of his gaze doesn't shift; I feel like his eyes are eating me for breakfast. 'Do you need help with that?'

I nod towards what was my mum's rose garden. 'Do you know how to fix it?'

'Zac might be able to help.'

'As in the owner of the couch you were meant to be sleeping on?'

'He's a mate of a mate. Someone from the city, actually.' He takes a deep breath. 'I did tell the cabbie thirty-six Jubilee Drive.'

'This is thirty-*three*.'

'Tosser.' He rubs his face, flicking yellow eye crust. 'I could hook up a towrope and drag out the Kombi for you? I know someone with a car who could help.'

I think about it, not sure if I should trust him. Then again, I don't really have another plan. 'Okay, sure. Thanks.'

He winks and walks off, up the driveway. 'Consider it rent and board. See you soon, Tara.'

———

13

Inside, I find Amy squatted against the toilet wall. Her freckled face is a blended shade of green. Dark, unruly hair sticks limp to her forehead.

'Ames?'

She wipes her dripping nose with a scrap of tissue and drops it in the bowl. 'Have I told you I'm *never* drinking again?'

'Once or twice.'

'This time I mean it.' She draws her knees to her chest and buries her head. 'How bad is the van?'

'It has a charming new grille: front gate, circa nineteen fifty-six.'

'Dad's going to kill me.'

I sit on the tiles; they're soothing like the kitchen bench. 'That guy, Justin, said he'd come back and fix it.'

'But what if –'

'Your dad won't find out.'

'But –'

'I promise.'

She looks at me. 'What are you going to tell your mum?'

'The same thing I told myself when I woke up this morning: Corey came over and hit the gate by accident. Mum already knows he's a hopeless driver. He almost rear-ended her in the supermarket car park the other day. Her insurance will cover it.'

'Wow,' Amy says admiringly, 'you have an answer for everything.' She swipes her phone, scrolling. Something catches her attention and she giggles.

I peer over her shoulder. 'Any good pics from last night?'

'A few . . .' She keeps scrolling. 'Check this out.'

She shows me Cammo's Facebook post – a photo of chunks of concrete and dirt scattered across a lawn. The area is swathed with yellow police tape. I quickly realise it's been shared from the official police site.

Amy reads aloud the accompanying text. 'Police are investigating the wilful destruction of property at Nichols Point Cemetery. During the early hours of Sunday morning, a grave was desecrated and a body disinterred. Witnesses are being sought. Family members are being notified.'

'Disinterred?'

'Someone dug up a body.'

'Are you for real?'

Amy puts down her phone. 'I guess that's Dad taken care of. He definitely won't notice the Kombi now.'

I lean my head against the wall and stretch my legs flat, bookends to Amy's. 'Digging up a body is a pretty sick act. Who would do something like that?'

She shrugs. 'Dunno.'

'Do you think it was someone from the party?'

'Maybe.'

We sit there for a while, not saying anything. Then Amy slaps her forehead. 'God! My head is killing me! Tell me again why we do this to ourselves?'

''Cos when you're thumping your body to the music nothing else matters.'

She smiles weakly. 'I wish it could stay like that.'

'Me too.' I don't really mean it, though. There's a limit, you know? Friday and Saturday night is respectable. The occasional

15

triple-header is also okay, but every Sunday is getting a bit try-hard. And during the week? That's just sad. I knock my knee into Amy's. 'What time do you have to be home?'

'I've got to be at Margo's by two.'

'Margo Bonney? *Why?*'

'Vermont paired us for the History assignment. I didn't get a say in it.'

I whistle long and loud.

'Stop it . . .' Amy laughs.

'Spending an afternoon with Margo Bonney on the back of a hangover – now, *that's* cruel.'

'She's not that bad, Tara.'

'You think?'

Amy rolls her eyes.

'I'm surprised Vermont didn't offer you a three-week extension. He *loves* the Abo kids. You should milk it. I would.'

Amy is about to say something, when her face turns an even greener shade of green. She gets on her knees and hangs over the toilet bowl. I hold back her hair. I'm about to go out in sympathy, but I swallow hard and manage to keep it down.

Hovering over the spew-spattered porcelain, Amy wipes her mouth. 'Tara?'

'Hmm?'

'Kylie Martin's eighteenth is next Saturday.'

'Is Corey fixing us up?'

'He said he would.'

I get to my feet. 'Take your time. There's a couple of bits you forgot to coat.'

'Oh, you're hilarious . . .'

'I should get dressed before Justin comes back.'

She reaches up and flicks my undies. 'Why do that?'

I rifle through my tallboy, pushing aside piles of tank tops and denim cut-offs to unearth last season's bikini. I hold it up. The blue fabric is faded and smells manky, but a spray of Impulse should do the trick. Justin couldn't take his eyes off me. It felt good to be noticed. *Really good.*

I shove my clothes back in the drawer and, as I do, nudge the photo frame I keep buried at the bottom – I'd almost forgotten it was there. I pull it out. It's the picture of us on our first family holiday to Cairns when I was six years old. I'm sitting on Dad's lap, cuddling him by a sparkling pool. Palm trees sway, the sky bluer than blue. Mum smiles a huge smile. So do I. Dad looks as happy as a pig in mud.

Photos lie.

I put it back and head for the shower.

When the water hits me, I start to feel human again; the churning in my stomach subsides and my head feels clearer, calmer. I've ridden the scariest ride in the fun park and come out the other side a survivor. Nothing on this planet could make me feel better than that.

Not even my dad remembering I exist.

Or my mum.

Justin

That Tara chick. *Wow.*

I leave her house and make my way up the footpath, sun smacking my face. The street is dead, no cars, no one around. Heat pulses my skin. Sweat pours rivers down my forehead, stinging my eyes. I'm surrounded by a haze of fruit trees. Fallen oranges rotting in the soil. Polka-dot sunspots burning scars on my retinas.

I'm full of scars.

When counsellors tell you to give up the junk, they conveniently make it sound like you'll get a whole new life, be reincarnated – new head, new body, new attitude, the works. No one tells you you'll have to crawl back to the hellhole you grew up in just to get your life back on track, or how humiliating that will be.

Mildura is my hellhole and today the Devil has turned up the heat. The sky was bucketing the day I skipped town. From the back seat of the coach, it looked like Mildura was under water. *Sinking.* People were drowning – they just didn't know it. I was one of the lucky ones who'd made it onto a life raft. It didn't matter which way I floated, somewhere –

anywhere – would do. What I didn't know then was that I'd end up drifting for the next ten years.

Last night I told the cabbie to take me back to Melbourne. He said I couldn't afford the fare, nor could he afford the serve he'd get from his missus if he was home late from work. So I told him to take me to Zac's place instead. That's the last thing I remember. How I ended up on a sofa in Underwear Heaven is anyone's guess. My empty pockets give no clues – no receipts, no money and definitely not the address I'd scrawled on the back of a coaster. All I have is my phone, even if the battery has been dead for two days.

I turn the corner, headed for town.

I walk past a yard full of children's toys lost in sky-high grass. A rusted petrol drum and a stained, moth-eaten lounge grace the front porch of a turn-of-the-century bungalow. I don't recognise the street or the house. I thought the landscape of Mildura was mapped to my soul. Time has marched on, marched all over the things I thought I knew, reminding me I know nothing. I'm still the same clueless dirtbag I was at fourteen, still without a cent to my name. I have to get my hands on some cash. Short of pulling a fasty on the chemist gift shop, my old man is the only one I can hit up for a loan.

I'll find him where he always is: propping up the bar at his local. If there's one thing that's a sure-fire bet, Dad won't have moved a muscle in the last ten years. He'll be sitting under the TAB sign, racehorses galloping past on an overhead flat screen, a near-empty pint glass in one hand, stacking and restacking a pile of coins with his other. That's how I'd seen my old man every day of my childhood: barely upright, surrounded by printed dreams in the form of white race-bet cards. The barman never asked and neither did the old man. It's what's called a silent agreement – the beer is poured and the record tallied. Dad paid his tab with the TAB. There's irony in that, I reckon.

'You bushed, mate?' The kid bounces a red footy and grins a gob full of neon-white teeth at me. I have no idea where he came from; it's as though he fell from the sky. 'You not from round here?'

I could tell him I was once, in another lifetime.

He laughs. 'Didn't think so.'

'What gave me away?'

'That T-shirt you got on. No one wears that city-boy dance clobber round here.' He drops the ball on his foot and flings it up. His limbs are gangly like a baby giraffe's, skin browner than burnt syrup. 'Where you headed, mate? Maybe I'll show you the way. Us blokes good trackers, mate. Find anything you want,' he adds, taking the piss.

The kid's wearing new sneakers with no socks. For no good reason, I wonder if he lifted them. Then I want to smack my head for being a racist pig. Jesus, that's the old man coming out in me. You can run, but you can't hide.

A girl catches up to him, head down as she speaks. 'Bradley, stop messing around. We gotta get this stuff home.'

Here's the thing. In the movies, when a guy sees a beautiful girl, his heart stops and he gets all breathless and awkward and shit. I thought that stuff was bogus. Not any more. My heart blows up like a solar flare. She's even more gorgeous than that

Tara girl – and that's saying something. Her skin isn't as dark as the kid's, and her eyes are brown and soft, arms muscular and strong. In Melbourne, she would have been plucked off the street and sent marching down the catwalk.

'Come on, Bradley. *Move.*' She carries five plastic shopping bags bulging with groceries. Her arm is curled under one stretched taut by loaves of bread and cartons of milk.

The kid bounces his ball. 'What's the hurry, Margo? It's not like the milk's going to go off, is it?'

Margo. Her name is Margo.

'The milk's not going to curdle, but –'

As if on cue, the bag bursts and my shoes are bathed in white. Other products thud onto the asphalt. Margo bends to collect them. She stuffs them into the remaining bags. To help her out, I reach for a little pink box. Our hands lock over it. *Shit.* It's a box of tampons. I let go, stung.

She turns and charges up the road, bags swinging pendulums at her sides.

'Margo!' Bradley yells. 'Wait!'

But she marches on, tumble of glossy hair swaying in the sun.

'Gotta go,' he says, flashing a cheeky smile. 'You should know better than to touch that women's gear. She's not gunna speak to me for a week.' He runs after her, football tucked under his arm. 'Maybe you've done me a favour, mate!'

I look down at my T-shirt. *Dance clobber.* The kid's right – I do look like an outsider. I rip it off and leave it hanging on a fence post.

My lips are leather. It's strange how you can drink yourself into oblivion the night before and wake up thirsty. A hose lies running on someone's lawn. I grab it and spray my shoes, my head, slurping like a dog.

'Whatdaya reckon you're doing?' A screen door slams and a blur of blue singlet and denim shorts flies my way. Poly pipe waves in my face. 'Go on, get outta here, ya flamin' mongrel!'

Ducking for cover, I realise I'd know that voice anywhere, no matter how many years have passed. It's my dad's mate Tiny Johnson.

'Go on with ya! Bugger off, ya hear? And yer put that hose down! We're on water restrictions, ya know! Ya can't go round drinking other people's water whenever ya feel like it!'

'Tiny?'

He squints through gaffa-taped glasses, bulbous nose sniffing. 'No! It can't be . . . Sparksy's boy?'

'Yeah. Surprise!'

'Well, damn it, why didn't ya say so?'

I'm engulfed by a sea of hairy armpit, layers of belly fat and cold sweat. Just as quick, I'm thrown to the lawn. Tiny towers over me, ready to strike.

'Yer poor mum wasn't even cold in the grave and ya just buggered off and left!'

I scramble to my feet, but Tiny is strong for an old bloke and he pins me flat against the fence.

'Where ya been, boy? Where ya been, eh?' His hot breath reeks like week-old roadkill. The hose struggles under his feet, spurting a useless protest. One lingering look and he drops me into the quagmire. 'Ah! I'll get ya a shirt and take ya up the pub. No shirt, no service, these days. Bunch of men gone soft, if you ask me.'

If I thought the old man would recognise me, I needed to think again. Cirrhosis of the liver must travel to the brain. His cloudy eyes swim with prescription gel as he leans in to evaluate me. He produces something white from the bowels of his pocket, pops it on his tongue and takes a swig of beer. 'I ain't got no son,' he slurs.

His words stab and stab again as I curse myself for allowing him to get to me. I'm out of practice. Was I expecting him to roll out the red carpet? Soppy backing music? Nothing's changed.

Tiny parks his considerable arse on a rickety stool and slaps the counter. 'Oi! Coupla beers over here?' The old man shifts his glass under Tiny's nose. 'Make that three!' Tiny corrects. He stuffs a handful of nuts into his mouth and talks through them. 'Sparksy, it's Justin.' He slaps my shoulder. 'Remember? He took off after Martha died.'

The old man shudders at the mention of my mother. 'Don't know what yer on about. Martha cooked me dinner last night. She did, I tell ya. Cooked me rump and three veg exactly the way I like it.'

'Ah, ya stupid old coot!' Tiny roars. 'Ya missus is dead and you know it. Now, turn around and take a good look, man. It's the prodigal son returned. He's your mixed bag of genetic tricks through and through. Swear it blind, I do.'

23

Tiny's a poet who doesn't know it.

The old man gives me the once-over. 'Boy's wearing yer shirt, Tiny. Got that stray dog look about him too.' He pokes my belly. 'Hoping for a free feed, are ya?'

The barman plonks a pint on the beer mat. 'You look like you need this, mate.' His thick fingers are cracked and his smile is exactly the same – a thick, cracked marriage of amusement and disgust.

I push the beer at him. 'I'll have a squash, thanks.'

He tips the beer down the drip tray.

'Sacrilege,' Tiny mutters.

'Name's Graham,' the barman says. 'And for what it's worth, I remember you.'

I don't remember him. Nothing about the place looks the same. The pub had undergone a facelift since I'd seen it last. Sparksy's Saloon, as the old man affectionately called it, now sports a red-gum bar with twenty-something beer taps. Sticky floorboards and cigarette trays have been replaced by commercial-grade carpet and brass foot rails. Fox Sports and MTV play on flat screens, and poker machines sing from where the dining room once was. I remember the old man saying he and Tiny performed a civic duty: they kept the pub solvent and, therefore, the beer flowing. No wonder when it came to me and Mum, his wallet was a dried-up well.

I pick up the squash. There must be a hole in the bottom because I'm soon begging for more.

'See that, Sparksy?' Tiny says. 'Boy has your elbow action.' He shoots up a hand and flags another round. This time

Graham waits for him to produce payment. Tiny hands over a bent-up credit card and Graham hands it back.

'Where am I gunna swipe that, Tiny? That slot poking out the top of yer trousers? Cash or nothin', sunshine.'

Tiny grunts and throws bunched notes onto the counter. 'Happy? Gas'll probably get cut off now.'

'With the amount of hot air you create, I'm sure that won't be a problem.'

'Bloody barmen got an answer for everything,' Tiny grumbles.

The old man rocks on his stool, thumbing the edge of his pint glass. He mutters my name and fumbles for something in his shirt pocket. He pulls out a tattered polaroid and throws it on the counter; a link in his alcohol-riddled chain of broken memories. Mum's pretty face shines up at us. She's pushing me on a swing in one of the local parks. I'm laughing. I'm seven, maybe eight years old, and I'm laughing my head off. I feel a sudden urge to dive into the picture and swing back into her arms. I'd swing and swing forever if it meant being caught by her again.

The old man picks up the photo and holds it by my face. 'Yer look nothin' like him.'

'I need some money, Dad.'

He shakes his head. 'Ain't got none.'

'I'm broke. I need somewhere to live.'

'Find a woman.'

'I've come back from Melbourne.'

'Melbourne, eh?'

'Yeah. To live with you.'

He throws his arms wide. 'Welcome to the palace, then! Got a pool table and everything.' He gestures to Graham. 'And I'll be damned, a butler to sweeten the deal. See what a success I've been without ya?'

'That Uni of Codswallop degree is working out for you, Sparksy,' Graham cracks.

The old man salutes him. 'With honours, sir!'

Graham places another squash in front of me. I drink it fast, quashing the fire burning inside me, dissolving it back to where it came from – deep, deep in the past. 'You haven't moved in twenty years, Dad.' My fingers itch, begging to punch sense into him. 'You wouldn't move. Not even when Mum told you to come home.'

'Yer mother understood.'

'Yeah. She understood so well she killed herself.' Too late, I realise I've said it out loud.

He grabs me by my throat. 'Yer shut up, ya hear!'

Graham bangs a fist on the beer mat. 'Sparksy! Pull your head in!' He points to the sign above the bar: IT'S ILLEGAL TO SELL ALCOHOL TO INTOXICATED PEOPLE. 'One more stunt like that . . .'

The old man backs off. 'S'right . . . kid's gotta know where he stands, is all.'

Tiny laps his foamy beer. 'Ya got a girlfriend, Justin?' He pokes the old man in the ribs. 'Been a while since we had an excuse to talk to a young filly.'

I think of that Tara chick and the Kombi van. The term 'girlfriend' is a technicality. 'Actually, I do.'

Tiny bangs his glass on the bar, slopping beer. 'Where

26

ya hiding her, boy? Didn't yer father ever teach ya to share? Come to think of it, he probably didn't teach yer nothin'.'

The old man shoves Tiny so hard he almost wobbles off his chair.

'Got a ute with a towrope, Tiny?' I ask.

'What's it to ya?'

'Need to borrow it. Girlfriend's in a spot of trouble.'

'Yer not pulling calves, are ya? 'Cos that's not how you do it with the human ones.' He slaps his knee.

'How about it? Can you help?'

'Yeah, righto. Give me a few minutes. Gotta catch up to yer old man. Cast-iron stomach, he has. Can store it up like a flamin' camel. I ain't seen nothin' like it.'

The old man downs another pint and belches. 'I'm just farkin' gifted.'

Margo

Of all the things that guy could've picked up, he went for the box of tampons. Talk about my luck. He probably thinks I'm a complete moron.

He was kind of cute, though . . . Okay, *really* cute.

I stuff groceries into the cupboard and make a start on the mountain of dishes. I have to get it sorted before Amy arrives; I don't want her seeing the mess. Who knows what Mr Vermont was thinking pairing us up. Amy hardly speaks to me. If she does, it's a one-syllable 'hi' or 'bye'. I already know I'm going to do all the work. It's a pity my study partner isn't that guy I just met. Now, *that* would be something to look forward to.

Mum comes in and dumps her handbag on the only free bench space. She adjusts her uniform and brushes her greying hair, drawing it into a tight ponytail. 'What's that dreamy look on your face, girly? Wouldn't be about a boy, would it?'

My cheeks get hot. How do mums know these things?

She snaps her hairband and pulls the lumpy bits flat. 'You know, I've seen that look on your face before. You were knee-high to a grasshopper and his name – if I remember it right – was James Truscott. Cutest boy going. You two was inseparable. Always huddled tight, plotting who knows what – probably a fairy-bread heist. Too cute for your boots, the both of you.'

I roll my eyes. James Truscott dunked my braids in a jar of craft water and pulled down my pants.

'What's this one's name, then?'

'No one,' I say, busying myself by tipping self-raising flour into a plastic container. Half of it lands in a snow cloud on my shoes.

'He must have a name.'

'Mum!'

'Oh, come on, Margo. Don't try to hoodwink me. I can read you like a book.'

'That's original.' But I'm smiling and she is too. Her smile lights her face.

Mum's pretty, but the years are starting to show. Dark circles frame her eyes and deep lines weave her forehead. She's carrying a few extra kilos, but she still looks fit. She has to be – working in the hospital geriatric wing is a really demanding job. She loves it. No one could keep her from cleaning bedpans and shovelling vitamised food into slack, toothless mouths. *Completely harmless, those old folk. Don't cause you no grief. Too blind to care about skin colour. Treat you nice. Well mannered too. No such thing as manners these days.*

I look at the microwave clock. It's half an hour slow. I do the maths. 'Won't you be late?'

Mum snorts. 'Jaqueline Weidenhurst waltzes in ten minutes late for every shift and no one says boo to a gooseberry to her.' She rubs supermarket moisturiser into her split and weeping skin. Washing with hand sanitiser up to a hundred times a day takes a toll. 'I do my share and they know it. No other nurses do half the work I do.' She plants a juicy kiss on my cheek and grabs her handbag. 'Hey, did you hear the news? Nichols Point was vandalised.'

'The cemetery?'

'Someone dug up a body.'

'They *what*?'

'Bloody drunken idiots, they reckon. Up to no good.'

I wonder if it was someone from Craig Carter's eighteenth. I didn't go; I didn't get an invitation, but then again I never do. It wouldn't surprise me if it *was* someone from the party. The people that hang around in that crowd aren't going anywhere in life, except maybe SuniTAFE, and it'll be a small miracle if they make it that far. The sooner I'm at uni and the people around here are a figment of my distant past, the better off I'll be.

'Do they know *who* was dug up?'

I can see Mum thinking it over. It's obvious she doesn't know the ethnicity of the person involved, nor how long it's been since they passed. In our culture, we're not supposed to speak the name of the dead. But our family has never really followed that; many in the southern and eastern states don't. Mum is simply mindful because some of her relatives get a bit thingy with her about it.

'You know what?' I say, before she can answer. 'Never mind. Doesn't matter. Forget I asked.'

Mum gives me a thankful smile. 'Don't spend too long

on this mess.' She eyes the cereal boxes littering the kitchen bench. 'It comes back faster than an ageing rock star's concert tour.'

I grin. Mum's got a way of saying things.

'And don't be thinking about boys.' Concern crosses her face. 'My girl is too good for the boys round here, you got that? Too good. Bunch of yobbos in this town. This latest cemetery debacle is proof of that. Wait till you're out of here. There'll be ones in the city worth waiting for. Ones that go to uni, just as smart as my girl.'

I think about telling her *this* boy doesn't look like he's from Mildura, but I don't. The less she knows, the less she can tease me.

'Trust me,' she adds, blowing me a kiss. 'I'm old and wise. Well, not *too* old.'

As soon as Mum's gone, my stepdad, Ralph, comes in and dumps his coffee mug in the kitchen sink. He's been cocooned in his study, writing a government job application. 'This stupid thing's cooking my head.' He throws papers in front of me. 'I don't get why they tell you you've got the job and then make you apply for it in writing. Could you write it for me, Margo? You're smart with that mumbo-jumbo stuff. Smart with most stuff, my soon-to-be dux of Year Twelve.' He ruffles my hair.

'Year Twelve has just started, Ralph.'

'Even so, I'm betting you'll be the first of our mob to have the honour.' He opens the biscuit tin and fishes for a Monte Carlo. I whisk the tin away and he pouts. 'Not even one?'

I shake my head. He has diabetes.

'You're as bad as your mother.' He looks around. 'Where's Bradley?'

'Where do you think?'

Since arriving home, my brother has been in the back-yard, driving home legend-status goals between the veggie patch and the chook shed. He wants to be a football star. He thinks the AFL will get his mug on TV and he'll be famous and everyone in town will have to kiss his footy boots — including me.

Ralph grins. 'Cyril Rioli started somewhere.'

'Not in our backyard, he didn't.'

'Give him time, give him time . . .'

Our front door rattles, under siege from a pounding fist.

'Yeah, yeah, keep ya shirt on,' Ralph grumbles, heading off to answer it.

Tiny Johnson leans against the doorframe, scratching his Rudolf nose. I don't know why they call him Tiny; he's the size of a truck. 'Ralph, mate, I need a favour.'

Tiny doesn't come here often. He and Ralph meet up for the annual speedboat competition, but other than that my stepdad keeps his distance. Tiny's fond of the booze and Ralph has no interest in the stuff.

'Me towrope's busted,' Tiny says. 'Can I borrow yours?' He cocks his head and whispers out of the side of his mouth, 'Got a young filly to lasso.' He punches Ralph's arm and gives him a less-than-subtle wink.

Ralph peers out the door. 'You and Sparksy been at the pub?'

Tiny places a hand over his heart. 'Dunno what you mean, Ralph.'

Oh no. Old Man Sparks must be sitting in the car. Ralph hates Sparksy with a passion for reasons I don't really understand. The mere mention of Sparksy's name gets him all wound up.

Ralph eyes Tiny. 'What do you want with my rope?'

'See that boy out there?' Tiny points unsteadily. 'He's got a *girl* problem. Boy's gotta pull a Kombi off a mailbox or something chivalrous like that. You know how deese women drivers are, mate. Crash into a bag of Allsorts, if ya let 'em.'

Ralph shakes his head. 'Why are you even driving, Tiny? You can hardly stand up. Come inside for a minute and have a seat. I'll go out to the shed. But I'm driving, you 'ear? Sergeant McGovern will bust your chops if he catches you tearing up the asphalt.'

Tiny gives Ralph an army general salute. 'Hey, you lot! Come in 'ere!' he yells over his shoulder.

Ralph goes out to the shed.

Tiny comes in and plonks himself on the couch. It groans under his ample weight. He tips a non-existent hat at me. 'G'day, love. How's things? You still in my boy Hamish's class?'

'Yes.' Unfortunately.

Hamish Johnson is a complete tool, just like his father. He got done for drink-driving not so long ago, and now his best mate, Corey, has to drive him around. Sometimes I see them cruising with Tara Ramsey. *That* girl is my worst nightmare. Tara acts like she excretes lavender-scented bath bombs. If she could turn her nose up any higher, she'd be doing a backflip. I have no idea what her problem is. Her friend Amy McGovern, the policeman's daughter, is the one I have to do the History assignment with.

I smell Old Man Sparks before he's even in the room. He staggers about, looking confused. 'Where's the trough, love?'

I point to the hallway and pray he has good aim. 'Second door on the right.'

He walks in one direction, then the other, a man on a rocking boat.

'You again!'

I turn around. It's him – the guy who got third-degree burns from a tampon box. What's he doing here?

'Margo, right?' He smiles and holds out his hand. 'Justin.'

I shake his hand and this time his touch doesn't burn – it feels good. 'You're wearing a different top.'

He looks at his chequered flannelette shirt. It's faded and too big. I wonder where he got it from. 'Your brother was right,' he says.

'My brother? About what?'

'He said I looked like an outsider.'

'Are you?'

'An outsider? Guess it depends on who you ask.'

I'm not sure what that means. 'Well, I don't know if I'd be taking fashion advice from Bradley. He's been known to wear his T-shirts inside out. And once he wore my mum's undies to footy training.'

Justin laughs. 'For real?'

'Sadly.'

He's about to say something when Sparksy staggers back into the room, a stupid grin plastered over his stupid, plastered face. 'Geez, I took a slash that'd give Black Caviar a run for her money.' As he fumbles to do up his trousers, I catch a glimpse of his greyed forest. *Gross!*

'Dad . . .' Justin moans, turning red.

It takes a moment for the penny to drop. *This* is Justin Sparks?

He must know what I'm thinking, because he nods at me. 'Sadly.'

There were all sorts of rumours back when Martha Sparks died. Some said she killed herself and took her son with her to the grave. Others said it was Justin who killed his mother and he was secretly sent to juvie. Some say Sparksy became an alcoholic because of his wife's death and his son's disappearance. Ralph reckons it's all a romantic bunch of bulldust. He says Sparksy's greatest love affair was always with the bottle, before and after Martha. Justin was sent away because his father was incapable of caring for him. End of story.

'Got any home brew, love?' Sparksy asks.

I go to the kitchen and hold up a coffee mug, perfectly aware of what he's referring to.

He screws up his nose. 'You know what Burke and Wills died of, don't ya?'

Ralph comes inside holding a snatch strap. 'Right, you lot, ute's stacked. Was quicker than I thought I'd be.' He spots Sparksy standing in my personal space and gives him a glare to end all glares. 'Let's go. I haven't got all day.'

Sparksy does this weird boxer-in-a-ring-type dance under Ralph's nose. He pretends to take a few swings and ducks once or twice, dodging imaginary blows. He wavers sideways, almost falling over.

Glancing at Sparksy, Ralph says through gritted teeth, 'Sorry to ask you, Margo, but do you think you could come with us?'

He has to be kidding. It's not like I have the muscle to be pulling a vehicle. 'Why?'

'I'll drive Tiny's bus, but I need you to drive the ute. Bradley will stay here.' As if to prove it, the football crashes onto the roof. Ralph flings open the window and presses his nose to the flyscreen. 'Bradley, you break another tile, boy, I'll be breaking you!' He turns to me. 'Margo?'

'I'm on my Ls. I need a fully licensed driver.'

'I'm licensed,' Justin offers. 'I haven't had anything to drink.'

'It would've been a top-up from the night before, if you did,' Tiny quips.

'But Amy is coming over . . .'

'The policeman's kid?'

'We have an assignment. It's due on Monday.'

'Fair enough. Well, we won't take long. I promise you'll be home in no time.'

Tiny hoists himself up. 'Come on, let's sort this mess out. You'll owe us a few rounds for our trouble, young Justin.'

Justin nods. 'Dad owes me a loan.'

'Your buy, Sparksy,' Tiny redirects.

Sparksy belches. 'Always is.'

———

36

'So . . .' Justin says, as we trundle up the road in Ralph's dusty rust-bucket ute. 'A History assignment on a Sunday. That's gotta suck.'

I shrug. 'It doesn't bother me.'

'You like school?'

'I have to like it if I want to go to uni.'

'Uni, eh? Smart chick.'

'Not *that* smart . . . I work at it.'

'Good for you. I never finished school.' He rifles through the glove box, searching for something. 'Had your Ls long?'

'No.'

'How old are you?'

'Seventeen.'

He pushes aside driver-owner manuals, tissue packets and a bowerbird collection of ballpoint pens. 'Does your old man smoke?'

'Ralph's my stepfather and, no, he doesn't smoke. Doesn't drink either, if he can help it.'

Justin grabs a CD and fiddles with the cover, opening and closing it. 'Where is he?'

'Sorry?'

'You said Ralph's your stepfather. Where's your *real* father?'

'He died,' I say quickly, hoping he'll drop it. All I know about my real father is that he's a white man, and the only reason I know that is because my skin colour tells me so. I don't even know if he's alive or dead; Mum won't tell me. I gave up arguing a long time ago. She says he's dead to her and that's all that matters.

37

Justin frisbees the CD case and slams the glove box shut. 'This street. Turn left here.' We pass four or five houses before he says, 'My mother's dead too.'

I adjust my seatbelt. 'I know.'

'Yeah. Right. I forgot the whole bloody town knows.' He raps his fingers on the window ledge. 'I should visit her grave, take her flowers. Is your dad buried here too? We could visit them together.'

I cough, clearing my throat. 'I heard you went to live with relatives after your mum died.'

'Something like that.' He slaps his thighs, clocking a beat. 'So, what do people around here do for kicks?'

'You're asking the wrong person.'

He looks at me, curious. 'You don't go out?'

'Not really.'

'Why not?'

Because some girls around here are racist bitches. 'It's not my thing.'

'You must do something. Do you play sport?'

'Netball.'

'What else?'

'That's it.'

'Do you get high?'

He's joking, right?

He runs a hand through his greasy brown curls. 'Actually, that's what I'm doing here. I'm trying to stay clean, get my life back together.' He taps the dashboard, as if playing a drum set. 'Dodge the polar ice cap.'

'You did *ice*?'

He nods. 'I threatened to jump off the Westgate Bridge. It's how I ended up in rehab.'

'Wow. That's intense.'

His eyes go dark. 'Killing yourself is nothing *but* intense. I don't know how my mother did it.'

His pain is shiny and raw; he's varnished with it. I'm desperate to ask why his mother did it, but I know it's a question that can never be asked.

He thumps his head against the car seat. 'I kept telling myself I was better than the old man, you know? Drugs are cleaner than booze, blah, blah, blah. Really, I was exactly like him. I needed something that took the edge off. I still do. The counsellors would cut sick if they knew I was drinking last night.' He stops talking and touches my arm. 'Sorry, Margo. I'm not sure why I'm dumping on you like this.'

There's something natural about him, something open. I smile. 'It's okay. I don't mind.'

'Really?'

'It can't have been easy.'

'It wasn't. Just about everyone in rehab had family helping them. Me? I was lucky when the tea-trolley guy rolled in.'

My chest aches for him.

'You're easy to talk to, you know that?' He points. 'Turn here. That house . . . *there*.'

I pull over. A Kombi is parked – if you can call it parked – on top of a pile of bricks and rosebushes. I recognise it straight away. It belongs to Amy McGovern. This is Tara Ramsey's house.

The ute is suddenly unbearable. I wind down the window.

'You know these girls?'

'Long story.'

'Fill me in.'

'Not now.'

After a lingering look, he gets out of the car.

Tara swans across the lawn like she's strutting down a catwalk. A voice-over plays inside my head, telling me she's wearing a cobalt-blue bikini with diamante trim, teamed with a see-through cheesecloth dress made entirely of imported Egyptian cotton – *perfect* for those lazy afternoons on the beach. She leans against the driver's door, boxing me in, completely ignoring the fact that I'm sitting right under her armpit. I wish I could say her armpit is pimply and unshaven, but it's smooth and perfect-looking, just like her.

'Back for more?' she croons.

A sinking feeling grips me. *He stayed the night with her.* So what. Why should I care? I only just met him.

Justin leans against the passenger's side door, talking to her across the roof. 'I brought the cavalry.'

In the rear-view mirror, Ralph, Tiny and Sparksy pull up behind.

'That's not Old Man Sparks, is it?' Tara's tone suggests Sparksy crawled out of a sewer pit. 'Been recruiting at the pub, have you? Why'd you pick him? He's not the full loaf, you know.'

Justin doesn't answer, instead he beats his hands on the ute roof. Something inside me rises. He can't be himself with her. He's acting different.

Tara doesn't get the cue to drop it. 'Well? Why him?'

'A job like this requires manpower.'

She twirls a strand of hair. 'Bet you have a lot of that.' Tara leans down and whispers, 'How'd you end up part of the deal, Mabo? Your mob good at pulling things off?'

I spell my name slowly, as though she's mentally challenged. 'It's Margo. M-a-r-g-o.' I shove the door with all my strength, ramming it into her as I get out. She wobbles back, almost losing her footing. 'And I'd say *you'd* be the expert at pulling things off.'

Ralph comes over and tips his cap. He scratches his head, averting his eyes, trying to avoid Tara's revealing outfit. He's failing miserably. 'How's things, Tara? Bit of a pickle. What happened?'

'I was just saying to Margo how nice it was you came to help.' Tara smiles graciously at me. 'Corey was moving Amy's Kombi into the driveway and his foot got stuck on the accelerator. Mum is going to have a fit. She's been on a camping trip, rejuvenating . . . after her illness.'

'Illness?' Ralph says. 'Geez, love, I'm sorry to hear that. Sounds serious.'

'Oh, I shouldn't talk about it.' Her eyes roll skywards and she turns her back, covering her mouth. Her voice cracks. 'I can't do it to her.'

Cate Blanchett couldn't have delivered a better performance. Tara's mum is fine. I saw her at the gym a couple of weeks ago. I knew Tara was a piece of work, but this is something else.

Ralph's soft heart buys it. 'Don't you worry about it, love. We'll help you out. We'll fix it so good your mum won't even know what happened.' He lifts the tarp. 'Righto, folks, let's get started.'

Tiny crosses his legs. 'That beer went right through me. I need to take a leak.' He heads off to the nearest tree.

'Me too,' Sparksy says. 'Me back teeth are floatin'.'

Justin watches on, shaking his head. Shame floods his face and he can't meet my eyes.

'I'll have to think of a way to repay you,' Tara says, linking her arm through his. She steers him away, but not before flashing me one last smug grin.

Corey

'You're a friggin' goober, Cammo!' Hamish's head drips with beer foam. 'You're gunna cop it for that, ya hear?'

Cammo falls from his armchair and rolls on the shaggy carpet, holding his guts, pissing his pants. 'Sucked in, Johnson! Sucked in!'

Wednesday-arvo Russian roulette.

My turn. I grab another sixpack from Mrs Johnson's holiday-magnet-infested fridge and clear the coffee table, pushing aside magazines and chip packets. I dump the tinnies in the centre, pick a can and shake the absolute crap out of it. Boys are cheering. I put it down and swap cans, mixing them up until I have no idea where the shaken can is. 'Round and round and round she goes. Where she stops, no one knows.'

'You're a poet, Corey!' Hamish reaches for the homemade bong nestled between his feet and settles into his mum's doily-clad armchair. 'Lay a beat on me.'

'Mary Rose sat on a pin. Mary Rose.'

Hamish wipes his face with a pair of blue Bonds jocks. 'What the fuck does *that* mean?'

'It's poetry.'

Cammo reaches for a can. 'It's wussy shit, is what it is.'

I smack his head. 'Hey! I'm not ready yet.'

'Twist 'em round any more and they'll *all* be shook up!'

'I'll shake *you* up, if you're not careful.'

'Hey, Corey,' Hamish says, 'got some more of that poetry stuff?'

I place my hand flat across my chest. 'T'was in a pub they first met, Romeo and Juliet. Romeo went broke, you know, 'cos Romeo'd what Juliet.'

Cammo's face is a screwed-up dishrag. 'I don't get it.'

'You never get it,' Hamish hoots, lighting a smoke. He tosses the lighter and Cammo cops it smack in the nose. Cammo hurls an empty beer can at Hamish's head.

I repeat the punchline: 'Romeo *owed* what Julie *ate*.'

Cammo clicks the lighter on and off, running a finger through the flame. 'I still don't get it.'

'She was fat,' Hamish explains.

'Who was fat?'

'Juliet. Romeo went broke feeding her. That's what it means.'

'Nah, Juliet wasn't a chubster. I saw her in a play. She was hot. Total package.'

'You saw her in a *play*?' Hamish says, cracking up.

'Rack off, Johnson! Just 'cos I had an education, you povo dickhead!'

Education? Cammo Gibson spent one year at a private college in Melbourne and he won't let any of us forget it. His dad reckons all Cammo did was learn to smoke and drink and he could have done that here. Would've cost less.

Cammo turns to me, his blond, bronzed features curled into a sneer. 'You'd know all about big chicks, wouldn't ya, Corey? What happened on Saturday? Keita not hungry for a chow on Corey-sausage? Had she already eaten three buckets of KFC?'

I'm never going to live that down. These boys are like the National Library when it comes to storing shit for reference.

'Keita wasn't available,' Hamish jumps in. 'Aunt Flo came for a visit.'

Cammo takes the bong from Hamish. 'Huh?'

Hamish grabs a can. 'Even if it *wasn't* a red dot on the calendar, I don't reckon she would've put out. She's a massive tease. *Massive*, full stop.'

'Get stuffed, Hamish. Just 'cos she won't give *you* the time of day,' I say. 'Besides, the only bone you've had lately is the one under your bed.'

Shit. That's what happens when I've had a few – I start shooting from the lip.

The scar on Hamish's forehead, from when he got glassed a couple of months ago, puckers. 'I thought we weren't gunna say anything about that?'

It's too late. Cammo's suss. 'What are yers on about?' he asks. Trust him! Most of the time he can't understand a simple joke and next minute he's Sherlock Holmes.

'Nothin',' I say quickly.

'Nah, come on. Tell me!'

'I said, nothing!' I hurl a magazine at his head.

Hamish thinks we should dump the bones somewhere out of town, like by the roadside or in a paddock, but I'm not real down with that idea. It doesn't seem right. What if some farmer finds the bones on his property? Or if some truckie pulls over for a leak and gets more than he bargained for? That'll only create more heat from the cops. At least if we put the bones back and we get busted in the process, it'll look like we actually gave a fuck. And I do. What we did ain't right in anyone's book.

'We'll talk about it later,' I tell Hamish. He shoots me a look. *'Later.'*

He drops it. Good thing he knows when to put a cork in it.

'Right, are you lot in or what?' Everyone grabs for a can. 'On the count of three. One, two, three!'

We pop caps. Beer sprays in Cammo's face, up the wall and all over the lounge room. Hamish doubles over. 'Unlucky. Too unlucky!'

I scull my can. It'll take the boys another minute to finish theirs, bunch of try-hards. It's a lonely place when you're standing in a league of your own.

Hamish crushes his can and lobs it at Cammo's head. 'Wanna do shots?'

Cammo catches it and throws it back. 'Will you stop tossing stuff at me? What've you got in stock, Mummy's boy?'

Hamish grabs a key and opens the crystal cabinet. At the bottom, hidden from view by a dark wooden panel, is a selection of dusty bottles. He takes one and clicks his fingers. 'Tequila! Worm and all!'

'I wanna know the guy who thought it'd be a good idea to stick a grub in a drink. What's that about?' Cammo muses.

'Aristotle probably pondered the same thing,' I say.

Cammo must be hearing whooshing sounds. 'Arse's bottle? Who the –?'

Hamish snorts and loses it.

'Geez, you talk some BS, Corey,' Cammo grumbles.

Hamish plants the tequila bottle on the table. 'My olds don't drink this. They just store it in the cabinet to look good in front of their friends at dinner parties and stuff.'

'Let's do it.'

My phone buzzes. Hamish's head snaps up at the sound. 'Is that Keita?' He stuffs his face with Cheezels until he looks like a set of barbells. 'Keita Sanders shags Ned Flanders!' He cracks up, showering bits of mashed yellow across the room. 'Who's the poet now, Corey?'

But it's not Keita. It's my sister, Felicity. I put the phone on loudspeaker. 'Yeah?'

'Where are you?'

'Out.'

'Hey, baby!' Hamish calls. 'What are you wearing?'

I cover the mouthpiece. 'Dude, that's my sister.'

'Is that Hamish?' Felicity asks, her voice thick with righteousness. She's the missing offspring of the British royal family. 'For your information, Hamish Johnson, I just got home from work at the bakery. I'm wearing my *work* uniform. Does that interest you, Hamish? 'Cos it's *work*, so I'm guessing probably not.'

'Oh, baby!' Hamish laughs. 'Keep talking.'

'Do you know what *work* is? It's this thing you do to earn money instead of skipping school and getting shit-faced.'

'We had a student free,' Hamish argues.

'Amazing. And the rest of the school didn't get the memo?'

'Sorry, didn't catch that.' Hamish makes the sound of an old TV that's lost reception. 'Gotta go, you're breaking up.'

'When are you coming home, Corey?'

'When I'm good and ready.' I hang up. The home number flashes. This time I ignore it.

The old girl reckons if I'm not working, I've got to do stuff around the house. She won't pay me, though, and who wants to work for nothing? Truth is, I've tried. I've applied to most places in town, but no one wants to give me a go. It's always the same: *No vacancies. Register your interest. Try again later.* That's all I hear. Centrelink isn't enough – they pay you chicken feed. It covers smokes, fuel and a few other little luxuries, but that's it. The rest of the time, I'm busy bumming favours. It gets tiring. The only thing keeping me sane is playing footy. That, and having a sesh with the boys. If it weren't for arvos like this one, I'd go mad.

'Up for a few slammers?' Hamish says, tearing off the wrapper.

'Yeah.'

He twists the cap. 'Kylie Martin's eighteenth this Saturday – you going?'

I nod and light a smoke. 'You?'

'Course. You're fixing me up.'

'Am I now?' Hamish's eighteenth is still a couple of months away. In the meantime, I'm a goddamn walking supermarket. I see the bottlo attendant more than I see my own reflection. 'You sure your credit's good?'

Hamish flashes a toothy grin. 'Defo.'

I blow smoke in his face. 'Not what I heard. I heard you're about to be blacklisted.'

'Aww, come on! You can spot me, can't you?'

My phone rings. Private number. For a split second I wonder if it's Lawson's Panel 'n' Paint. I had an interview there last week.

'Hello?' I say in my best voice.

'Corey?'

'Yes?'

'This is Tara's mum, Caroline Ramsey.'

I slide back and prop my feet on the coffee table. 'Yeah?'

'Don't *yeah* me. You trashed my front yard.'

'Huh?' What the hell is she talking about? Did we do something to her place the same night we did over the cemetery?

'Let me remind you, Corey. You drove Amy's Kombi through my front gate and into my garden bed.'

I'm about to ask her what crazy pills she's popping when it occurs to me that Tara's pulled a fast one. She's dumped me in it for something she did and it sounds like she's covering for the copper's daughter, no less. She's going to owe me. Like, mega owe me.

'This phone call is to let you know I've sorted it,' Caroline says. 'You don't need to do anything, but I'm warning you that's the last time you pull a stunt like this. Understand? Stay away from my daughter.'

She doesn't need to tell me twice. If Hamish's credit rating is about to be blacklisted, Tara's is as good as there.

Tara's got fuck-all chance if she reckons I'll get her grog after this. Sweet fuck-all.

'You hear me, Corey? Stay away from my daughter.'

'Yeah, I heard ya. Trust me, no problem there.'

She hangs up.

Hamish eyes me. 'Keita?'

I shake my head.

He glances at Cammo, who's messing with the iPod dock. Confident he's not paying attention, he mouths, 'Cops?'

'It's not about the bones, okay? Leave it alone, will ya?'

I'm in no mood to explain. I'm not even sure what I'm more peeved about – Tara's lies or for getting my hopes up about the Panel 'n' Paint job. One thing's for certain: Tara will have some explaining to do. I'm not about to let this one slide.

Hamish gets the shot glasses ready. 'Line 'em up, fellas. Line 'em up.'

I toss down a tequila and wait for it to creep through my veins.

Tara

'So you're not coming home?' My voice bounces back from the walls. The phone connection crackles, as if Mum is calling from the moon. She may as well be.

'Trevor says we've got enough supplies. We've come all this way, so we should make the effort to enjoy it. The scenery is spectacular, Tara. The Flinders Ranges are incredible. Ah, the colours! Red, orange, blues at sunrise *and* sunset. It's constantly changing. I'll take you with me one day, I promise. We'll do a holiday together, just you and me. Something special. A mother–daughter thing. Oh, and I almost forgot to tell you, Trevor says . . .'

Trevor says. Trevor says. Trevor says.

I watch an ant make its way up the kitchen wall. Instead of going in a straight line, it zigzags one way then the other. Then it doubles back and stops, twitching, lost in a gyprock desert.

'I've spoken to Corey.'

I zone back to what she's saying. 'You what?'

'Listen to me! I don't want to have to keep repeating myself. Corey. I spoke to him. I rang him this afternoon. I told him to stay away from you.'

So Corey didn't argue with her. Thank God. I can't believe the neighbours dumped me in it. They rang Mum as soon as they saw the Kombi getting towed.

'Tara? Did you hear me?'

I hitch my dressing-gown and draw my knees to my naked chest. 'Yeah, I heard you.'

'Did you go to school today?'

'It's Wednesday. What do you think?'

'You don't have to be like that, Tara.'

'Like what?'

'Tell me . . . what else has been happening?'

'I took a shower.'

'Exciting stuff.'

'I need to get dressed,' I say, ignoring her sarcasm. 'I'm behind with my homework. If there's nothing else you want to –'

'You'll be all right, won't you?'

'Sorry?'

'While I'm away. You'll be all right, won't you, honey?'

Honey. Sticky, saccharine-sweet. She feels guilty for leaving me at home. It never occurs to her that the guilt might mean something.

'Tara?'

The ant moves with purpose now, scurrying along the window, searching for a gap in the frame – an escape route, a taste of fresh air.

'Tara, don't be like this . . .'

I imagine her shoulders drooping, eyes rolling, chest caving as if I've stabbed her.

'I know you're cross. You're *always* cross with me.'

I reach up and crush the ant with my thumb. It smudges – a shock, black streak.

'Tara, I thought this is what you wanted? Lord knows when I was your age I wanted freedom from my mother.'

I've heard it before. How when she turned sixteen, my grandmother made my grandfather hammer nails into the window ledge to prevent her from climbing out. How Mum liked attention from boys and that's *why* she got pregnant with me so early, and that's *why* her parents don't speak to her, and that's *why* things between her and Dad were so strained, and that's *why* their marriage ended up in the toilet, and that's *why* she had to quit her job to look after me, and that's *why* we barely scrape by, and that's *why* she needs a new man who can support us. And, oh, don't forget how she's doing all of this for me and how I should stop behaving like an ungrateful brat and how I should stop and think about what she's been through and what she's had to overcome and how other people in life get an easy ride and how I couldn't possibly even begin to understand because I'm way too young.

I hang up. The phone rings. And rings. She gives up after the fifth try. I switch on the iPod dock and crank it full blast. Heavy metal rips through the house. In the living room, I pull back the curtains and bunch the lacy scrim into a knotted ball. Sunlight floods the room and warms my skin. Across the street, Mr Detloff is mowing his lawn, as he does every Wednesday afternoon. He's wearing his usual gardening get-up: earmuffs, floral gloves, Akubra and sunnies. I concentrate on the rhythm of his mower, gliding back and forth. As if he can sense me watching, he looks my way.

I let my dressing-gown slide off my shoulders.

He stops the mower and removes his sunglasses.

His wife appears, passing him a water bottle. When he fails to take it, she follows his gaze and her mouth hangs open. She seizes his arm and drags him inside.

I close the blinds and turn off the music. I go to Mum's bedroom, crawl into her unmade bed, pull the covers over my head and breathe hot, trapped air.

'Tara!'

Bang! Bang! Bang!

'Tara! Are you in there? Open up!'

I wait for my eyes to adjust, but it's pitch black. I search for the red glow of the alarm clock, then realise I unplugged it the day before. The pounding continues.

'Tara!'

I drag on my robe and stumble into the hallway, feeling for the light switch.

'Tara!'

I open the door. Corey stops knocking, fist midair, swaying on his feet. 'So you *are* here.' He punctuates this with a healthy burp. 'Found you.'

'Congratulations, James Bond. I live here.'

Dazed moths dance above his head, drunk on porch light. His car is in the driveway, headlights on, door wide open, keys dangling in the ignition. An empty beer bottle lies on the footpath halfway between his car and the porch. Another is in his hand.

His glazed eyes narrow. 'You screwed me over, Ramsey.'

'I didn't have a choice.'

'And you thought I'd save you?'

'You did, didn't you?'

He belches and screws up his face at the aftertaste. 'I'm done. I'm *so* done.'

'What do you mean you're "done"?'

'I'm done fixing you up, that's what. D-O-N.'

'E.'

'Huh?'

'You forgot the "E".'

He kicks the doormat, edging thonged toes underneath, flipping it. A cockroach runs for the sanctuary of a pot plant. 'You're fresh out of favours, Ramsey.'

'But you promised you'd get our stuff for Kylie's party. Amy said.'

'Amy said, did she? Yeah, well, that was a week ago.'

'*Before* my mother rang you. Doesn't count.'

'Like hell it doesn't.'

It occurs to me he might actually mean it. I go for a different tack. 'Look, I'm sorry, okay? Mum's already had a go at me. She's already got it out of her system. Trust me, she's probably forgotten all about it. You're in the clear.'

'How do you know?'

'She doesn't care. She's not even here.'

'She's not?'

'Do you see her kicking you off the porch?'

He clears his throat. 'Where is she?'

'Camping. She's been away for ...' I stop, realising I've lost count of the days. 'For a while.'

Creases form in the corner of his eyes. Concern, perhaps? 'So you're all alone?'

'I'm fine, Corey – great, in fact. Never better. Especially when some lunatic is belting my door at ... What's the time, anyway?'

He squints at his watch. 'After one.'

I twirl my hair into a bun. 'You've been partying.'

'Maybe.'

'On a Wednesday?'

'Hump day.' He smirks. 'Had a few at Hamish's.'

'A few?'

'Slabs.'

'Hamish was drinking too?'

'Why?'

'He wasn't at school. Vermont was asking.'

Corey snorts. 'Vermont? Good old Vermont, eh!' He turns the doormat the right way up. 'Make sure you say hi to Vermont from me. Give Vermont my very best regards, won't ya?' He flips me the bird.

'I'll be sure to pass on the message.'

'Thanks.'

'So, you'll get my stuff?'

He thinks about it, massaging a crack in the corner of his mouth with his tongue. I have a sudden vision of my father standing at the kitchen bench buttering toast. *Tara, when you get a crack in the corner of your mouth, you need to eat Vegemite for vitamin B. Without it, you'll end up with a gaping slash like the Joker, and we don't want Batman on our doorstep, do we? So eat it, okay? No arguments.*

Without really thinking about it, I reach out to touch Corey's mouth. He backs away, giving me this look. 'Red Cliffs, Year Seven. You weren't that good from what I remember.'

He's talking about the boat race. I kissed him once, years ago. Pash and dash. It was over faster than the race. 'Ancient history, Corey.'

He eyes my chest. 'What are you – a D cup now? Damn. My timing was off.'

I smile. Corey might behave like a total tool, but somewhere under there is a good guy.

He grins, pleased with himself. 'So, what'd the policeman's princess say to her old man? Did she tell him it was me who took out your garden?'

'Amy's dad doesn't know anything about the accident. The Kombi was pretty dinged up to begin with, so another few scratches didn't make a lot of difference.'

'The cops aren't coming after me?'

'Not unless you've murdered someone and hid the body.'

His cheek twitches. He shakes himself, as if he just got out of a swimming pool, turns and staggers to his car.

'Corey –'

He waves his hand. 'Gotta go. Places to go, bodies to bury.' He gets in the car and talks through the open window. 'Don't worry, I'll get your stuff. Forget everything I said.'

But that's not what I wanted to say. I wanted to say it wasn't a good idea to drive, that maybe he should come inside and sleep on the couch. But before I can get the words out, the wheels squeal, reversing onto the road.

He drives off, a set of swinging red tail-lights disappearing into the dark.

Justin

'Are you sure you want to do this?'

Margo's brown eyes dart over the concrete headstones, hovering somewhere just above. Cemeteries must weird her out. Maybe it's an Aboriginal thing. Hell, maybe it's a *normal* thing. I don't know what I was thinking, inviting her here. It's right up there on my list of stupid ideas. Hardly the kind of thing you ask a girl to do, especially one you've just met.

We stand by the wire fence of the Nichols Point entrance gate. I've parked Dad's pathetic excuse for a car on the roadside. Stupid clapped-out Holden Gemini practically died on the way here.

Margo's fingers curl around a signpost. 'Are *you* sure?'

'Sure I'm sure.'

We're invaders about to set foot on foreign soil. The place is deserted, but if we walk just a few metres inside we'll be far from alone. She kicks the gravel, digging at it with the tip of her sneaker. 'We can do this another day if you want.'

'It was my idea.'

'So?'

'So we're here now.'

She twists the stem of her posy of flowers, breaking off pieces one by one.

'We can visit your dad's grave first?' I offer.

'Let's go to your mum's.'

I get the feeling visiting her father's grave isn't something that gives her inner peace, more like something that brews an inner storm. 'Are *you* sure?'

She smiles. 'It was your idea, and we're here now.'

We walk up the main path. Burial plots stretch as far as the eye can see. For some ridiculous reason, I'm sure I can smell the aroma of freshly baked scones. My mother's wake was all about scones – plate upon plate of the puffy little buggers – as if the women who baked them thought they'd fill the massive void my mother left behind with a bit of milk, flour and sugar.

'How long is it since you were last here?' asks Margo.

'I haven't been here, not since her funeral.'

'When was that?'

'Ten years ago. I was fourteen.'

'Oh,' she says after a moment, 'I thought you were younger.'

'Does it matter?'

'No ... it's just ...'

'You know what? I'll take that as a compliment, after all the drugs I've done. I hope people think I look young when I'm fifty.'

She smiles.

'If I make it that far,' I add.

'You will.'

'You think?'

'Of course.'

'Sometimes I wonder.'

A grin spreads across her face. 'You're safe for now. No big bridges around here.'

'That was dark.'

'Cemetery humour.'

I take my chances and tease her, digging her ribs. 'Well, we are in the *dead* centre of town.'

She wriggles away, laughing. The sound is magical.

We keep walking. As we near a patch of graves, her smile disappears. 'How much further?'

'Not far.' But I'm not really sure where my mother's grave is. My memory is fuzzy. 'I bet my mum's wondering where I've been.'

'You think she's here?' Margo stops and corrects herself. 'I mean, I know her body's here, but I wonder if they stay put – you know, spirits. Or do they follow us?'

'I hope she hasn't followed me. There's stuff I've done a mother should never see.'

Margo gives me an inquisitive look but doesn't pry. 'What's her full name? So I can look for it.'

'Martha Joyce Sparks.' I lift my T-shirt sleeve and show her my tattoo; her name is written underneath.

Margo's fingers lightly brush my mother's image. Her touch gives me aftershocks. 'She's beautiful,' she whispers.

So are you.

We continue along the asphalt path. A row of saplings sprout from the back of the cemetery, where the crowd of mourners at my mother's funeral had gathered; an army of people wearing navy-blue and black suits. I remember how my old man stood out in his creased R. M. Williams moleskins, his blue-and-white chequered shirt buttoned wrong, tie askew, hanging like a limp noose. He'd washed his hair and combed it – made that much of an effort. He couldn't make the effort to stop swigging his hipflask throughout the service, though.

Anxiety rises. 'Ten years. Maybe she's forgotten who I am?'

'A mother doesn't forget her child.'

'Does a father forget his?'

She looks away.

'Till now, I reckon my old man had pretty much forgotten about me.'

When she looks at me, her eyes are brimming. 'Yeah?'

'Come on, Margo. Everyone knows what my dad is like.'

She presses her lips and nods.

'Stupid bugger is lucky if he remembers his address. To tell you the truth, I can't believe he's still standing. Proof only the good die young.'

We head towards a patch of burial plots covered with reddish-brown scoria. Bursts of colour are everywhere in fake flowers, garden gnomes, teddy bears, ceramic angels and bottles of wine. An in-built vase at the head of one of the graves contains the skeletal remains of roses, tributes from visitors long since been and gone. The gifts remind me of the items I laid inside my mother's coffin. The funeral director said it was a nice way to farewell someone – to bury them with things that meant something to them. I chose a batch of birthday cards Mum had collected, a perfume bottle so she'd smell nice, and a painted white jewellery box that contained a string of brown beads. The beads had belonged to her mother, and Mum used to put them on and stare into the mirror. She'd done it my whole life – no explanation, no reason, it was just her thing. Her little ritual. Sometimes I wondered if she saw her mother looking back at her. I never got to ask.

I pause to look around. I know it's somewhere nearby.

Margo walks on with her head down, reading names. Then she's moving with purpose. I assume she's found her father's grave, but instead she's pointing at something flapping in the wind. Yellow crime tape. A grassy area has been cordoned off. Lumps of smashed concrete scatter the ground. A gravesite is boarded with MDF. There's a piece of paper protected by a plastic pocket stuck crudely to a post.

Margo holds it steady and reads, then she looks at me, shocked. 'Justin, I'm so sorry. I heard about it, but I didn't stop to think it could have been . . .'

'What?' But deep down, I already know the answer. It rises inside me like heartburn.

In my mind, I'm hanging upside down from the Hills hoist clothesline in my childhood backyard. Trees, headstones, blue sky and green lawn whiz past me in a swirly blur. Margo's voice calls to me from the sidelines.

I can't stand it any longer. Before I know it, I'm back at the entry gate, fury scalding me, trembling hands digging my pockets for the car keys.

Behind me, Margo calls, 'Justin! Wait! Please wait!'

But I don't wait. I don't want her to see what I do next.

The pub is busy for a Thursday afternoon. I find the old man hunched over the bar, watching the overhead flat screen, several empties lined up like soldiers in a row.

I grab him by the throat. His neck is a wooden ruler – one snap and he's kindling.

Graham makes his way down the bar, ready to kick me out. It's a good thing the bar is long and it'll take him a few seconds to reach me.

'Where is she?' I shout into my father's face. A spark of recognition flickers and he grunts, wrinkled hands on my wrists, trying uselessly to pull me away. I clop his sorry mug. 'Where the hell is she?'

Blood trickles from his lip and down his shirt, an angry, scraggly line. Graham's hands yank me back. The old man shrinks away, wiping his face. Milky eyes evaluate me as if *I'm* the crazy person in the equation.

'You wanna have a family reunion, son?' Graham bellows. 'You take it outside! I got enough problems today. Bloody plumbing is banked up again. I've got crap everywhere!'

The old man turns back to the bar and reaches for his drink.

'Where is she?'

Graham pushes me across the room, a good distance from my father. The rest of the bar has stopped watching the greyhounds. 'Who are you talking about, son?'

'She's been dug up!' I choke.

Sighing, Graham draws up a stool and steers me to take a seat. 'So that's what this is about. Look, mate. The coppers were here the day after it happened. They told your father what was going on.' He gives the old man a sideways glance. 'Not sure how much of it he absorbed, though.'

'Told him what?'

'That some idiots did over the cemetery on Saturday night. From what I understand, your mother's remains – or what's left of her – have been moved to the morgue. I'm sorry.'

'What's *left* of her?'

'They'll find her, don't worry. The cops are on to it. They'll have her back – I mean, the bits of her that are missing back – in no time.' He strokes his chin, considering something. 'Not sure if this officially makes her a missing person?' He can tell I'm not appreciating the humour. 'Look, why don't you sit down and have a beer with your old man? Work out a plan to catch the buggers.' He stuffs a twenty into my hand. 'Drinks on me. If the manager catches me pouring freebies, I'll be out on my arse.'

I throw his money at him and walk out of the pub, kicking over a chair and ripping a poster off the wall on the way. What I *really* want is to rip someone's head off. I want to smash someone's face in. The desire eats at me. I jump up and punch a 'No Parking' sign so hard it bends, metal reverberating with my blow. My hand stings even more than it did when I hit the old man.

I do a burnout and head for the police station. Whoever raided my mother's grave had better pray the cops find them before I do. If I get my hands on them, *they'll* be the ones looking at the world from six feet under.

It's only when I'm halfway to the cop station that I remember I've left Margo at the cemetery. *Damn.* I chuck a U-ey and drive back to Nichols Point.

I search everywhere, but she's gone.

I end up parked in Tara's driveway. It happens.

At the sound of the engine, she comes to the door to investigate, lithe body leant against the security frame, lips locked over a red icy pole. Glossy, bare legs stretch from under an oversized T-shirt.

I quickly find myself so close I can breathe her in.

She flashes her baby blues. 'Lost again?'

I come up short for an opening line. She curls a finger and I follow her inside.

The curtains are drawn, the room dim except for the glow of a television flickering in the corner. Cushions are strewn across the tiled floor. Empty bottles, cereal bowls and tattered magazines litter the furniture. A cockroach darts under the couch.

A creeping vine of regret stretches out to grip me. What am I doing here?

I gravitate to what was an open fireplace, now filled by a gas heater. On the mantle is an ornament of Uluru. I pick it up and trace its famous curves.

'Mum bought that thing at a garage sale.'

'Yeah?'

'She loves it. I have no idea why.' Tara sits on the coffee table, T-shirt scooped between her open thighs; a performance curtain begging to be lifted. Her tongue runs the length of her icy pole. She points the confection at me. 'People like us don't get to go to Uluru.'

I turn the ornament over. Remnants of glue are stuck to its base. It looks as if it's been snapped off something else. 'And why don't people like us get to go to Uluru?'

She shrugs, a red trickle running down her wrist. 'This is as far as we'll ever go.'

I put the figurine back and move to the black ottoman opposite her. My hand, still smarting from when I hit the street sign, hovers above her knees, fingers itching to connect with her skin. My mouth is dry, each breath unbearably needy. This is how I felt before having a bump: equal parts dread and desperate anticipation.

'You didn't tell me Sparksy was your father.'

'So?'

'So I wouldn't have made the "he's not the full loaf" comment if I'd known.'

'He isn't the full loaf.'

She doesn't argue.

'How'd you find out he's my dad?'

'Doesn't take long to find out stuff around here.' She licks her icy pole.

'Hey . . . fill me in,' I say, changing the subject. 'What's with the Bonney girl?'

There they are again – blinking innocent eyes. 'Huh?'

'The other day we came here, Margo seemed . . . I don't know . . . uncomfortable.'

Her lips curve – a confirmation of something. 'Why do you care?'

'I don't. I do. I don't know. I was just wondering.'

She flicks her blonde locks.

'Well?'

Tara rolls her eyes. 'If you really want to know, she's an Abo, that's all.' She says it like that. Like, racist. Fully out there, no apology. For a moment I'm so stunned I don't know what to say. She holds my gaze, unfazed. 'What?'

'And being Aboriginal is a crime because . . .?'

She rolls her eyes again. 'It's not a *crime*. It's just . . . Well, you should see her at school. She's up herself. She gets all this stuff regular kids don't.' She sucks her fingers one by one. 'The teachers fall all over her. She gets better grades than the rest of us. It isn't fair.'

'Maybe she's smart.'

'Maybe they give her more attention.'

'Maybe they're trying to make up for years of inequity.'

'Maybe they should get over it.'

I simmer inside. 'Get over it? Haven't you ever lost something? Do you just "get over it"?'

She gives a care-factor shrug.

'Do you?'

Eyes ablaze, she leans forward. 'No one falls all over *me*, trying to fix *my* problems, do they? I don't see a queue of people offering to help *me*.'

I can tell there's no getting through to her. I'm torn between staying and leaving, between caring and indifference. I'm like this town: on the border of three states, not sure in which I really belong.

'What?' she says again.

'Nothing . . . Where are your parents?'

'Mum's away.' She skims her tongue across her top lip. Her mouth is an intoxicating distraction. 'How old are you, Justin?'

'Old enough to know better. How old are you, Tara?'

'Old enough.' She rests her sweet treat in the fruit bowl and sips a mouthful of a pineapple-flavoured vodka. She wiggles closer until my lips edge the crevice of her thigh. 'I keep finding you on my couch,' she says, her fingers trailing through my hair, tugging my head down. 'Mum likes to go camping.'

I kiss her thigh. She's no good for me. I knew that when I pulled up in her driveway. Knew that when I followed her inside. Knew that when I sat my weak-as-piss arse on her couch. *This* is how it feels to self-destruct by non-chemical means. I lift her T-shirt. 'And your dad?'

She leans back, hand resting across her face. 'Lives overseas.'

I blow and watch as tiny goosebumps rise, little hairs on her flat belly stand to attention. Her fingers dance on my shoulders, dig in as my tongue glides to her navel and back down. She sits up and cups my face, lifting it to hers. 'You owe me.' Her lips brush my forehead. 'There's a party this weekend. Come with me?'

I clench her T-shirt and reel her in. 'Is this your dad's?'

'It was in the washing basket when he packed his things.' She pulls the T-shirt over her head and drops it by my feet. 'I don't like to take it off.'

I kiss her full on the mouth. She kisses me back. It's good at first, but then something about it becomes robotic, *honed*.

'Do you feel close to your father when you wear his shirt?'

'Something like that.'

'Miss him?'

'Hate him.'

A familiar sentiment. 'Where's your room?'

She picks up her drink and leads the way. She's everything that's hopeless, everything that hurts and everything that needs to be medicated.

Like me.

I'm with her, and all I can think about is Margo.

Margo

Justin left me. He drove off and left me. In the middle of a bloody cemetery. What's wrong with him? He knows how far it is to walk home.

'Margo! Wait!'

I turn around to see Amy McGovern following me up the footpath. She breaks into a laboured jog, schoolbag bouncing on her back. Then, like some cartoon character in slow motion, she trips on a tree root sticking up from a crack in the concrete and goes down, stumbling, arms flailing, face ending up an inch above the ground.

I rush to her side. Her right hand is cut and bleeding, knees dirt-smudged and grazed. 'Are you okay?'

'Terrific,' she mutters, getting to her feet. Items from her unzipped bag are strewn over the footpath. I collect the scattered books, pens and papers and shove them back in the bag.

She wipes her bleeding palm on her school dress. 'I don't think they'll help,' she says, eyeing the box of tampons I have in my hand. Like an idiot, I'm thinking about Justin and the moment we met.

I hurriedly put the box in her bag and dig some tissues from my pocket. 'Here. Use these.'

She accepts, smiling. 'I've been following you for two blocks.'

'You have? Why?'

'Um, well, I wanted to thank you for what your stepdad did for me the other day.' When I don't answer, she adds, 'You know, helping me out with the Kombi. I should've thanked you the afternoon we did the History assignment, but I was tired and sick and a bit . . . preoccupied.'

I hand her the bag. 'Don't mention it.'

'Can you carry it?' She inspects her hand. 'Just while I sort this out?' One of her nails is split and bleeding. She holds it out to me. 'It might be enough to get me out of Phys Ed. What do you think?'

'Maybe.'

She looks me over. 'Where's your bag?'

'Oh. I've been home already.'

She folds a tissue into a neat square and dabs her finger. 'I've been at the station. I had to butter up Dad for some cash.'

I wonder if she saw Justin ranting about his mother's grave. 'Was it busy?' I ask. We start walking. 'For an afternoon, I mean.'

Her gaze lingers, as if wondering why I'm interested. 'Nah, it was dead. I think the phone rang twice – that was it.'

So if Justin didn't go to the police station, where did he go? 'What's happening with the cemetery case? Have they found out anything new?'

72

Amy squeezes her bleeding finger and winces. 'Um, the cemetery thing. Yeah, to tell you the truth, I don't know much about it. Mum goes spare at Dad if he brings up work at home. She reckons there's an invisible line on our front doorstep and, once Dad crosses it, the uniform comes off.' Then she adds, turning red, 'Metaphorically speaking, of course.'

I smile. 'Of course.'

I consider telling her that the grave belongs to Martha Sparks, but then I think better of it. Maybe Justin doesn't want everyone to know.

We keep walking, neither of us saying anything. The silence grows uncomfortable.

'Are you headed home?' I finally ask.

'Actually, I'm headed to Kylie Martin's place to help her put up decorations.'

'For her eighteenth?'

'Yeah, it's this weekend.'

'Kylie lives a few doors down from me.'

Amy elbows me and laughs. 'You won't have far to stagger home Saturday night, will you?' When I don't answer, she says, 'Hang on. You're not going?'

'I have something on.'

'Margo, people don't send birthday invitations any more,' Amy says. Apparently, I need to be socially educated. 'Word gets out a party is on and the gang just shows up after the footy club calls last drinks. Dad reckons it's why these parties get out of control – because of the gatecrashers.'

She stops walking and looks at me. *Gatecrashers.* We burst out laughing.

73

'I can't believe I said that!' Amy squeals.

I giggle, thinking of her Kombi sitting in Tara's rose garden, with the driveway gate attached to it. 'I can't either.'

She wipes her eyes. 'Too funny!'

We laugh some more. Despite all I know about Amy, I feel myself relaxing.

'It's going to go off.' She beams a megawatt smile. 'Kylie's eighteenth will be huge. One of the biggest this town has ever seen.'

'You think?'

'Her parents are letting her have the place to herself.'

'They're brave.' Or stupid.

She laughs. 'I know, right?'

We turn the corner, headed for my street.

'How do you do it, Amy?'

'Do what?'

'I mean, with your dad being who he is. How do you do stuff and get away with it?'

She shrugs. 'What he doesn't know can't hurt him.'

'Aren't you worried he'll find out?'

'Sometimes.' But the look on her face tells me she's letting on less than what she's saying.

'I'd be terrified of getting busted.'

'It's not like I do anything *that* bad.'

I wonder what she thinks the Kombi accident was – just a little prang?

Then her face lights up. 'Hey, you should come with me to Kylie's party.'

I'm not sure I heard her right.

'Come on, Margo. Please? It'll be fun.'

Part of me is flattered she's asking – what would Tara think? But another part tells me Amy can be kind and generous when she's alone, but add Tara or Keita to the mix and things quickly change. If I turn up to the party, they'll spend the whole night paying me out. It's not an *if*, but a good-as-sold guarantee.

'Thanks, Amy, but I can't.'

'Why not?'

'Year Twelve. My folks are heavy about my grades.' I roll my eyes for effect. 'You have no idea. They're super strict.' But the truth is, *I'm* strict. If anything, my parents are supportive. Sometimes they even pull me away from my desk and tell me to relax. 'I need a good score to get into uni.'

Surprise etches Amy's face. 'You're going to uni?' She lets out a flaky laugh. I'm not sure what it means. Then I wonder if it's because she thinks my people don't go to university.

We walk past four, maybe five houses before curiosity gets the better of her. 'What do you want to do at uni?'

I hesitate, knowing that telling Amy might provide her friends with ammunition.

'Come on,' she urges. 'It's not some national secret, is it?'

I shift the weight of her bag on my shoulder. 'I want to do Aboriginal Studies.'

'Oh.' She says it like she figured as much. 'Sure. Of course.'

And right then I officially decide I don't care. If Amy thinks that's stupid, that's her problem. I learnt long ago to shrug off the idiots in this town. What they think of me means nothing. 'I want to learn more about Mildura's original inhabitants,' I say proudly. 'I'm of the Catfish people – that's our totem – the Kureinji, and of the "Baaka" Darling River people, the Bakandji.'

She thinks about it. 'Hey, didn't we go on a school excursion to some Aboriginal place when we were in primary school?'

She's talking about Willandra Lakes, the Mungo Lakes meeting place where the forty-thousand-year-old remains of an Aboriginal woman were discovered. It's a World Heritage site not far from Mildura. It's thought to be the oldest cremation site in the world.

'Yeah, we did.'

Amy squeezes her bloodied finger. 'Well, I think that's really cool, Margo.' And bizarrely, it sounds like she means it. 'I wish I knew what I wanted to do after school.'

I'm confused. Maybe she *is* being genuine. 'Really?'

'Yes, really. I hope you get to do it.'

'Thanks.' I smile, relieved. 'So, you don't know what you want to do?'

She bites her lip and her eyes fill with shame. I thought Amy didn't care about anything; I thought all she cared about was mucking around with her mates and the next party. But maybe she does care. Maybe I'm the one who's wrong.

'Have you thought about doing police work like your dad?'

'Because I'm such a shining example of lawfulness?'

I laugh. 'Okay, perhaps not.' I try to think of something else she's good at, but all that springs to mind is her and

76

Tara sitting up the back of class, laughing and gossiping and being the talk of the night before.

'I thought hairdressing?' she says. 'But Dad says it doesn't pay very well and you can get all these weird skin diseases from the products you have to use.'

'What does he think you should do?'

'Oh, you know . . .'

We turn the corner. Houses with glaring window-eyes and long judgemental door-mouths seem to say: *What are you doing with her? This is Amy of Tara and Keita ilk, the same girl who stands by and lets her friends call you Mabo. Are you seriously going to trust her?*

'I should get home,' I say, handing over her bag.

'Thanks.'

'Well . . . see you at school, Amy.'

'Margo?'

'Yeah?'

She reaches for my hand. 'Come to Kylie's party with me? I'll take care of you, I promise. Please, Margo?'

'I'm not some charity case, Amy.'

'I know you're not. I didn't mean –'

I tilt my head to the sun, feeling its warmth on my face. It gives me the energy, the guts to say what I say next. 'Why do you hang out with Tara?'

'She can be a lot of fun,' Amy says meekly. 'You just have to get to know her, that's all.'

'Believe me, Amy, I know her. I've known her since Year Two when she locked me in the boys' toilets.'

Amy cringes.

'Tara has it in for me.'

'That's not true.'

'Um, yeah. It is.'

'If you talk to her, if you get to know her, she'll change. You'll see. She might even be sorry.'

'Saying sorry doesn't always cut it.'

We stare at each other. After a moment, she tries again. 'Come on, Margo. The party will be worth it. I won't let anyone hang crap on you, I promise.'

Every cell I'm made of is screaming *No!*, but my silence makes her think she's won.

She links her arm through mine. 'I knew you'd say yes. We'll have the best time, Margo. The best.'

And that's how I end up at Kylie Martin's party.

And as part of the nightmare that follows.

Corey

We're in for another legendary Saturday night on the piss. Kylie's olds have gone bush and left her with the keys to the kingdom. Champions. Totally their funeral. If this place doesn't get trashed, we're doing something wrong.

'I'm getting laid!' Cammo declares, stubby held high. He points at two girls sitting by the bonfire. 'One of them. *Both* of them.'

'Dream big, Cammo. Dream big.'

'You don't reckon I could?'

'I reckon you've got as much hope of bagging those two as you've got of winning the club best and fairest.'

'Fuck off,' he grumbles, and sucks his beer.

He knows it's true.

Kylie's backyard is going off. Kids crawl under the porch, in the tool shed, by the bonfire and in the carport. The whole high school's here. Some takers are already smashed and it's not even nine-thirty. Most look barely out of nappies. Geez, I feel old.

'Maybe I'll do that blonde over there,' Cammo says. 'The one by the bonfire. She's sculling her sixth bottle of tart-fuel now.'

'You counting?' I eyeball the girl. 'How old is she?'

'Dunno. What's the world coming to if a guy has to ask for ID before he has a crack?'

As if Cammo would ever ask for ID.

'They should have their birthdate tattooed on their wrist,' he adds. 'That way, no guy could ever get strung up again.' He slaps my back. 'I should run for the White House with that as my policy.'

'Um, culture fail, Cammo. This is Australia.'

'Well, what's the name of that fuckin' flagpole thing in Canberra, then?'

'Parliament House?'

'Yeah, I could run for President of Parliament House. Plenty of guys would vote for me. Chick ID as my platform. *Vote One for the ID tramp stamp: Cammo Gibson.*'

Hamish stops pashing an exchange student long enough to weigh into the conversation. 'Are you soft cocks talking politics?'

To show Hamish I couldn't care less, I hoick a big juicy one and spit the beast over his shoulder. It launches a good two metres onto the lawn. 'Whoa! Check the range on that!'

He's totally unappreciative. He turns his attention back to the girl.

'Have a look at this.' Cammo points to a kid slumped by the shed. The little trooper has coughed up his breakfast, lunch and dinner in a pizza box. Now, that's what I call home delivery. Someone's pulled his T-shirt over his head and written 'FREE RIDE' across his chest in thick, black texta, complete with a crooked arrow pointed to his groin.

Another kid is sprawled facedown on the lawn, a stubby neck in his butt crack. A bunch of other kids are half naked, swimming in a plastic paddling pool, feeling each other up. This I don't mind watching.

'Were we that bad at their age?' Cammo asks.

'Worse.' I light my last ciggie. I'm out because Kylie keeps floggin' them. I suppose I'll be right to drive to the servo if I leave soon. I've only had three beers. That wouldn't register, would it?

Cammo chugs his dregs. 'Man, I love this. Girls everywhere. *Drunk girls*. Falling out of their tops with their legs in the air and skirts over their faces. Exactly the way I like them served: primed and ready for my special sauce.'

'Aw, dude, mental image . . .' Here's the thing. I reckon I treat women with respect – not like Cammo. The guy is a lion hunting a gazelle; he gets this look in his eye like he's excited by the kill, not the meal. I wouldn't leave my sister alone in the same room as him, that's for sure.

I dig my pockets for cash. Tara owes me a fifty. She's clueless her grog cost me ten bucks less. Pre-mix is on special this week – I checked the catalogue. I wish she'd hurry up and get here so I can go to the servo. Right now is the best time to go. Coppers are on their rounds of the primary school and golf club, hunting down graffiti-scribbling little pricks and giving their olds a serve for letting them out this time of night. That's what happened to me when I was eleven. Copper dragged me into the pub by my ear after he sprung me tagging a street sign. My old man said, *Yes, officer. Three bags full, officer*, and when the copper left, the old man sent me off with a fist full of coins so he could finish his flagon of port with his mates. Geez, I loved playing pub arcade games. Going to the pub with my old man meant packets of chicken chips and an endless supply of raspberry soda. The old girl loved it too. She was glad to see the back of me.

'Oi, Cammo, wanna come to the servo?'

'What about the cops?'

'They never get the witches hats out till after midnight.' I check my phone. Texting's champ when it comes to avoiding roadblocks. 'I haven't got a text either.'

Hamish extracts his tongue from the exchange student's ear. 'Hey, Corey, I heard there's a job going at the bank. You're looking for a job, aren't ya?'

'What'd ya say?'

'I said, there's a job going at the bank! You can make money hand over fist!' He puts his beer bottle between his legs, circles the neck and pretends to jerk off. The blonde laughs like he's bloody Tim Minchin.

I unzip my pants. 'Want a deposit now?'

'Put it away, Corey.' The policeman's princess slides her silky hand onto my shoulder. I want to slide it down south, but I need my junk for a lot of things and handing it to her father on a silver platter is not one of them. Amy is one chick I'm never going to touch, no matter how tanked I get.

'Got my stuff?' she asks.

Margo Bonney is with her. I'm surprised to see her here; she's not exactly the partying type.

'Red esky, bathtub. Where's my thankyou kiss?'

82

Amy flips me the bird. Talk about ungrateful. No manners at all.

'Where's Tara?' I ask.

By the look on Amy's face, you'd think I'd asked her to chew a cigarette butt. 'She was on her way here when I last spoke to her.' She pulls out her phone and starts typing. 'Why?'

'She owes me and I'm out of smokes. Can you spot me a fifty? Tara can pay you back.'

Her eyes narrow. 'Did you get her stuff?'

'It's all in the esky.'

Amy sinks her hand into her jeans pocket, pulls a yellow one and slaps it into my hand. Finally, I'm cashed. 'How're you getting to the servo?'

I swig my beer and read the label.

'Cor-rey,' she says in a singsong voice. 'You're not planning on driving, are you?' She turns to Cammo. 'Did he say he was driving?'

'Nah, don't think so.' But Cammo couldn't lie straight in bed.

Amy glares at me. 'You're on your red Ps.'

'You didn't seem to care last weekend. I heard you were off your trolley.'

Her face plummets. 'How do you –'

'*Everyone* knows. Plus, I copped the blame from Tara's mum. I didn't even get a thankyou for that either.'

She looks sideways at Margo. 'Maybe I learnt a lesson.'

'Yeah, you learnt a lesson,' I say. 'You learnt how to get away with it. Anyway, it's not like your old man's out yet, is he? Know any inside information? What street he's targeting?'

Margo jumps in. 'It's not about getting caught, Corey.'

Fair whack. Now they're ganging up on me. 'Of course it's about getting caught. Hames knows that, don't ya, Hames?'

Hamish pulls his head from a sea of blonde hair. 'Whazzat, mate?'

'I said, how about you give her other ear a clean-out?' The girl gives me a guilty smile and twists her body into Hamish's. He's copping a feel, the lucky dog. 'Chuck me a ciggie, will ya?'

He flicks me a bent-up smoke; it lands in the dirt at my feet.

Amy picks it up and hands it to me. 'What if you get caught, Corey? It'll be my dad who busts you. You gunna blame me?'

I straighten out my ciggie. How did I get myself into this? I'm pinned in the corner, getting whipped by two do-gooder girls. Girls and lectures – they don't do it because they care, they do it to let you know they're good girls. Good girls aren't slags. They have a bit of style to them.

'How are you going to feel if you hurt someone?' Amy persists.

'I'm not gunna feel anything 'cos I'll have passed out by that stage.' Both girls give me the death stare. I guess they don't see the humour. I neck the rest of my stubby and reach for the one I stored in the pot plant behind me. 'Don't get ya knickers in a twist. I've only had a couple.'

'Margo will drive you,' Amy announces.

Margo turns to Amy, her voice strained. 'I can't. I'm on my Ls. He's not even fully licensed.'

'If anyone asks, we'll tell them you thought he was,' Amy says.

'If you're so worried, why don't you drive?' Margo counters.

I take a long swig of beer and massage Amy's tense shoulder. 'Once bitten, twice shy, eh? You gotta get back on the horse sometime.'

Cammo grabs his crotch. 'You could start with this.'

Amy ignores him. 'I can't, Corey. Not yet.' She turns to Margo. 'You're sober. I've already had a drink. If my dad picks you up, I'll sort it out – honest. He'll believe me. I'm his daughter.'

Margo looks hurt. 'Is this why you invited me? So I can drive you and your friends around all night?' She walks away. Amy follows her. I stand back and watch them argue. I can't hear what's being said, but whatever it is, it's intense. I think Margo's going to pike, but then she comes up trumps, walking back and announcing, 'Okay, I'll drive. Let's make it quick.'

I shrug. 'Whatever.'

Amy smiles, satisfied. 'Impressive,' she says, giving me a playful punch in the abs. I feel her hand rebound – those three hundred sit-ups a day are really paying off. 'I thought you'd keep arguing.'

'I would if I thought I was gunna win.' I've watched my old man in enough scraps with the old girl to know when to put up and shut up. 'I guess you don't have wheels, so we'll take my bus.' My wagon's got stuff-all fuel in it. I've got a job interview on Monday for some fruit-picking gig sixty clicks out of town. I probably won't make it there now. Who gives a toss? I won't get it, anyway – never do. 'Come on, then.'

Margo hesitates. 'I need my plates. I have to walk back to my place to get them.'

'I'll come with you,' Amy says.

Chicks. They have to hold hands everywhere they go. They can't even go to the shithouse alone, they have to do it as a team.

I swig my beer and watch some pimple-faced player make his move on a chick wearing a strappy Pocahontas-style top. Good luck getting into that thing, buddy.

'Hey, Corey . . .'

Keita. And is she dressed to kill or what? I kiss her cheek, breathing in her mint-scented shampoo. She pulls away, hands pinned flat against my chest.

'Got my stuff?' she asks.

I light my smoke. *Got my stuff? Got my stuff?* Girls are only ever interested in one thing. I feel so used. 'Red esky. Bathtub. Where's Tara?'

'Dunno. I thought she'd be here already.' She goes to the back door but stops and calls out to me. 'Did you and Kylie really get it on last Saturday?'

I tip my head at her. *As if.* 'What do you reckon?'

She shrugs. 'You tell me.'

'I have standards. Get me another beer while you're in there, will ya?'

She gives me the finger, but I know she'll get me a brew. She's good like that.

'The party has arrived!' someone shouts.

Queen Tara Ramsey, reigning monarch of Milduraville, is finally making an appearance. She stumbles across the lawn in an almost-there miniskirt, tottering dangerously close to the bonfire. Her unco stagger has little to do with the six-inch heels she's wearing; the girl is ticking over big time. Some dude is on her arm.

He puts out his hand. 'Justin.'

I slap it. 'Corey.'

'Justin, meet my supplier,' Tara slurs. 'I want my drinkies, Cores.'

'Well, show me the money, honey.'

She flashes a knowing smile and lifts her top so I glimpse her pierced belly button. She pulls a fifty from her G-string. *Oh dear God in heaven, why can't all ATMs be like that?* I pocket the cash. I won't tell Amy that Tara has paid me too. They can battle it out later, preferably in their underwear and with lots of jelly. I point at the house. 'Find Keita. The esky won't be far.'

Tara heads inside with Justin.

I skittle my empty stubby across the lawn. 'Cammo! Ya ready or what? Let's case this party and find true love.'

Cammo scoffs. 'I'll settle for a root, thanks.'

'Works for me.'

Tara

I'm so smashed right now and it feels *amazing*. My head's full up with nothingness. Kylie's birthday is the bomb. Lights flash, music blares, people swamp the house: dancing, laughing, making out, arguing, getting totally shit-faced. This is where I belong. These are my people.

Party on.

Justin tugs my hand, leading me past a labyrinth of rooms, past shouting people, tinkling glasses and glowing cigarettes bobbing in thick, smoky fog. 'Hurry up, Tara!'

'I'm *trying*.'

'Well, maybe if you took off those heels, you could walk faster.' He bends to remove my shoes – Prince Charming making off with my magic slippers – and lines them neatly against the hallway wall. 'I'll put them in the car afterwards,' he promises.

The car. I lied to him. I told him my mum wouldn't mind if he borrowed it, but the truth is, she would mind; she'd go apeshit if she knew. And you know what? All I can say to her is *Sucked in. You want to rack off with Trevor on a whim? You get no say in what goes on when you're not here. None.*

Justin tugs my hand again. 'Move, Tara!'

God, he's bossy. I thought he'd want to make out before the party, but when I kissed him, he pulled away. He wouldn't even have a drink. How's he supposed to have a good time?

I try to keep up with him, but my feet crisscross and I lose my balance. I crack up, making it harder to walk. I can't stop giggling. I'm stumbling and dribbling, and I have these gross dark stains streaked across my top from my drink missing my mouth. Part of me cares, but the part of me that doesn't care is a whole lot stronger. Giving a fat rat's about anything when I'm this far gone is practically impossible.

Justin opens the laundry door, flicks the light switch and peers in. A spinning haze of green tiles. I put a hand over one eye and squint in an attempt to see straight. There's a wall-mounted clothes dryer hung so crooked a cross-eyed tradesman must have installed it, an overflowing clothes basket on top of a beige washing machine time-travelled straight from the seventies, and a wash trough with barely a foot of floor space in front of it.

'In here,' Justin says over the thumping music.

I'm way ahead of him. I shove him inside, kick the door closed and turn off the light.

'Hang on a minute . . .'

I push him against the washing machine and kiss him, my teeth smashing into his. Something tastes salty; I've cut my lip. The blood doesn't mix well with the nausea swimming in my gut and I swallow hard on an acidic burp.

Justin pushes me away. 'We're supposed to be cleaning you off, remember? You sat on a slice of pizza. You've got cheese and tomato stuck to your bum.'

Oh yeah – that's the reason he dragged me in here.

He reaches for the light switch. Blinding yellow stings my eyes. The washing basket crashes to the floor and a sea of soft material engulfs my feet. I laugh – I can't *stop* laughing. I feel the urge to pee and have to squeeze. A twinge of embarrassment passes over me, so I swig my vodka to wash it away.

'Come here,' Justin says, trying to steer me to the sink. Instead, I back up to him, pressing my bum into his crotch, pushing him against the washing machine. He groans and slips his arms around my waist, pulling me against him harder. 'What are you trying to do to me?' he whispers.

I turn and kiss him, this time on target, shoving my tongue deep into his mouth. He lifts me onto the cold metal lid of the washing machine, grasping my thighs, clawing me to him so he can wrap my legs either side of his hips. His hands roam my top, down my waist to my thighs, where he pushes up my miniskirt. His fingers nudge aside my knickers and work their way inside me. I bury my face in the crook of his neck, biting prickly skin, boring my nails through his T-shirt. His face is in my hair, his breathing heavy. He slips a hand inside my bra. I twist to bite his earlobe. It feels good to have him close. Good to have anyone this close.

Then, without warning, he stops.

Hands on my cheeks, forehead pressed to mine, he says, 'You're a polished act, I'll give you that.' He turns on the tap, reaches into the trough and swishes a cloth. He grabs my wrist and wrenches me down from the washing machine, spinning me so my belly is caught against the lip of the trough. He wipes my backside the way my dad did when I was a kid, after I'd been playing in our sandpit. The memory is enough to bring the contents of my stomach rushing into my mouth. I vomit into the trough.

Justin doesn't notice, or if he does, he doesn't say anything. He tosses the cloth over my shoulder and slaps my bum. 'You need to learn how to behave, Tara Ramsey. Let's get out of here.'

I wipe my mouth, annoyed that my never-fail sexy-girl act hasn't worked on him. If I want his attention, I'll have to go for old faithful: unleashing my inner drama queen.

Tears come on cue. I slap his chest, pointing my bottle in his face. 'You're nothing but a user!' I want him to feel bad. I want him to suck up to me. I want him to *want* me. 'User! User! User!'

He crosses his arms and smirks. 'Really? Who used who?'

I hear words coming from my mouth all slurred and jumbled, and the harder I try to make them come out straight, the harder I have to concentrate on making it happen. In the end, I give up midsentence.

'You should drink some water,' he says, like some condescending arsehole schoolteacher. 'You're going to have the headache to end all headaches if you don't.'

'I don't give a toss what you think!' I push him aside, throw open the door and head for the bathroom – and for Corey's esky. It's a last-ditch effort to have him follow me, but when I look over my shoulder, it hasn't worked; he walks off in the other direction.

Kylie's toilet is next to the bathroom. With the door open, skirt bundled around my waist and hands pressed flat against the wall, I squat over the bowl and pee, sighing from the release. Some of it misses the bowl and lands like iridescent fairy dust sprinkled on the seat. Torn-up newspaper is piled next to the empty toilet-roll holder. The hell I'm using that! I do a bum-wiggle and drag up my undies.

Cammo appears in the doorway. 'I arrived a second too late, didn't I?'

I tug down my skirt and try to push past him, but he shoves me back so I land with my bum wedged in the bowl; pee sticks to the backs of my thighs.

He closes the door and locks it.

I struggle to get a footing. 'What are you doing?'

He unzips his pants. 'What do you reckon, genius? I need to take a leak.' He's swinging his limp dick in my face. Somehow I manage to roll myself forward and duck under his arm. He pins me to the door and belches in my ear. 'What's the problem, sweetness?'

I kissed Cammo once in Year Eight. *Once.* We played spin the bottle at Keita's birthday while our parents were at the shop, picking up the cake. I never would've kissed him if it wasn't for that stupid game. We went into a bedroom, he kissed me and I let him put his hand down my pants for, like, thirty seconds. I didn't even *feel* anything. He's hinted at getting it on with me ever since. He can keep hinting as long as he likes; it's not going to happen. Cammo, Hamish and Corey are good for one thing and one thing only: booze. All I have to do is flirt a bit and I get what I want. I have no intention of being *with* any of them.

I knee his groin. 'Get off me!'

I obviously didn't do it hard enough because he lets go, laughing. 'Don't try to fight it, Tara. You are what you are and, personally, I love it.'

I fling the door open.

'Meet you in fifteen?' he calls.

In the bathroom, I plunge my hand into Corey's esky and come up empty. Someone's pinched my drinks. Arseholes. I feel around in the blue esky instead, cursing when I almost topple into the bath. I find a cherry-flavoured vodka, crack the top and scull it. A sharp pain shoots through my head and dizziness overcomes me. For a moment I panic I'm going to have a heart attack or something, but the feeling passes.

I catch a glimpse of myself in the mirror: smudged black eyeliner, pink lipstick smeared halfway up my nose, knotted hair. I wink and blow myself a kiss. Then I throw my drink at the mirror. Crooked red rivers distort my face.

I look sad.

Maybe I am.

But if I drink enough, I won't be.

Justin

I'd planned to leave after Tara's meltdown, but this guy has me bailed up in the kitchen, chewing my ear about interleague footy. He's a footy-record savant. Knows every goal, every statistic, players' guernsey numbers, quarter-time biff-ups, grand-final sob stories, right down to who won the bloody chook raffle. And here I was thinking *I'd* wasted the past ten years.

'So in round eighteen, Rick Parsons copped a cork thigh 'cos Clacker Jackson was benched, so they had to use –'

He's drowned out by someone shouting, 'Cammo, you're a fucking legend!' Hooting laughter emanates from the next room. It's the perfect opening.

I thumb at the doorway. 'What's all that about, then?'

Guy Whose Name I Can't Remember looks crushed I've interrupted his trip down memory lane.

'Think I'll check it out.' I make a break for it.

In the living room I'm confronted by something that stops me dead. Cammo kneels by the sofa, phone poised, a cheering crowd behind him. Tara is sprawled out, miniskirt riding high, undies stretched taut into a string around her ankles, inviting a full view of Mildura's Promised Land. Her bra has been yanked down, exposing her breasts.

Spotting me, Cammo leaps to his feet. 'Busted!' he shouts.

I grab a throw rug from a nearby chair and sweep it over Tara. I turn, ready to smash in Cammo's stupid skull.

'Hey, dickhead!' some guy yells. 'You're blocking my view!'

'Yeah? Get a view of this!' I hurl a cushion at his head. He ducks with surprising dexterity and pirouettes to drop his pants, displaying a hairy white crack. 'Are you going to take a photo of that?' I ask Cammo.

'Hell no!' He fiddles with his phone. I lunge for it, but he dangles it out of reach. He's a tall guy – probably a footy ruck – and with his phone in one hand, hipflask in the other, he jumps around the room, taunting me. 'You want it? You want it?'

'Give me the phone!'

He holds it high. 'No way. This is gold!' The screen lights up like a halo above his head. He texts, keeping me at bay with one arm. 'Absolute gold.'

'Delete it!'

'Or what? You can't tell me you're going to defend her?'

'Someone has to!'

Cammo shrugs. 'Hey, she was offering. I'm just showing my gratitude.'

'She wasn't offering you squat! She's off her face. Can't you see that?'

'Oh, go tell the Give-A-Fuck Fairy.' He quickly types on his phone and shoves it in the front pocket of his jeans.

95

Somewhere on the other side of the room, a phone beeps. Seconds later, a bunch of guys are huddled in a circle, laughing, slapping one another's backs. He's posted it. For all I know, he's probably filmed her. In another five minutes it'll have scored fifty likes.

Something inside me snaps. I shove Cammo, catching him off guard. He staggers back, the impact launching his hipflask into a nearby fish tank, where it sinks to the bottom.

'No!' He plunges his arms into the water. Fish scatter. The tank wobbles, a swaying boat soon to capsize and serve up a sushi banquet. He manages to hook the flask before flinging it wildly, smashing it into a glass buffet cabinet. Fired up, his eyes burn as he hauls me close and shouts in my face, 'I just refilled that!' He punches a hole in the patch of wall above my head.

'Are you right?' I yell, my nose inches from his. He may have redecorated Kylie's living room, but something tells me he won't redecorate me. Without losing eye contact, I slip my fingers into his pocket, pull out his phone and drop it. Plastic and glass crunch satisfyingly underfoot.

He falls to his knees, picking at the ruined pieces.

'Justin?' Tara's voice is a croaky whisper.

The throw rug has slipped into her lap and vomit flows down her bare breasts, pooling on the floor. The crowd of onlookers quickly disperse. A dull chant of *fight, fight, fight* comes from somewhere outside and Cammo leaves, drawn by the siren call.

'Tara?'

'I want Justin,' she moans.

I use the throw rug to mop up the mess, trying all the while not to gape at her chest. I've seen it before, granted, but looking at it when she's in this state makes me no better than the clowns who were just using her for their private strip show. She lays her head on the neck rest, eyes closed, parted lips smeared with the gloss of fresh vomit. She has drinking horns: those little dark stains you get in both corners of your top lip from red wine.

I adjust her bra, pull up her top and draw down her miniskirt before untangling her undies from her feet. I shove them into my pocket; it's easier than trying to get them back on. I need to get her into a bedroom where she can sleep this off.

'You need to move,' I say, easing her body forward.

'I want Justin,' she mumbles again.

'Exactly how much have you had to drink?'

She gives a slight shrug and her head lolls to one side, sleepy eyes wandering. It occurs to me she may have had something other than booze before I picked her up. Pills? Dope? I saw a bucket bong upturned in the front garden on my way in.

It's only 11 pm and, if anything, Tara should be just starting to tick. Instead, she's skipped the trailers and gone straight for the main feature: fucked-up and fully trashed.

I touch my nose to hers. 'Tara, answer me. What've you had to drink?'

She doesn't respond.

'Did you take something?'

'Vodka,' she slurs. 'A few tinnies. Some reddies.'

A Devil's cocktail. I could take her to the hospital and have her stomach pumped, but given the mess I mopped up, I wonder if that's pointless.

I slap her cheeks. 'You need to move.' Looping her floppy arm around my neck, I hoist her up. Who knows what else that pack of morons could've done if I hadn't found her.

'I can't.'

'Try.'

The weight of her body falls against me, blonde hair cascading over my shoulder. Something warm and wet trickles onto my thongs. *Fuck!*

She shakes with fits of giggles.

'Tara, I want to help you.'

'I'm trying . . .'

'Try harder. A minute ago you were in la-la land and Cammo was up your skirt.'

She casts a lazy hand. 'Oh, he's been there before.'

Her admission doesn't surprise me.

'Justin . . . doing . . . what have I . . . what are you . . .' She speaks like a crossword puzzle. 'You don't like me, do you? That's why you left me . . . before . . .' She slaps my face – hard.

I steer her to a slightly ajar door and spy the end of a double bed. *Bingo.*

'Ooh, it's dark!' She giggles as I ease her onto the bed. She drags me down and we end up side by side: her on her back, me facedown, buried in her tangled hair. 'I peed.'

'I'll get something.' I fumble by the bed, feeling for a box of tissues. Instead I find what I suspect is a T-shirt. Music thumps outside and a choir of voices scream a drunken chorus of 'Teenage Dream'. By the light of the thinly veiled window, I gently dry her.

Tara rests a hand on my cheek. 'Thank you,' she whispers.

'You know Cammo was taking photos of you, don't you?'

'He's in love with me,' she sighs. 'Annoying.' She rolls onto her side, mumbling, 'I'm tired.'

'I'll get you some water. I'll be back in a minute.'

'I want to go home.'

'I think you should stay here and sleep it off.' Before the words have left my lips, she's snoring. I get up and walk out, closing the door behind me.

My phone beeps. It's a message from a number I don't recognise. *CHECK THIS OUT*. Attached is Cammo's handiwork: a photo of Tara slumped near naked on Kylie's couch.

Was I this big of a jerk when I was on the gear?

I hit *Delete* and head for the kitchen to get Tara a glass of water. I have to sober her up and get her the hell out of here.

Margo

'Margo!' Amy calls. 'Wait!'

But I don't wait. I charge up the road, determined to forget this night ever happened. Behind me, music booms. The street is crammed, cars parked bumper to bumper. Frosted mag wheels glint in the moonlight, moths swarm under street lamps and a stereo thuds as a bouncing car pulls up and births five people from the back seat. Clutching bottles, they stumble into the gutter, shouting slurred words I can't understand. Their laughter all but drowns out Amy's repeated calls for me to slow down.

'Margo! Will you *please* stop?'

'Why? I have to get my plates, remember?' But I have no intention of getting them. I'm just saying that so I can go home.

Amy catches up and falls into line. She swigs her drink. 'This isn't exactly how I saw things working out. I thought we'd have a good time.'

'I'm having a swell time so far.'

'Don't be like that.'

'Like what?'

'Like, bitchy. Uptight.'

I stop and face her. 'Why did you even bother inviting me, Amy?'

She grabs my arm and pulls me close. 'I invited you because you're a stiff and you need to learn to get messy once in a while.' She lets go. 'Sorry, it had to be said.'

Her words are little arrows biting my skin. 'I'm not . . .'

'A stiff?' Amy sculls the last of her drink and tosses the can into someone's garden. 'See? You can't even argue with me. You know it, I know it.'

She's right. I *am* a stiff. Compared to her.

'Margo, just chill. It's a short drive – a few blocks. A quick trip to the servo, staying under sixty clicks the whole way. No biggie.'

'But what if –'

'If we get caught, I'll take care of it. I told you that. Come on, I'm the copper's daughter. What's the worst that can happen to me?'

'You drive into someone's flowerbed?'

'After that.'

'Amy!'

'I'm kidding! Look, it won't happen again, I mean it.' She gives me this earnest, pleading look.

'Do you remember when your dad came to school to give that talk?'

Her eyebrows pucker, as if she doesn't know what I'm talking about.

'After Hamish got busted for DUI? Remember?'

'Oh. Yeah, um, I think so.'

'Did any of it sink in?'

'Margo, the stuff Dad talked about – the pictures of the car wreck – it didn't even happen in Mildura. It didn't happen anywhere near us. He pinched it from the net. Trust me. He's technologically inept and he asked me to help him make the PowerPoint. That mangled car you saw was from some American website and it wasn't even related to drink-driving. I think there was a bear on the road or something.'

'A bear?'

'He wanted to scare us.'

'Yeah, well, it worked.'

'No, I mean he wanted to scare us out of living.' She places a hand on my face, fingers tracing my cheek. 'Live a bit, Margo. Feel the rush of doing something crazy. You don't know how alive you are until you're living close to the edge.'

She leans in and kisses me. On the mouth. Soft. Wet. Tongue and all. It happens fast, too fast for me to do anything other than stand there, frozen. Her lips are silky and then they're gone.

'You never know,' she breathes, pulling away. 'You might actually like it.'

'Amy . . . I think you have the wrong idea . . .'

'No, I'm pretty sure I have the right idea.'

'You know I'm straight, right?'

'I know.'

'Then why . . .?'

'I thought I'd try it, feel the rush.' She smiles that killer smile of hers and I can't help but smile back. She's so sure of herself. Surer than I am.

'Do you always get away with everything?'

She threads her fingers through mine. 'Mostly.'

'Amy, I've got a bad feeling about this . . .'

'Come on, let's get your plates.'

Corey

Heidi Hillier sits up and massages her jaw. 'Is it any good?'

Honestly? It's the worst BJ I've ever had. She's a total rookie. All over the place: no rhythm, all teeth, no tongue. If I don't give her some pointers, she'll spend her whole life serving up duds. Better to nip the problem in the bud. Service to my fellow man and all that.

I'm about to educate her, when Kylie's bedroom door swings open and Toohey Marshall belts in. 'Hey, Corey, you wanna mixer? Macka's got the blender out and . . . Oh! Sorry, man!' He slams the door, yelling, 'Hey, fellas! Corey's up to his nuts in it in there!'

Heidi jumps to her feet, wiping her mouth. 'He saw me! Corey, he saw me!'

I zip my jeans. 'Calm down. He saw the back of your head.'

Her eyes are like nail guns firing at full speed. 'He knows who *you* are, he'll see *me* walk out of here.' She hurriedly fixes her shirt. She told me she was a Year Twelve student. I sure as shit hope so. You can never be too sure about these things, though.

The door opens again and Kylie flounces in, wearing

a pink feather boa and plastic silver tiara. She's sipping from an oversized 18-emblazoned novelty wineglass and smoking a joint. She opens her closet door and pulls out a coat, tossing the hanger at me without meaning to.

I duck to miss it. 'Hey! Go easy!'

Her surprised eyes flit from me, to Heidi and back to me again. 'Corey, tell me you weren't just doing it on my bed.' She sinks her arms into her coat with the vigour of a boxer strapping up for a fight.

I give her my best guilty grin. 'Good mattress. Very firm.'

Heidi fires up. 'In your dreams, Corey Williams!' She climbs onto the bed, heaves up the window and pushes the flyscreen free. One filthy look my way and she's gone.

Kylie blinks, amazed. '*What* was that?'

I kiss her cheek. 'Happy birthday, baby.' I push past her and out into the hallway. Two steps later, I collide with Cammo exiting the bathroom.

He chucks me a stubby and slaps my back. 'Scoresheet?'

I zip my lips and toss away the key.

'That bad, huh?'

'A gentleman never tells.'

He sniggers. 'So it was crap, then? Commiserations, dude.'

We clink bottles and head for the room adjacent to the kitchen. Five guys are planking across the glass dining table. Cameras flash, people cheer.

Kylie walks in and goes troppo, pink feathers flying. 'Get off it! You're going to break it!'

It's like she gave the universe permission. There's an almighty crack and the table caves. Glass shatters into thousands of tiny cube-like chunks. Three guys are dumped on the floor, while two are still balanced across the steel frame. Kylie turns ballistic, running around in circles, fist stuffed in her mouth, muffling freaked-as-shit screams. Everyone is laughing. One guy's leg is losing blood at the rate of a half-slaughtered pig. Someone rushes in with a white bath towel.

Hamish holds up the wall, watching the circus unfold. 'Let the entertainment begin . . .'

'Hey, Hames,' Cammo slurs, 'Corey just put one on the scoreboard.'

Hamish winks at me and sucks his stubby. 'That's one more than you'll get, Gibson.' He points at a Chris Hemsworth lookalike picking his way over the broken glass. 'Who's that?'

It's the guy I met earlier – the one with Tara. 'Justin something.'

Cammo's sour as. '*That* is Old Man Sparks's son. He just got back to town.'

Justin Sparks. Why didn't I put two and two together? I caught the olds saying something about Sparksy doing nothing to deserve such a ratbag for a son. Geez, I'm slow on the uptake sometimes.

'What I heard, he used to be an ice addict,' Cammo says.

'Well, he'd fit in fine with the meth heads in this town.'

'Yeah, but not with this crowd. That shit's for losers.'

'True.'

'He stopped a good show before,' Cammo grumbles.

'What are you on about?'

He points at Hamish. 'Ask him to show you the pictures. My phone's cactus, thanks to that tosser.'

But Hamish isn't paying attention. 'Yo! Sparksy!' he yells. 'Over 'ere!'

Justin gives him a broad, toothy smile. 'Hamish Johnson? Tiny's son?'

'Hey! How big is *your* johnson, Hamish?' Cammo jeers. 'Is it *tiny* too?'

Hamish smacks Cammo's head. 'Fuck off! That joke's as old as your mother's twat.'

Justin shakes Hamish's hand. 'You were a little fella running round in junior colts when I saw you last.' He looks at me. 'We met before. Corey, right?'

I slap his outstretched hand. 'I hear you've been up to no good.' Can't help but indulge in a shit-stir. Born with a mixer in my hand is what the old girl reckons – didn't even need the recipe. 'You got some on you or what? Share and share alike.'

His face twists into a dirty glare. 'Nah, mate, I gave up the gear a while ago.'

I lift my stubby. 'This is all you need anyway. So . . . you and Tara.'

'What about it?'

'How do you know her?'

He glances at Cammo. 'I met her last weekend.'

'Is that right?' I swallow my beer. It slides down as easy as a box of nails. How's his style? Waltzes into town and snags the hottest chick going. Not that I'm interested – I'm not – but it'd be nice to see Tara hook up with a local.

The hottest chicks always end up with some rich, educated blow-in.

'Where is she? Has she dumped you already or what?'

'Why don't you ask your mate here?' Justin looks at Cammo like he might thump his head in.

I quiz Cammo. 'What's he on about?'

Cammo is suddenly interested in the wonders of wallpaper design.

'Tara's resting,' Justin adds. 'I was headed to the kitchen to get her some water. Catch you later,' he says, and walks off.

I grab Cammo's shoulder and make him face me. 'What'd you do to Tara?'

He's distracted by a brunette plonking herself on the couch in front of us. 'Hey . . . I saw this chick before,' he whispers. 'She was searching the esky, bending over so far I could practically see what she had for breakfast. Ab-so-fucking-lutely maggoted.'

Whoever she is, Cammo wastes no time seating himself in prime position. 'In for a big one?' he asks.

The girl's head tips, eyes half closed. 'Piss off, will ya?' she slurs.

'What's yer name?' Like Cammo *needs* a name.

'Sally.'

'Well, telling me to piss off isn't real friendly now, is it, Sally-wag?' He slides his hand along her inner thigh and mouths 'like velvet' to us.

Hamish hoots, but I don't say a thing. It turns my guts, watching Cammo leech all over her. Cammo ranks on the shag-worthy list where he ranks in footy tipping: last place.

He knows it too. He's got zero chance of getting with a chick like this, sober or not. I might play the field, but at least my girls are conscious and consenting when I have a crack.

Cammo works his magic despite Sally-wag slapping his hand away. Her head falls, skimming his shoulder. He necks his stubby and spits a mouthful into her cleavage.

She grabs him by his hair. 'Will you get off me?'

Cammo eyes his brand-new silver watch. Reckons it cost him twenty pineapples on eBay. He got ripped off, if you ask me. 'Guess what, Sally-wag?' he says. 'My watch says it's time you get *me* off.'

Blokes say some stuff when they're on the turps. Most of it is hot air; we don't mean what we say, we just say it to put the wind up each other. But there's something about Cammo that suggests he *does* mean what he says. One day, sooner or later, he's going to get his head smacked in for overstepping the mark. I'm definitely not going to be the one waiting around to bail him out.

Sally's pretty head wobbles one more time then slumps into Cammo's lap. I wait for her to pull herself up, but she's down for the count. I remember the old man telling me you have to work for stuff, it doesn't just fall in your lap. I wish he was here to see this.

'Leave her alone, Cammo.'

'Nah, she's good. She's *good* . . .'

'She's a corpse.' I put out my hand to help drag him up. 'You need your head read if you're gunna try that shit on.' I wave my hand. 'Take it. Get up.'

He pulls himself to his feet without my help. 'Cock-blocker.'

'Call me what you want. I just saved your arse. Now, go to the esky and get us another brew.' I shove him into the hallway. He walks off, mangy dog, tail between his legs.

I'm about to slap Sally-wag's cheeks and get her breathing again, when I notice Margo and Amy watching me. L-plates dangle from Margo's hand. She gives me a strange half-smile.

I look away, not real comfortable with playing the good guy. 'You two took your sweet time. Ready or what?' I turn to Hamish. 'You coming?'

'Where ya going?'

'Servo.'

'Nah, I'll stay here.' He digs my ribs. 'Try to even the scoreboard.'

I point at the girl. 'I hope you don't mean with her.'

Hamish scoffs. 'Give me some credit.'

'Do you think you could keep an eye on her? Make sure she doesn't – I don't know – face plant off the couch?'

'Do I get paid for babysitting?'

'Do it out of the goodness of your heart, mate.' I ditch my empty stubby and follow Margo and Amy out to the car.

Margo keeps looking at me as though she's trying to figure me out.

'What?'

She smiles. 'Nothing.'

Something warm sings in my chest. I've never had a girl look at me like that. Ever. I wonder what it means.

Tara

I wake, head throbbing; a string of knockout punches to my skull. There's distant shouting. Bottles smash. Trap music jack-knifes as one track intercepts another. A car door slams and wheels spin.

Slurred voices argue. 'Hold her still . . .'

'Hurry up then . . .'

A dark outline of a man hovers by my feet. Another figure looms closer, moonlight hugging his shoulders. He grabs my wrists and pulls my arms over my head.

I struggle. 'Hey! What are you doing? Get off me!'

His hot tongue weaves its way into my clamped mouth. I thrash my head and spit into the dark. He slaps me – *hard*. Tiny bursts of light dance behind my eyes. 'Shut up,' he growls through stale breath.

I try to kick but my feet are caught in a vice. I'm skewered meat on a spit, flipped and driven into the mattress. 'No! Let me go!'

A bourbon-soaked tongue probes my ear. 'Let's see if you live up to your photo.' He stuffs something soft in my mouth. The suffocating stench of urine fills my nostrils. I squeal as his prickly skin bites down on the back of my neck.

A zipper unzips and his mate laughs, 'Now she's gunna get what's coming to her . . .'

'Keep an eye on the door, would ya?'

I buck, trying to fight him, but this only excites him more. He pushes, pressure delivering fiery pain, ripping me apart.

'Yeah, that's it . . .' he moans, grunting breathlessly.

Useless words form: hollow arguments dissolved by the bitter taste of bile rising fast, burning the walls of my throat. Fighting, pointless. Crying, useless. I feel myself slipping, spiralling, *disappearing*.

He strokes my hair. 'That's it . . . There's a good girl . . .'

Time leaks away and the world stops. Blaring silence. I'm suspended inside a black, empty void. I am nothing. I am no one.

His indifference leaks between my thighs.

He yanks the material from my mouth and, as he does, something on his wrist catches the moonlight. 'Don't say a word.'

I vomit, firing a geyser into his hand.

He jerks away. Laughter. 'Hey, you wanna have a go now?'

'I'm not touching your leftovers,' his mate crows.

'Screw this for a joke.'

'Thought we did.'

Zipper zips. Hands high-five. Bedroom door slams. Music thumps. Someone sings out of tune.

A wet sheet sticks cold to my skin.

Justin

This friend of Tara's – Keita? – has no shame. Sweet FA. The girl is throwing herself at me. She's got me pinned in the corner of the kitchen, side-show breasts bobbing in my face, baby pink tongue circling the rim of her bottle, eyelashes skipping like bugs in the grass. Back in Melbourne, if she'd have tottered past, I'd probably have given her a second inspection. But I'm not smacked off my face. She looks pathetic, exactly like every other drunken idiot at this party.

'Tara thinks you're hot.' Spidery eyelashes bat. She sinks her tongue inside the neck of her bottle and pokes it about. 'You won't tell her I said anything, will you?'

I fill a glass with water, thinking I should check on Tara.

'Will you?'

'Will I what?'

'Say anything. About Tara liking you.'

'Why are you telling me?'

'I thought it might speed things up.'

'Speed things up?'

A cheeky wink. 'If you're into her too?'

113

I know what this is about. Keita's got the rod out and she's fishing with bait. If I say I'm not into Tara, she'll have a crack herself, no trouble.

Glass of water in hand, I make my move.

She blocks my step. *'Are you?'*

'Am I what?'

She rolls her eyes. 'Into her.'

'Now, that would be telling, wouldn't it?'

She leans in close, ready with a secret. 'You know . . . Tara's high maintenance.' Girls like Keita are predictable and this one's wearing her training wheels. She's warning me off, planting a seed to make me think twice about pursuing Tara. 'Of course, she can be a lot of fun too.'

'I'll keep that in mind.'

She smiles, satisfied. 'It was nice, what you did.'

'Huh?'

'Helping them out with the Kombi. My friends might've got into a lot of trouble.'

'Oh. That. Sure. I'm a regular Superman.'

Stealthy fingers creep up my arm, stroking my shoulder. 'I should find a way of thanking you . . .'

'You don't need to do –'

'Of course I do, silly.' She leans in further, breasts squashed against my chest, legs straddling mine. As her lips loom, I'm saved by a panicked scream.

'Get out of the way!'

We're shoved aside. Water gushes from the sink, spraying up the window and across the kitchen. The ceiling rains, soaking everything – including us. A wispy, limp-haired girl, probably thirteen or fourteen, holds a boy's hands under the water. He's got the dodgiest haircut I've ever seen – that, or someone has hacked off his fringe to spite him. He tries to wriggle away as the girl turns up the water pressure.

Keita creeps forward to peer into the sink. Her hands start flapping. 'Oh my God! Oh my God!'

'He fell into the bonfire,' Wispy Girl explains. 'Someone dared him to hurdle it. He tripped and his hands went into the coals.'

The boy grins a lopsided grin. 'Doesn't hurt much,' he slurs.

I push the girl out of the way. 'Give me a look.' I carefully lift the boy's arms from the water. It's not a pretty sight. Peeling, blistering, bloodied lumps cover his palms. I once worked in a burger joint in Melbourne where a guy burnt his hands so bad that there was nerve damage and he couldn't feel any actual pain. Either this kid is in the same boat, or he's so off his face he has no sense *and* no feeling. 'What's your name?'

'Jackson,' he says.

'You need to get to a hospital, Jackson.' Up close, I see his fringe has actually been singed off. 'You need to see a doctor.'

'Nah. She'll be right, mate.' He stumbles to the fridge and elbows open the door. 'Just put a bit of ice on it.'

'I'm telling you, dude, you need a doctor.' I nudge him sideways and dig into the freezer. 'Keita?'

'Yeah?'

'Soak a tea towel. Lay it flat on the bench so I can crack ice cubes on it.'

She nods and searches for a towel.

'Just cover it up,' the kid argues. 'I wanna get back outside.'

The ice cubes scatter the floor and I find my fingers wrapped around his throat. 'Listen up and listen good, you little twerp. I'm taking you to the hospital, you idiot. Your hands are roasted, get it? You need a doctor tonight – *now* – or you're gunna spend the rest of your life wiping your arse with your foot.'

Freaked, the kid squeaks in agreement. His girlfriend edges from the room. 'I can't . . .'

Jackson's head, locked in my hands, swivels to look at her. 'What do you mean "you can't"?'

'I can't come with you to the hospital,' Wispy Girl says, hopping nervously from foot to foot. 'They'll find out we've been drinking.'

His remaining hair seems to poke up with comic fright. 'Will they?' he asks me.

The hospital staff will smell it on him the second he arrives in Emergency. He's totally screwed. 'Not if you don't tell them,' I lie, letting go. I help Keita pick up the ice cubes.

''Cos I got busted at Apex Park a few months ago and I can't go down a second time.'

Keita laughs. 'Oh yeah! That was you and that Carter kid, right?' She piles ice cubes onto the tea towel, smiling like she's in the company of greatness: a town celebrity. 'The paper couldn't print your names because of your age but everyone knows it was you.'

Jackson smirks. 'Dad'll use my balls for bait if he finds out I've been partying again.'

116

I turn to Keita. 'I'll drive him to the hospital. I need you to hold the ice on his hands.'

She looks pleased – too pleased – like I've asked her on a date. 'I'll grab a couple of roadies for the trip.'

———————

Halfway to the hospital, I slam my hands on the steering wheel. 'Shit.'

'What?' Keita says from the back seat.

'I should've told Tara I was taking her mum's car.'

'She won't care.' She slaps Jackson's head. 'Would you sit still? I can't hold the ice on your hands if you keep moving!'

'I don't feel so good,' Jackson mumbles. If that was supposed to serve as a warning, it wasn't much of one. Next thing I know, he's hurling all over the back seat.

Keita shrieks, winding down her window. 'Oh my God! That's foul!'

Jackson follows up his technicolour yawn with another one, bigger and brighter than the first.

'Screw this!' Keita climbs into the front, hand digging into my shoulder for leverage. The car swerves across the road.

'Hey! Watch it!'

'I'm not sitting in the back with that! He puked all over me!' She rips off her T-shirt and throws it over her head. I hate to admit it, but her sitting next to me in her bra *is* kind of distracting.

In the rear-view mirror, Jackson is now horizontal, Keita's T-shirt covering his face. The stench of his vomit fills the car. I wind down the windows with the knowledge

I'm going to spend the best part of tomorrow cleaning up another mess – one that's not even mine. The thought strikes: this is what people used to do for me.

'Turn here,' Keita instructs, sucking on her vodka. 'Park over there.'

She's pointing at the rosebushes a short distance from the main hospital entrance. Mildura's public hospital is situated across the road from the town rubbish tip. It crosses my mind to dump the little brat there. Maybe that's what the town planners were thinking – put the rubbish tip opposite the public hospital and give the scrubbers a choice. The decent population can go to the private hospital around the corner.

A wheelchair rests against a 'No Smoking' sign. Cigarette butts litter the ground.

'Drop him at the door and I'll ring the night bell,' Keita says. 'We can't hang around or they'll ask questions.'

'You sound like you've done this before.'

She shrugs. 'Corey was mucking around with a nail gun one night. He shot a four-incher through his hand.' She opens the car door. 'Keep the motor running.' She jumps out, grabs the wheelchair and guides it to the car.

I pull the handbrake, get out and help her lift Jackson into the chair. Keita steers him up to the entrance, pushes the green button and bolts to the car. I swing past, barely stopping, and she jumps in. We fly onto Ontario Avenue, Bonnie and Clyde reborn in country Victoria.

Keita swigs her drink and sighs. 'Caroline will have a cow when she smells this car.'

'Caroline?'

'Tara's mum.'

'Oh. Don't worry about it. I'll clean it up.'

'You can do it at my house, if you want? My parents are at the pub celebrating. Dad won five hundred bucks on the greyhounds. Turn at this street. It's the second on the right.'

We pull into Keita's driveway. Her house is a brick veneer framed by conifer trees and a green hedge.

'Move the car onto the lawn,' Keita instructs. 'The hose is twisted round that post over there, see? There's a bunch of old newspapers stacked by the bin that you can use for the lumpy bits.' She digs her pocket and dangles a key. 'I'll be back in a minute.'

By the glow of the interior light, I clean up Jackson's recycled innards, gagging on the stench. I hope the little shit wakes up tomorrow in so much pain he's pissing in his pants and crying for his mummy. I should've rubbed his nose in it like you do to a dog, but I know from experience it achieves nothing. In a few days he'll be parading his battle wounds in front of his mates, laughing off the night he turned himself into a roast pig on a spit. Then he'll do something else stupid and something else and something else again, and get pissed so many times he loses count, and ten years down the track he'll wake up one morning and wonder what the fuck he's done with his life.

Keita returns to the car, sipping from a cleanskin bottle. She holds it out to me. 'Want some?'

'Nah, I'm right.'

She takes another swig. 'How'd you go?'

'Stinks like wet dog.'

'Thought it might.' She throws me a can of air-freshener.

I spray it, emptying the can, then take another whiff. Now it smells like I took a dump and tried to cover it up. I climb into the driver's seat and Keita gets in.

'Tara's probably wondering where we are. She's not stupid, you know. She'll think we snuck off together.' Keita gives me a sideways glance, gauging my reaction.

I can't help but smirk. You'd think she'd give up. I admit it would be easy; easy to pull the car into a quiet little parking bay and stick my tongue down her throat. But there's something about her that tells me filling her up won't make her full. Besides, I've complicated my life enough with two chicks. A third is getting greedy.

I reverse the car onto the road. 'We'd better get back.'

She gulps more wine. 'You think I'm fat, don't you?'

'Huh?'

'That's why you're not interested. I'm huge. I look ridiculous next to Tara.' She's crying too.

I turn the car onto Ontario Avenue. 'I don't think you're fat.'

'Hamish says I'm fat.'

'Hamish Johnson?'

She nods. 'He said something to Corey.'

Knowing Hamish's father, Tiny, like I do, I don't doubt Hamish fell out of the same cookie cutter; it wouldn't surprise me if he said stuff like that to girls. 'Maybe you heard him wrong?'

She perks up. 'Maybe.' She rests the bottle between her legs and gazes out the window. 'I dunno . . .'

There's something a bit desperate about this girl. She's looking for approval from someone – *anyone* – and I'm not sure if I'm the one to give it to her. 'For what it's worth, I think you're attractive,' I tell her, despite my better judgement.

Her smile lights the night. 'You do?'

'Sure.'

Her light quickly dims. 'You're blind.'

'Sorry?'

'You're blind.' She covers my eyes. 'You need a walking cane.'

I wrench her hand away, but not before the car straddles the white dividing line. Bright headlights fly past, horn honking. My heart hammers. I correct the vehicle and attempt to make light of the idiotic thing she just did. 'Hey, go easy, Keita. You want them scraping us off the road?'

She reaches out again, this time waving her hand in my face. 'Tell me the truth, Justin.'

I catch her hand and push it back. Now I'm driving one-handed. 'I *am* telling you the truth! Will you stop that?'

'Tell me the truth! Tell me the truth!' she chants, wriggling free. She waves both hands in my face. She's a loose cannon, tickling my chest, my stomach, my groin.

'Keita! Cut it out!'

The road stretches before me, flickering black and white. Wheels rip at the gravel and my body rocks as the car swerves. She struggles, laughing. I push her away and she lets out a yelp. *Shit!* I've punched her. I'm my old man – I punched a woman! 'Oh God, I'm sorry, Keita. I'm so sorry! I didn't mean to –'

Her eyes widen. 'Look out!'

Bright white lights up the car's interior. Our capsule becomes a private disco.

The world slows as an apparition floats past my window: a girl draped in a white Grecian dress, blonde tendrils whipping in the wind. I hear her voice, a breezy whisper in my ear.

The sound is all but drowned out by the thunderous applause of groaning steel and shattering glass.

Margo

I can't believe I'm parked outside a servo, waiting for Corey to buy cigarettes. How did I let Amy talk me into this? If her dad catches me, I'll lose my licence for sure. I shouldn't have listened. I should have gone home and stayed home. This is stupid. Stupid, stupid, stupid.

Amy's dark hair swings from side to side as she strides towards the toilets. Maybe she *is* using me. Maybe that kiss was just another part of her act. Something to distract me. This night isn't turning out the way I thought it would. All I need now is for Ralph to pick up a late-night litre of milk. He'll have a fit. He won't even stop to ask questions. He'll haul me out and drive me home. Maybe that wouldn't be such a bad thing. Maybe a small part of me secretly hopes he will.

Amy's drink sits in the console, a partner to Corey's half-empty stubby. I think about taking a sip, but then remember I'm supposed to have a zero blood-alcohol reading. What a joke! I'm driving on my L-plates without a fully licensed driver *and* carrying peer passengers. How many laws do I want to break in one go?

Eventually, Corey swaggers to the car, clutching two cigarette packets and a large bag of potato chips to his chest. He gets in and tells me to fire up the engine. I think he's going to get me to drive off and leave Amy behind, but he depresses the cigarette lighter and fiddles with the stereo. The radio blares the familiar riff of an AC/DC song. He sculls the rest of his stubby, belches and disposes of it behind the seat. In the same movement, he extracts a bottle of whisky, unscrews the cap and necks it.

'Christ!' he curses, resting the bottle between his legs. 'You know, when I woke up this morning, my throat killed like it does when I'm gunna get tonsillitis, so I downed half a bottle of this stuff.'

'You drank whisky for breakfast?'

'Nah, I had Weet-Bix, but I drank whisky to get rid of my cold. That's what my old man does when he's coming down with a bug – he drowns it. By lunchtime, I'd never felt better.'

I wonder if Corey feels anything – he's constantly anaesthetised.

He lights up, a haze of smoke filling the car. I cough and wind down my window. He takes another drag, smirking. 'Want one, princess?'

'No.'

He turns up the radio and AC/DC lyrics thump. His phone beeps and he flicks the screen. Then he groans in disgust. 'Have a look at this,' he says, holding the phone out to me.

At first I think he's showing me some kind of porno, but then I realise it's Tara Ramsey – practically *naked*.

I can't conceal my shock. 'Who sent you that?'

He shoves the phone in his pocket and belts the car door. 'Idiots. What were they thinking?'

'Who?'

'Whoever took that photo.'

'You think someone *made* her do that?'

He looks at me, dark eyes shadowy under the glow of the fluorescent servo lights. 'Hey, I know Tara gets up to a lot of stuff, but she wouldn't do that. She's got more class than that.'

'That's what *you* think.'

'Yeah, well, I know you're not her biggest fan . . .'

'How do you know?'

He shrugs. 'Stuff she's said.'

'She's the one who has a problem with *me*, not the other way round.'

'Sounds like it goes both ways.'

'She started it.'

Corey laughs. '"She started it." You sound like a five-year-old.'

I don't bother arguing. How do you explain the years of snide remarks, dirty looks and underhand behaviour? It's not any *one* thing, it's the weight of all of it. Tara was a pile of steaming muck heaped on top of me day after day; she never went away.

'Where's Amy?' Corey asks impatiently. 'Did she fall down the shitter or what?'

'I'll get her.' I open the car door, but he leans across me and closes it.

'Leave it. She'll be out soon enough.' He passes me the whisky. 'Drink up, princess.'

I push it back at him. 'Stop calling me "princess".'

'How come you're not partying, princess?'

I tap the steering wheel. 'Gee, I don't know . . .'

He swigs another mouthful. 'I can drive, if you want.'

I don't bother honouring that with a response. I look up and see Amy running to the car. 'Hey, you two! Thanks a lot! The bloody toilet door got stuck. Couldn't you hear me yelling for help?'

Corey turns up the music, thrashing his head, as if that should serve as an answer.

Amy shakes her head at him, climbs in and reaches for her drink. I rev the engine and turn the car out of the service station, headed in the direction of Kylie's place.

'Nah, do a U-ey,' Corey commands.

'Why?'

'Just do it.'

Reluctantly, I turn the car around. 'Where are we going?'

'Jaycee Park.' He drags on his smoke. 'I need some fresh air.'

'I don't think that's a good idea, Corey,' I argue. 'It's amazing we've got away with this much.'

'Just do it.'

I look at Amy in the rear-view mirror. She rolls her eyes and shrugs. So I drive to the park, convincing myself we'll stay for maybe twenty minutes and then head back to the party, where I'll make my apologies, leave and walk home.

While I'm sober and behind the wheel, Corey and

Amy are alive and safe. What happens after that is not my problem.

At the park, entry signage displays a list of council by-laws. Some have been defaced. 'No Alcohol in the park' reads as 'No A-hols in the park'. 'No Dogs Allowed' appears with a stick figure walking a dog, except someone has redrawn it to look like the stick figure is taking advantage of the animal. It's stupid and juvenile, but for some reason I find myself laughing.

Corey wastes no time settling himself on the play equipment. He straddles a swing seat and taps his lap. 'Fancy a ride?'

Amy groans. 'Keep it in your pants, Corey.' She sits on the other swing and waves me over. 'Push me, Margo?'

I go and stand behind her and give her a heave. She launches into the air, arms spread wide, laughing.

Corey rocks sideways and takes a swig. Half the bottle is gone. 'Like my wheels?' He points unsteadily at his car. 'It belonged to my gramps, but the old dude is cactus now ... lawn fertiliser. Anyway, me and Hames took the beast out last weekend and laid tracks with it. Did some pretty spec circle work on the road out've town too. Hames reckons he did that mega long one, but he's trippin' if he thinks he did. He can't control the wheel like I can.'

'Hamish lost his licence, didn't he?' Amy says.

Corey smacks his head. 'Whoops. Shouldn't've told you that.'

'You let Hamish *drive*?'

'Well, it's not like he can lose his licence again, can he?' His logic is undeniable. 'Hey, can you keep a secret?'

Amy doesn't hesitate. 'What?'

'You wouldn't dog on me, would ya, Margo?' he says, looking at me.

I'm unprepared to commit to anything when it comes to Corey. 'It depends . . .'

He swings a while longer, weighing up his options. Finally, probably emboldened by the booze, he comes out with it. 'We did over the cemetery the same night.'

My insides sting. 'What?'

Amy digs her feet into the dirt, grinding herself to a halt. 'That was *you*?'

'Actually, that was Hamish. I thought we'd go there for a bit of a laugh, freak each other out and stuff, that sort of thing. But Hamish went mental, eh? You should have seen him smashing stuff left, right and centre. Pure psycho. I had to duck for cover or he would've knocked my head clean off.'

'The body?' Amy asks. 'The one that got moved?'

Corey rolls his shoulders and sighs. 'Yeah, that was us. And I'd hardly call it a body. It wasn't juicy or anything. Hamish has the bones under his bed.'

My ribs constrict. *Justin's mother!*

Amy's mouth hangs open. 'Fuck . . .' she breathes.

'It wasn't my finest moment, I admit.' Corey looks as though he's telling the truth. 'When I woke up the next morning, I felt guilty as hell. I wanted to take the bones back, but Hamish wouldn't let me. He reckons whoever we dug up is as dead as a doornail, so why should it matter?'

'What about their relatives?' Amy says. 'They're not dead. The report I saw on Facebook said they had to be contacted.'

'Yeah, well, I was kind of hoping we'd dug up an old one. I was hoping the whole family was dead, actually. That way, they'd be none the wiser.'

He's wrong. He couldn't be more wrong.

'Besides,' he adds, 'it's not like we *meant* to upset anyone. We were drunk. We were mucking around.'

Amy is unsympathetic. 'Digging up dead people *isn't* what I'd call mucking around.'

Corey gives her a menacing glare. 'We *were* mucking around.'

'What about the bones?' I ask. 'Are they still under Hamish's bed?'

'Yeah. Why?'

I turn and walk in the direction of the road. I have to find Justin. I have to tell him. I can't even begin to think how I'll do that. He's going to kill Corey. And Hamish. Maybe even me, for hanging out with these people in the first place.

'Hey, Margo!' Corey yells out. 'Where's the fire?'

I don't stop.

Amy catches up to me. 'God! He's such a moron! Slow down. I'll walk back with you.' She reaches for my hand. 'It was a dumb idea to make you drive. I'm sorry.'

I shake her off. She thinks I'm angry about Corey. She has no idea.

'Hey, Amy!' Corey calls out. 'Are you gunna tell your old man?'

'You just confessed to a crime!' Amy yells back.

'Oh! And you're so bloody innocent, aren't you?' He sways on his feet, holding the bottle high, as if it's a beacon of truth. 'What about last weekend?'

Amy stops.

'What about driving around with me *now*, princess? What about all the booze I buy for you and your friends?'

'There's a difference,' she mumbles. 'It's about respecting others . . .'

Corey marches up to her and sticks a finger in her collarbone. 'Hey. No one in this town bothers to respect *me*. Why should I respect them?'

'When you do stupid things like trash the cemetery, what do you *think* is going to happen?'

'Screw 'em!' Corey shouts. 'People round here got plenty of money to replace headstones. People round here got plenty of money for everything.'

'What does money have to do with it?' Amy counters.

'What've I got? Stuff all − that's what I've got!' His voice is bitter, his fists clenched with rage. 'I tried to get a mechanic apprenticeship and, even though my grades were all right, they wouldn't take me on. I applied at Lawson's Panel 'n' Paint, but the manager took on Holden Swinburg instead − you know, Jackson's brother? Holden's grades are no better than mine. Bert took him on 'cos his dad plays golf with him, the toffee-nosed old sod. Bet he took him 'cos his name's Holden and he's fixing cars, so he probably thinks that's funny. I've tried everywhere in town. No one wants to throw me a line. What am I supposed to do?'

Despite what I know – the fact it's Justin's mother Corey has dug up, and the fact tonight's little expedition could get me in a lot of trouble – I feel myself warming to Corey. His pain is genuine. It's plain for anyone to see. I don't know why I haven't noticed it before.

He kicks the dirt. 'Couldn't even make it to the big league with footy. Got picked for the coaching clinic, but that's as far as it went. Teachers were right. They said I was gunna amount to nothing. Vermont was always twisting my ear when no one was looking, saying stuff like he went to school with my old man and I was gunna turn out just like him: a no-hoper. That I came from shit and I'm always gunna be shit.'

Amy folds her arms. 'You need to try harder, Corey. Don't give up so easy.'

He takes a mouthful. 'And that's exactly what I'd expect from the copper's daughter. You've got it easy, haven't ya? Bet the policeman's baby gets whatever her little heart desires.'

Amy grabs the bottle from him and takes a long swig. 'Have you ever thought about what it's like to live with a cop?'

'Gee, it must be *so* hard!'

'Fuck you!' she spits.

'I think I know what you mean,' I say. Both of them stop arguing and turn to stare at me. 'About getting a fair go, I mean.'

Corey's all ears. 'Yeah? What would you know about that?'

I point to my bare arm.

He looks uncomfortable. 'What's *that* got to do with it?'

'Are you really going to ask me that?'

He rolls his eyes.

'What Vermont said to you was wrong, Corey. You should have reported him.'

He gives a cynical laugh. 'Report him? He was the one reporting me! I got detention every other day. And then I copped it again from the old man when I got home.' He takes a swig and gurgles. 'Anyway, screw school! School's over. All I wanna do now is have a good time. I want to forget this town and all the stuck-up turds who live in it.' His hand grapples for my pocket. He plucks his car keys and spins them on his pointer finger. 'You coming or what?'

I don't move. Amy also hesitates.

'Come on, we'll be back at the party in less than two minutes.' He shakes the keys. 'You're a good chick, Margo. You don't deserve to get busted. If anyone's gunna get busted, it's gunna be me. It might as well happen sooner than later. The suspense is killing me, anyway.' He goes to his car.

After a moment, Amy throws her hands in the air and follows him.

'Amy?'

'I can't be bothered walking,' she says over her shoulder. 'Like I said, Margo, if my old man catches him, I'll tell him I didn't know Corey had been drinking. Easy.'

Maybe Amy's had enough to drink not to care. Maybe, like me, she's gambling on the fact it's only a few minutes' drive to Kylie's and the chances of getting caught are slim. If Corey could be off his head laying tracks on the highway into Mildura last weekend without rolling the car or getting caught, surely he could drive a straight kilometre up the road at sixty clicks without too much trouble?

He holds the door open to the front passenger seat. 'We've got away with it so far,' he says.

I get in the car, telling myself it'll be a few short minutes; before I know it, we'll be back at the party and then I can walk home and pretend this night never happened.

Amy gets in the back. She grabs my shoulder for leverage and reaches into the front seat to turn up the radio. Country music blares. Corey fires the ignition and we turn onto the main road.

———

I see her coming out of the fog: a weightless, ethereal being. She glides past my window, mouth open, singing a muted serenade.

Wheels screech.

She swallows me whole in her luminous white light.

Corey

Someone's crying. He's wailing like a fucking baby. Shut him up, for God's sake. *Shut him up!*

Escaping gas hisses. A car radio crackles broken country tunes. Feet beat heavy on the pavement – frenzied bombs dropping one after the other. My breath rasps in my ears. The sting of a thorny branch slaps me, then another, then another. Sirens rip through the dead of night. Blue and red lights chase the shadows. I crouch like a feral cat hiding in a garden.

Flashing beacons fly past. A dog barks, then a porch light turns on and a door opens. 'Who's out there?' somebody growls.

I run, teeth snapping at my heels.

'Hey! Get back here!'

The dog, chained to the gate, goes nowhere.

'That's it! Run, you gutless wonder! If I find out who you are, the cops will be the least of your worries!'

The door slams behind me.

I keep running until a movie set comes into view; a strange outdoor stage lit up like a New Year's sky. Actors shout lines, scurrying this way and that. They carry props: white boxes embellished with green crosses, shiny silver blankets, white stretcher beds, two-way radios, saline drippers.

I was here. *Before.*

A megaphone blasts: *Get the cones on the road! Block it off! I don't want this to turn into a flippin' circus like the last one. You got it?*

I kneel behind a tree and watch. A car is on its roof, curls of smoke rising from its brown metal underbelly. Another car rests against a tree, groaning as large metal teeth bite into its chassis. Men in orange spacesuits spray white cotton and rake mounds of kitty litter.

A cop runs from stage right: 'Amy!' He falls on his knees, draping himself over the motionless body lying in the grass. He lifts her torso into his arms, howling. 'My girl! My little girl!' It's a midday soap opera. He's overplayed it. I wait for the director to shout 'Take two!', but the direction doesn't come.

A white van pulls up and men in navy-blue jumpsuits with silver leg reflectors pour from the sliding doors. One of them tries to peel the cop from the girl and has a hard time restraining him.

'Amy! *Why?!*' the copper chokes, fists swinging in the air.

Another copper rushes in to calm him. 'Easy, Brian, easy . . .'

'Dominic, tell me, who was it? Who was driving?'

'You need to hold it together, boss.'

'Who was driving?'

Dominic's throat is now caught in Brian's grip. Dominic points at a girl by the roadside, the one wrapped in a foil blanket. 'I'm doing the interview with her now. I've called for the Aboriginal liaison officer.'

His words are hot air. Brian grabs the girl by the shoulders. 'Tell me what happened?'

She doesn't speak.

'What's your name? What's your bloody name?!'

Her voice is small. 'Margo Bonney.'

'Were you driving?'

A shake of the head.

'Don't you lie to me! Tell me! Were you driving?'

Her answer is drowned out by a series of sharp cries coming from the tree-house car. Orange jumpsuit men fight with blue jumpsuit men in a battle for ultimate supremacy.

'We need to get in there . . .'

'We'll have him out in one minute . . .'

'That's a minute too long!'

'No, no! Too much force. Slow it down, Harvey.'

'You wanna do it, Frank?'

'That's it . . . Got him . . . Stand back . . .'

They lay the guy flat on the stretcher: sliced ham on sandwich wrap. He screams like a sissy boy. 'My leg! Christ, my leg!'

An ambo fusses with a gauze bandage. 'Would it be too much to ask to get some light over here?' He turns to his assistant. 'What about the girl?'

'Minor head wound. Airbag did the job. Sprained or broken wrist, not sure. Could be internal bleeding. We need to get her out. They're cutting the door now.'

Stretcher Meat tries to sit himself up. 'Is she okay?'

'Mate, you need to lie down.'

With one arm, he shoves the ambo aside and strains to see into the car. 'Is she all right or not?'

My insides twist. It's Pretty Boy from the party! God! Is that Tara in the car?

'Come on, buddy. Lie down, please. Anita, pass me the tape, will you?'

Pretty Boy fires up. 'Is she all right or not? Can't you people give a straight answer?'

'What's your name, champ?'

He stares at the ambo.

'Your name?'

'Justin.'

'Justin *who*?'

'Justin Sparks.'

'Well, you need to try to stay calm, Justin.' The ambo skilfully wraps his bloodied leg. 'What's your girlfriend's name?'

'Keita. She's not my girlfriend.'

Keita? What's she doing in the car with him?

Another cop car pulls up and the boys in blue pile out.

'Have you been drinking, Justin?'

'No.'

'Drugs?'

Pretty Boy laughs.

'Have you?'

'No.'

'What about Keita? It's important you tell us so we can treat her properly.'

'She's had a few drinks.' He struggles to sit up. His words sound lisped. 'Is she gunna be all right or what?'

'Don't know yet, mate. Let's concentrate on sorting you out. Do you know what happened? What caused the accident?'

He rubs his forehead. It's a while before he answers. 'I saw a girl on the road.'

He saw her too.

'A girl? What did she look like?'

'Um . . . she was wearing white. That's all I remember.'

The ambo looks around. 'Is she here? Did the car hit her? Where is she?'

Pretty Boy is drowned out by shouting. Metres away, Margo and the copper are going at it hammer and tongs. Behind Margo, Amy is being loaded into the back of an ambulance. Sirens wail and the copper curses, 'Where is he then? If you say he was driving, where is he?'

An orange-suited woman wraps her arm around Margo. 'Sir! Please! That's enough! She's suffering from shock. This is *not* the time.'

'Not the time? My kid is in that bloody ambulance!' the copper shouts. He shakes a fist in Margo's face. 'You tell me where he is right this second!'

Margo sways, her body shuddering. Her knees give out and she crumbles into a semi-upright heap. The copper towers over her, spitting ash and steam. 'I'll tell you why you don't know! Because Corey Williams wasn't driving that car! *You* were!'

When he says my name, none of it seems real.

I get up and leave my private theatre. I can't watch any more.

At home, the house is silent.

I open Felicity's bedroom door and see her sleeping, one leg hanging out from under the doona, blonde hair a knotted mess on the pillow. Earphones dangle from her ears. She doesn't stir, not even a twitch.

I creep down the hall and catch a glimpse of the old girl, flat on her back, open mouth sucking the darkness. The old man's snores are no contest; she's a garbage disposal unit on full blast.

In the bathroom, I look in the mirror. An ugly mug with a gaping gash to his forehead greets me. Blood stains my T-shirt in long, dark streaks. I peel it off, go outside and stuff it in the wheelie bin. Back inside, I rip off my jeans and turn on the shower. Steam clouds the mirror. I climb in and the water burns. The washcloth stings like murder and I waver, a hellish pain throbbing in my head, ripping me apart. I scrub myself raw.

There's that crying again . . . Some guy is whining his stupid head off.

Shut up! Shut up! *Shut up!*

The shower screen cracks under my fist. Come on, Corey! Pull yourself together, man! Crunching metal fills my head. The image of Margo swims behind my eyelids, her body crouched over Amy's, eyes pleading, mouth moving in slow motion, making strange shapes only I can understand: *Corey! Do something! Do something!*

But I couldn't do anything.

All I could do was run.

Tara

Morning sun seeps through the blinds, fingers of light creeping into the corners of my mind.

I stare up at the textured slab that is my ceiling. Subtle ridges, tiny variations in the thickness of the paint, long lines where roof beams hide beneath. If I slide sideways, twist my body and hang my head over the edge of the bed, it's like I'm up there, part of an upside-down world. Furniture, objects, mountains of things are glued fast, unable to fall. I'm untouchable. Unreachable.

My head throbs harder.

I let my head pound until my eyes water and silent tears run past my temples, dripping onto the ceiling. They form a lake, then a raging ocean. My room and everything in it swims. The boat rocks. My stomach clenches, releases, clenches again. A dull ache niggles down below. I swallow, tasting the bitterness of painkillers on the back of my tongue. My throat is sore, bled dry from vomiting. I smell of him. He's there, on my skin – stale breath, bourbon tongue, acrid sweat. He slithers, his fingers caught in my hair, yanking the roots, pulling, *pushing*. His voice scratches my ear: *There's a good girl. There's a good girl. There's a good girl.*

The phone rings.

I sit up and blood rushes from my head, draining me to an empty shell.

'Tara?' Mum's voice echoes. 'Pick up, will you? That police officer . . . What's his name again?' I hear Trevor's voice in the background. 'Dominic, yes, Dominic. He called a few minutes ago. He says my car was involved in an accident. He thinks it was stolen. He's looking at charging some blow-in junkie called Justin Something. Tara? Are you there? Tara?'

The edge of my bed is now a cliff face. Below me, an angry sea churns, tossing, turning, whirling. The cops called me too. They wanted to know if I let Justin borrow the car. I said I did. That was all they wanted to know. Like that was the only crime committed last night.

'I've tried calling your phone, Tara. Why won't you answer me? Why do you have to keep punishing me like this?'

Fragments of last night reel: Justin helping me to a bedroom. Voices arguing. Weight bearing down. Pain. Laughter. The slap of hands. My bare feet massaging a cold bitumen road. White lights. The explosion of steel on steel.

Drifting.

Running.

'There's money in a Milo tin in my undies drawer. If you need it, use it. We've decided to head home. Call me as soon as you get this . . . Please call me?'

Click.

I roll away from the edge of the cliff and press my face into the pillow.

———————

'Tara!' The bedroom window rattles. 'Tara! Are you in there?'

Through a crack in the slat blinds, I see Keita. She's standing on my front lawn, something green hanging from her neck – a scarf?

She steps away from the window, her ugg-boot feet dancing on the spot. 'Hey, Tara! Let me in!'

I go to the door. I'm about to open it when I'm jarred by the sight of a white sheet. It's stretched across the tiled floor like a giant bird-shit stain. Streaks of dried blood spatter it and a jagged tear in the corner practically screams. I quickly ball it up and shove it behind the couch before opening the door.

'Finally!' Keita breathes. She pushes past me, headed for the couch, where she dumps a plastic shopping bag and plonks herself down on the shagpile rug, kicking off her ugg boots. I see it now – it's not a scarf, but a sling, resting her right arm.

'I went to Kylie's,' she says. 'I thought you'd slept there.' Her eyes glow bloodshot red – a mini roadmap of last night's exploits. 'I found these in the bedroom.' She points to the bag of clothes and winks at me like I must have picked up, like I wore my boyfriend's oversized T-shirt home. 'Glad you had a better night than I did. Oh, and your phone's in there too. I can't believe you left without your phone! I mean, I'd be having a cow without mine.'

I grab the bag and fish for it. When I speak for the first

time, it sounds like I've swallowed sand. 'Did you speak to my mum?'

She reaches for a magazine and strums it, bending the corners into a pyramid of dog ears. 'She called my house. I didn't talk to her. Dad got it. They talked for ages. He's spewing about the accident. Have you spoken to your mum? Did she cut sick about her car? Is that why you're, like, I don't know, spacey?' She doesn't wait for an answer. 'I'm guessing the cops told you that her car's been towed. Everyone's talking about it. Facebook is going off. Amy's in hospital.'

Amy's in hospital?

'It's Mabo's fault, of course. Who knows what she was doing in a car with Amy and Corey. I didn't think anyone liked her.'

'Margo Bonney?'

'Yeah.'

'She was with Amy?'

Keita doesn't bother to explain. 'Justin and I were on our way back to the party, and we were having this totally killer time, mucking around and stuff, and then next minute –' her eyes widen – 'there was all this light and . . . *Boom!*'

'You were in the accident? You were with Justin?'

She stares at me for a moment. 'What planet have you been on, Tara?' She points to her arm sling. 'What do think this thing is? Dad went berko when he found out. He reckons Margo's as good as toast. He's gunna kill her.'

Flashes appear in my mind like still frames from a movie reel. The bonfire. Kissing Justin in the laundry. Cammo trapping me in the toilet. A dark figure at my feet. *Pain.*

143

Running from the party. Running from the accident, a sheet clutched to my chest.

'I heard an ambo say something about how Amy's dad shouldn't even be allowed at the accident scene. That's how I found out she was in the other car.'

'Is Amy all right?'

'I heard them say they were taking her to Intensive Care. That's all I know. It's pretty fucked up.' Keita skims her tongue across a split in her top lip. I didn't notice it before now. It's bloodied and bruised; it must have happened in the accident. 'You know what? Margo said Corey was driving. It was his car, for sure, but Margo was *definitely* the one driving. Corey wasn't even there. I didn't see him. And besides, I don't think Margo . . .'

Keita's voice falls away and I'm back there, standing on the road.

My teeth chatter. Each breath clouds in front of me like cotton candy. Wet runs down my inside leg. White headlights appear and a car swerves. A rush of wind snaps material against my bare legs. Eyes – *dark eyes* – peer from a frosted car window. The sound of ripping gravel fills my ears.

Keita pulls back her bandage to show me a bruise. 'It's sprained, but the doctor said it'll be okay. He reckons it was a good thing both cars were travelling at a fairly low speed otherwise someone could've been killed.'

'What about Justin?'

She touches her butterfly necklace, guilt swimming in her eyes. 'He sat with me in Emergency. His leg was injured, but it wasn't bad or anything. They gave him crutches.' Tentatively, as though she's treading a fine wire, she asks, 'Have you looked at Facebook? You know Cammo took photos of you, right?' Her face flushes red. 'I tried to stop them.'

I turn on my phone. Two hundred and forty-nine notifications. Countless PMs. I glimpse a thumbnail of myself with the tag 'Mumma's jubblies had too much bubbly'.

An uneasy heat radiates from the pit of my belly. 'Everyone's seen this?'

Keita looks at my phone as if to say, *There's your answer.*

My head spins.

'Tara, by the time I knew anything about it, they'd already taken the photos.'

My legs buckle. The shagpile rug falls away. I'm spiralling down between its thick threads, grasping at a woollen forest. Words try to surface. Was this why? Is this why they . . . they . . .?

Keita sniffs, holding back tears. 'It's not *my* fault, if that's what you're thinking. You're the one who got smashed.'

'Sorry?'

'I didn't pour it down your throat. You did it to yourself.'

I stare at her.

Her jaw stiffens. 'I'm just saying –'

'Get out.'

She sits there, not moving.

'I said, *get out!*' I drag her to her feet and push her to the door.

'Tara . . . I'm sorry. I didn't mean to –'

'Save it!' I push her onto the porch and slam the door between us.

Then I slump against it and cry like I'll never stop.

Justin

So I come back to get my life together and instead I end up in an even bigger mess. Car accident, body banged up, mother dug up, father the town joke. Maybe this is my life? My emperor's new clothes are *not* coming. They never were. The sooner I learn to wear the rags of my destiny, the less surprised by life's bullshit I'll be.

I balance on hospital-issue crutches, leaning against the front desk of the police station. A familiar itch hankers for a scratch. The voices nags louder: *One hit. One. That's all. One bump to take the edge off. One score, then back on the straight and narrow. One. One. One . . .*

The copper shoves a third pink form under my nose. Unlike the last two, this one has a whole lot of fine print. The Melbourne lawyer who got my sixteen-year-old backside off for flogging an old guy's wallet said you should never sign any legal form until you read it and you're satisfied you understand it. I scan the paper. It's complete horseshit. How is it that lawyers graduate when what they write is as clear as bloody mud?

The young copper points to the dotted line. 'Stick your autograph here and you can go.'

I scribble something resembling a signature. I don't have an official signature – you need to be a fully fledged adult to have one of those.

'Don't go leaving town.' He grins at his cliché and leans over the counter to inspect my bandaged leg. 'Guess you won't be going far.'

'Buggered ankle. Twenty stitches in my shin.'

'You're lucky. Could have been worse.'

He doesn't have to tell me.

I need to get out of here. I need to know how the others ended up. I know the policeman's daughter is in hospital – the cop told me – but I don't know what her condition is. I know Keita is okay because I was with her when she was discharged. I have no idea about Margo. I still can't get past the fact the cops told me she was driving Corey's car. *And drinking.* It doesn't make sense. The cops asked me if I saw anyone else at the scene and I told them what I could remember: I didn't see Corey, but that doesn't mean he wasn't there. They said they'd interview him when they could get a hold of him; he wasn't at home when they'd called around.

The copper smiles. 'Good thing speeding wasn't a factor and your result came up clean. Doesn't happen much around here.'

It's unusual for me to receive praise from anyone, much less from a cop. I have no means of processing it.

'I checked your story with the Ramsey girl. She confirmed she let you borrow the car. I've phoned her mother. The insurance mob will have to sort it out.' He slides a business card across the desk. I didn't know cops had business cards.

I wonder if he enjoys business lunches and goes on business trips too. 'That's my number.'

The card reads 'Dominic Carbone' – the name I was given last Wednesday when I called the station, looking for information about my mother. 'It's you,' I say clumsily.

'Sorry?'

'You're the one managing the investigation.'

A blank look.

'The graveyard robbery.' But as soon as the words have left my mouth, I realise they sound ridiculous – like a newspaper headline from the eighteenth century. 'My mother's grave was vandalised.'

He slaps his head as if he hadn't made the connection. 'Right, right. You called the station when I was out on my rounds. Sorry, mate. I haven't had a quiet minute to get back to you.'

'So you've found her?'

'No.'

'But you're looking?'

'In case you haven't noticed, I've been trying to keep people *out* of the cemetery, not put them back in.' Amusement flashes across his face. 'Look, you don't need to worry. We'll find her. These things take time.' He shuffles his paperwork into a neat little pile.

He hasn't started looking. I can tell. I turn and hobble to the door.

'Justin?'

'Yeah?'

He unlatches the desk gate and steps into the foyer,

carrying his clipboard. Looking over his shoulder to check there's no one within earshot, excitement rises in his voice. 'That girl you mentioned ... the one on the road before the accident?'

'Yeah?'

'Are you *sure* you don't know who she is?'

I've already told him what I know: I saw a girl and she was wearing white. She was nothing but a blur. I didn't even see her face. Apparently, the ambos couldn't find her. One of them suggested I'd dreamt her, said people see stuff like that when they think they're about to die.

He looks over his shoulder again, then leans in. 'Maybe it was your mother.'

My crutches wobble.

I must be looking at him as though he's a complete moron because he adds pointedly, 'Her grave got *disturbed*.' Now he's the one looking at me like *I'm* the moron. 'If her ghost didn't distract you, you might've hit that other car head-on. You might be dead too. She *saved* you.' He fiddles with his clipboard, scuttles back behind his desk. 'I'll be in touch.' Head down, not looking at me.

I leave the station, the officer's business card burning a hole in my pocket: *Dominic Carbone: Psychic Medium.* Could he be right? Was it my mother I saw on the road?

I'm a few metres up the footpath when I see Keita storming towards me like a bulldozer with no one at the wheel. When she spots me, she hesitates, feet twitching. Her eyes are full of dread. One look and I know she knows what she did. She *knows* she's responsible for the accident.

We stand at ten paces, weighing each other up.

'What'd you tell them?' she asks, nodding at the police station.

'What do you think I told them?'

She comes close, hand on her hip, her fingers digging the folds of her belly. 'It wasn't my fault.'

I nod.

'It wasn't,' she insists. I try to edge past, but it's like we're back in Kylie's kitchen and she blocks my path. 'Did you tell them it was my fault?'

There was no point telling the cops about Keita's passenger antics. She may have behaved like a total idiot, but I've been high off my arse enough times to know she wasn't in control. What good was telling the cops going to do? One look into her terrified eyes tells me she's already suffering. Nothing will change that.

'I didn't drop you in it, if that's what you're worried about.'

Her shoulders dip, her defences coming down. 'Why not?'

'Don't think I was protecting you. I wasn't.'

'What were you doing, then?'

I lean hard on one crutch, the other falls against the stone wall of someone's garden. 'I've stuffed up and *known* I've stuffed up. Believe me, there isn't anyone on this planet who can punish you better than you can punish yourself.'

If I thought empathising with her would break her down, I was wrong. Her defence shield springs back up. 'I did *not* stuff up,' she insists, enunciating each word clearly.

'I know what you did. *You* know what you did. Come on, Keita . . .'

She gives me nothing – she *is* the stone wall I've leant my crutch on. Steely determination burns in her eyes. 'Margo's going down for this, *not* me.'

I may have only just met Margo, but every cell I'm made of tells me she isn't capable of causing the accident. If Margo says she wasn't driving, then I believe her. When the coppers catch up with Corey, Margo will be cleared of any wrongdoing. I know it.

Keita turns on her heel and marches up the street, putting as much distance between herself and the truth as she can. 'My dad will make sure Margo pays!' she shouts over her shoulder. 'And I'll be the first person standing in line to watch it happen!'

I grab my crutches and hobble home. As I reach the front gate, I'm semiconscious of a car engine roaring up alongside me. The door opens. 'Young Sparksy?'

It's Hamish's dad, Tiny Johnson. Beads of sweat pour from his plump face. His nose glows like a hot bulb.

'Yeah?'

'Might be some trouble. Someone at the pub reckons your old man and Daryl Sanders are planning to take matters into their own hands.'

'Daryl Sanders . . . as in Keita's dad?'

'Yeah. You know the guy who helped us with the tow-rope? Ralph Bonney? Daryl reckons he's gunna give him a serve for what Margo did to you kids.'

Shit. Keita wasn't kidding.

He taps the car seat. 'Get in.'

Margo

'I thought I knew you, Margo! I thought you were better than this?'

The midday sun glares through our kitchen window: a powerful spotlight. I sit on a chair, fingernails digging the fabric seat, my head heavy and fatigued; I can barely keep it upright. Ralph circles me. Shouting. Ranting. Raving. Delivering parental justice in spades. I close my eyes to block him out, but instead the image of Amy's dad yelling at me burns. *Corey Williams wasn't driving that car! You were!*

'Maybe you're more like your no-good father than I first thought.'

My white father: the blackened core of my every mistake.

'What were you thinking? Margo? Answer me!'

Mum comes into the kitchen, peeling off her blue hospital-logo cardigan. She was meant to be at work more than an hour ago. She swapped shifts because they couldn't allow her any more than the morning off; they were already low on staff.

'I don't think speaking like that is necessary, do you,

Ralph? Can't we talk about this sensibly? Our daughter didn't have a personality transplant overnight.'

'Pull your head out of the sand, Jessie!' Ralph booms. 'Look at the evidence!'

Bradley appears in the doorway. 'Can I get something to eat?'

Ralph explodes – I've never seen him so angry. He shoves Bradley into the living room and slams the door. He looks at me. 'The *truth* this time, Margo. I want the truth.'

Hot tears hang on the end of my nose. One night – how can *one* night change everything? I'm no longer boring Margo, social nobody, straight-A student. I'm the drunken Abo bitch who nearly killed a bunch of innocent teenagers.

'Explain to me this little nugget.' Ralph's neck muscles are strung taut as a barbed-wire fence. 'Alcohol was in your blood.'

I close my eyes. I can almost taste Amy's vodka. How it slid down my throat. How it swelled and heated the pit of my belly. How she passed it to me in the car on the way back from Jaycee Park, telling me to shut up and just go with it. Tasting it made me feel reckless. One of them.

Mum shakes her head. 'You know the police said the reading was low. It was almost non-existent.'

Ralph slaps the kitchen bench. Plates jump. A mug falls into the sink. He holds a glass under the tap, fills it and swallows big, desperate gulps. 'I know what the report said, Jessie,' Ralph argues, drips flying from his face. 'But if Margo could do that – if she could taste a few mouthfuls behind our backs – what else is she capable of?' He turns to me.

153

'For the hundredth time, if you say Corey was driving, where was he when the police turned up? And why were you in his car in the first place?'

Tears come. Words are useless. He's already made up his mind.

'Don't think turning on the waterworks is going to sway me!' Ralph thunders. 'The service station attendant saw you! A witness! Tiny Johnson saw you sitting in the driver's seat of Corey's car! Another witness!'

Tiny Johnson saw me?

'Do you understand how serious this is? Alcohol in your blood. Driving unlicensed. Causing serious injury to passengers by dangerous driving?'

'I wasn't driving!'

'Ah! Now she speaks!' He lowers his voice. 'Tell me, Margo, if you weren't driving, how was it that Keita Sanders and Justin Sparks were injured? And the cop's daughter – of all people. Did I go to bed and dream it? Are you telling me I dreamt the police bashing on our door in the early hours of this morning?'

Mum looks at Ralph. 'Did you say Justin Sparks?'

Ralph won't meet her eyes.

'You didn't tell me it was *him* in the car.' She says it like it's a crucial piece of information.

Ralph tries to say something, but I interrupt. 'Mum, you believe me, don't you? I didn't –'

Ralph flings a dining chair against the wall, toppling it over. 'Don't you realise they expect this of us?' He points out the window, at the neighbour's fence. 'They expect it!'

He marches to the front door, throws it open and points outside. 'They expect it! *Everyone* expects it! Bloody alco Abos – that's what they call our people. That's what they call *us*. And you've just proven them right! Have you listened to a single thing I've –'

Mum puts up her hand. 'Have you talked to him?' she asks me. 'Have you talked to Justin Sparks?'

I don't get it. Is she mad at me for speaking to someone who used to be a drug addict?

She stands back, wringing her hands, her eyes darting from me to Ralph and back to me again. 'It was him the other day – the boy you were smiling about. It was *him*?' She looks at Ralph. 'Did you know about this?'

Ralph gazes up at the ceiling. His words are reluctant. 'Tiny turned up here out of the blue. He wanted my help with something. Justin was with him. And Sparksy.'

Her face is frozen. 'You let Sparksy into my house?'

I can't tell if she's talking about Justin or his father. Why is she so upset?

Ralph reaches for her, but she pushes him away. 'Get your hands off me!'

'Jessie, what was I supposed to do?'

Mum glares, lips parted as if she plans to argue, but then she catches herself. She takes a deep breath. 'I thought you understood how I felt.'

Ralph reaches for her again, but she takes another step back. They stare at each other. With her arms wrapped around her waist, Mum shakes her head at him. It's like they've forgotten I'm in the room.

What happens next comes without any warning. Her slap echoes long after the front door slams and the wheels squeal in the driveway.

Ralph rests a hand on his cheek.

I shudder, gripping the fabric chair as though it's some sort of lifeline. 'What was that about?'

He stares at the door a moment longer, as if willing my mother to reappear. Then he launches himself at me. 'Get out!' He pushes me so hard I stumble. 'I said, get out! *Go!*'

I'm forced out the door, ejected into my mother's tailwind. I stand on the doorstep, staring at the rosebushes. And then I'm running, cutting through the hot afternoon air, flying down the street, fuelled by a tank of despair. Houses, cars, trees blur. I run like I'm stuck in a tunnel that's about to cave and I have only seconds to get out. My exit narrows, shrinking to a small, white dot. Black walls press in on me. I run harder, willing my tunnel to cough me up and spit me out, to release me.

Finally, mercifully, I am delivered.

I collapse, hunched over the river's edge, gasping for breath. The riverbank is damp, soft, forgiving. Murky brown water laps at my shredded feet. Sunlight warms my skin and my breathing slows. The stitch burning below my right ribcage is a string pulling on me, threatening to make me unravel.

Why was Mum arguing with Ralph? I've never seen her hit him. *Never*. They rarely argue. They're always in each other's pockets, carrying on like a pair of lovesick teenagers. It didn't make sense. All I knew was that I was the cause of their argument. None of this would be happening if it weren't for me.

I swat a mosquito on my arm and a shock of bright red stains my skin. My head flashes to the night before: Amy lying in the grass, bleeding, and me calling out to Corey for help. How could he abandon us like that? Amy's dad said if I couldn't prove that Corey was driving, I would be charged. *Me*.

I have to find Corey. He has to tell the police. He *has* to talk about the accident. About everything.

Everything.

And that means the bones too.

Corey

The unmistakable rattle of spray-can ball bearings sings a familiar tune. Muffled laughter. Kids paint the town red.

I'm crouched inside a stormwater drain not far from the river, praying the taggers don't come looking. A trickle of freezing water runs the length of the pipe, my footy bag the only thing between me and a sopping wet bum. It's cold and draughty and a lame excuse for a hiding spot. I used to come here as a kid. My handiwork decorates the concrete arch above my head, slightly faded and partially covered by other tags but still there to be appreciated: *Corey Rocks*.

Corey did rock. Now he's a gutless wonder.

I have to suss my next move. Do I front the coppers and deny the accident? Margo told them I was driving, so they've got to be looking for me. It'd help if I could get hold of Hamish and find out what he knows, but he won't answer his phone; it keeps going to message bank. I'm not calling Cammo or the other lads. Those boys will dump me in it. Can't be trusted, that pack of marshmallows. Felicity has called me at least eight times *and* left a bunch of messages. She's probably got the olds in her camp by now, helping to hunt me down. Forget about the coppers. If the old man catches me, I'll never see the light of day again.

I could go to the station and fess, say I panicked and was in shock or whatever. It *is* the truth. I lost my trolley. Brain disconnected, legs carried me away without instruction. Good thing the cops can't breatho me. It'd be too late for that. I've spewed my ring up and taken a few slashes. There's nothing in me now except the half a packet of Tim Tams I grabbed from the pantry before leaving home.

I can't recall much from the actual moment I lost control of the car, but I remember what came after. Amy got shipped off in an ambulance. What if she ends up in a wheelchair for the rest of her life? What if she's *dead*? The idea makes me wanna hurl again. She doesn't deserve that. No one deserves that. And all for a night on the piss. If her father catches up to me, he'll shoot first and ask questions later. Sergeant McGovern will make it look like I went in for a scrap and he had to take me out in self-defence. Coppers do that sort of thing – crooked ones – I've seen it on TV shows. And who in this town would blame him? I'm good as fender meat. I might as well grab those bones from under Hamish's bed and head to Nichols Point right now. At least I'll have some company.

The lights go out in the tunnel as a figure blocks the entrance, then another. Fuck! Is it the cops?

'Hey, there's some dero in here!' Someone leans into my dark chamber. 'Corey?'

Welcome Mildura's next generation of pissheads to the stage: Jackson Swinburg and Michael Carter.

'It's the neighbourhood watch!' I yell. 'Busted!'

They jump like they've filled their daks.

'It *is* you!' Jackson laughs. 'How's it hangin', dude?' He's got the weirdest haircut, all tuft and random spikes. Must be the new style. He's wearing white gloves for some bizarre reason.

'Who the hell are you?' I ask. '*Michael* Jackson?'

The Carter kid cracks up at this, weedy body shaking with delight. Puberty might've passed him by if it weren't for his acne-ridden face. 'Jackson's gotta wear bandages.' He chews a massive cold sore on his bottom lip. 'He got maggoted and toasted his phalanges.'

I crawl to the edge of the pipe and scope the area. There's no one around, just a canopy of trees, long grass and random bits of rubbish blown here by the wind – me being one of them. 'Your parents know about it?'

Jackson gives a heavy sigh. 'Yeah, I'm grounded.'

I reach into the pipe for my footy bag. 'How come you're out here, then?'

'They've gone up bush for me cousin's wedding this arvo.' He smirks. 'No kids allowed.'

Michael bends over and plucks something rubbery-pink from the dirt. He dangles the franger in my face. 'Geez, Corey! Couldn't you afford a room?'

I belt his hand and the rosy sheath lands smack in the middle of Jackson's chest. He can't pick it off because his hands are practically useless. 'Get it off!' he squeals. 'Get it off!'

He's going to draw attention. I flick it onto the ground. I must look nervous because they cotton on fast.

Jackson's eyes narrow. 'Are you in trouble, Corey?'

'You *are*, aren't ya?' Michael laughs. He passes me a hipflask. 'Want some?'

For the first time in my life, my mouth doesn't water at the suggestion. If anything, I feel sick. I grab it and tip it out.

'Hey! What the . . .?' Michael watches the last of booze dribble at his feet.

I slam the flask into his chest. 'Your mate here is a human kebab and you still wanna drink?'

'When did you become the fun police?' Michael slips the empty flask into his pocket and reaches for the can of spray paint resting by the pipe. He paints a giant dick and writes my name in it.

'What'd you do, Corey?' Jackson asks. 'Murder someone?'

He hits a raw nerve. 'I've gotta go. You didn't see me. Got that?'

Michael salutes me, army-cadet style. Jackson attempts a moonwalk.

They're laughing at me: pathetic eighteen-year-old loser on the run. I swing my footy bag over my shoulder and take off, with no idea where I'm headed. I pull up my hoodie and keep my head down. On the road, every car that passes me leaves my head spinning. Every car is a cop car. Every car has blue and red lights in the back window. Extra aerials for two-way radios. A boot-load of handcuffs. Taser guns.

I should try to stay out of sight.

I head back to the river and weave past overhanging branches, dodging gnarled grey tree roots rising up like claws that want to grab me and suck me into the earth.

A cool breeze glides off the water. I tip my head back, feeling it, letting it wash over me. For a moment I forget where I am or why I'm even here.

Then I see her.

Margo.

I know she sees me too because her body heaves, exhausted. She's a shadow, no longer the strong girl who argued with me last night. She seems different now. *Broken.*

'Why?' she mouths.

Because I'm a useless dick. A coward. A screw-up. A loser. A fuckwit. A moron. Circle one, take your pick. Because the accident scared the absolute shit out of me and it was something no one could run from, least of all me.

I shrug.

Margo launches herself, fists clenched, eyes half-closed as though she's swinging in the dark. She cries words that make no sense. I ignore the right to defend myself, not bothering to shield my face or body. I let her belt me. I let her go hard until she's spent.

When she stops, I put my hand on her shoulder. 'I'm sorry.'

'Don't touch me!' she screams. 'They're saying I did it, Corey! They're saying I drove that car! You *left* us!'

'Is she alive?'

'Amy? Yes, she's alive.'

Rushing air escapes my lungs. 'Thank God for that.'

'No, Corey. Thank *the ambos* for that. Thank *the surgeons* for that. No thanks to you. And saying she's alive doesn't mean she's all right. She's in Intensive Care.'

'What about the others?'

'Their injuries were minor.'

I wonder what she's doing here, why the cops don't have her bailed up, why her parents haven't grounded her.

As if reading my mind, she adds, 'I haven't been formally charged. They want to speak to you.' Her voice cracks and she's crying now. 'I had to get out of the house. Ralph believes I did it. This just proves no matter how good I am at school – at *anything* – in his eyes I'll always be like . . . like . . .'

'Like who?'

She throws a stone into the river.

'Margo?'

'Doesn't matter.'

'It does matter. Who are you talking about?'

She sighs. 'My father.'

'Your father?'

'My *real* father.'

'Why would Ralph think that?'

'Because my real father left, okay? Because he's useless! Because he ran away and left some other guy to look after me and clean up his mess.'

She's shivering now. I go to her. I don't even think about it. I put my arms around her, as if it's something I've always done. She fights me to begin with, but then she lets go, sinking her body into mine. We stand on the riverbank in each other's arms. Nothing about it is right and yet everything is.

Eventually, she looks up, her eyes pained. 'You're hurt,' she says, touching the cut on my forehead.

'It's nothing.'

163

'Someone should look at that.' Absently, she traces the wound. 'I walked away without a scratch. Not a scratch. How does that happen?'

'I don't know. I'm glad you did, though.'

She stiffens and pulls away. 'We should get going.'

'We?'

'I'll go with you to the police.'

'You'd do that?' Wow. My own family wouldn't offer. This chick really is something else. 'Thank you.'

She bites her bottom lip and warmth flickers in her eyes. 'But you have to tell them about the bones.'

Shit. 'No . . . no, I don't think I can . . .'

'Corey . . .'

'I'm in deep enough as it is. If they find out about that too . . . I could be in some serious trouble. Like, prison trouble.'

'When then?'

'Soon, I promise. I'll figure out a way. Just not today, all right? If the cops find out, I won't get a fair go. You know I won't. They'll hang me.'

I hold my breath, waiting for her to make up her mind. Just when I think she's going to insist, she relents. 'Fine. Okay. I won't say anything.'

I let out a thankful sigh.

'For now,' she adds. 'Come on, let's get it over with.'

We walk by the roadside – me with my footy bag swung over my shoulder, her carrying her regrets. The streets are quiet. The good people of Mildura must be having a Sunday sleep-in.

A nervous tingle eats at my chest. I thought getting busted would happen to me sooner or later, but not *this* soon. I'm not ready to face the music. When Hamish got done for DUI, I figured it was bad luck. But it's got nothing to do with luck. How did I not see that?

'Do you remember the accident?' Margo asks.

'Sort of.'

'How did it happen?'

I was off my nut. I shouldn't have been behind the wheel. 'I can't remember exactly . . .'

'Did you see her?'

'See who?'

'Right before the accident I saw a girl walking on the road.'

It comes back to me: Justin had said something to the ambos about seeing a girl. But I can't tell Margo that, can I? She'll know I left and came back. *And left again.* That'll make me look like an even bigger coward than I do right now.

'I didn't see anyone.'

'Maybe she wasn't real.' But then Margo shakes her head. 'No, I *saw* her. I didn't dream it.' She grabs my arm, stopping me in my tracks. 'Maybe you swerved to miss her, Corey. Maybe she shouldn't have been walking on the road.'

'Does it matter? Distraction or no distraction, I shouldn't have been driving.'

'I think we should tell the police,' she says eagerly. 'It might change your case.'

We turn the corner and collide with someone.

165

Hamish's stunned face looks from me to Margo. 'Have you been home, Margo?' He doesn't wait for an answer. 'Keita's dad and Old Man Sparks are on their way to give your father hell. My dad's headed over there now to see if he can stop it.'

Margo doesn't need to be told twice. She takes off, running down the street.

'What are you waiting for?' I call to Hamish, chasing after her.

Tara

What I believe is this: deal with your own problems, no one else is going to do it for you.

These are my problems:

I need to see a doctor.

I need to lie, to say, *I was with this guy at a party. We had sex. The condom broke. I want the morning-after pill.*

I need for it to be done and then forgotten. A smudge on the rear-view mirror. A skid mark in the gravel. A grain of sand buried in the tallest dune or the deepest part of the ocean.

That's how it goes when I play it out in my head.

———

It's Sunday afternoon. The doctor's surgery is closed. I have to go to the hospital. At the main desk, I'm greeted by a grey-haired nurse.

'How can I help you?' she asks, sounding as if she couldn't give a toss. 'Are you here to visit someone?'

Visit someone. Amy.

'Did you hear me, lassie? Are you a visitor?'

I shake my head.

She looks me up and down. Frustration frames her weathered face; I'm a distraction from whatever it is she's doing. 'If you need a doctor, young lady, you need to go to the Emergency wing.'

'Emergency?'

'It's where patients are seen on Sundays. Down the corridor, to your left.'

At the Emergency desk, a middle-aged nurse snacks on an iced-pink donut. Bits of coconut are stuck to his top lip. Without looking at me, he shuffles files and pulls out a notepad, pen poised. 'Name?' He bites his donut. 'I need your name, champ.'

'Tara.'

He writes it on the pad. Pen hovers. He wants my last name, but I don't give it to him. He shoves the donut bag aside and brushes his pants. 'I'm guessing you don't want to tell me what the problem is either?' His eyes trail over me. I'm convinced he'll see the reason I'm here painted across my forehead like a big neon sign. 'I really should inform the doctor as to what you're here for, but, hey, management sprung for afternoon tea. I'm in a good mood.'

He shows me into a tiny room adjacent to the waiting area. 'Take a seat. Someone will be with you as soon as possible.' He closes the door.

I sit opposite a blue formica desk with a blank notepad on it. A blood pressure trolley stands in the corner. There's a poster of the cross-section of a woman's body pinned to the wall. I take a deep breath and recite cheer-squad lines:

You're here! You've made it! You can do this! It'll be over soon!
All you have to do is this one thing! One simple thing!

The door opens and Jessie Bonney walks in.

Shit.

I stand up, but she tells me to sit down. 'Normally, I work in the Aged Care wing, but Emergency is low on staff today.' She wiggles her ample bottom into the space behind the desk and gives a tired laugh. 'Like I don't have enough to worry about.'

She's talking about Margo. In the back of my mind, white headlights glide towards me.

'Tara, isn't it?' She writes something on the notepad. 'You're in my daughter's year at school, aren't you?'

Oh God, what has Margo told her?

When I speak, my voice sounds like it belongs to someone else. 'Is Margo all right?'

She seems grateful I've asked. 'Margo was unharmed . . . physically. Some of the other kids weren't as lucky.' She repositions herself as if she sat on something sharp. 'I hope you can forgive me if I seem a bit vague. I'm sure you'll appreciate I've had a long night.' She lets out a big sigh. 'Right. Now, the procedure is, I'll speak to you, then I'll brief the doctor and then she'll see you. Okay?'

I nod. 'Okay.'

'Right then. Does your mother know you're here?'

Does my mother know I exist?

Jessie moves on, as if my silence was expected. 'Well. What can I do for you?'

And this is the moment where I'm supposed to say the words: *I want the morning-after pill.*

169

I open my mouth and nothing comes out. *Nothing.*

I focus on the poster to avoid her eyes. Large red-veined breasts, pointed nipples, pink-skinned abdomen, thickened red uterus. Tiny arrows point to various parts of the woman's anatomy. No head, no limbs. This is the sum of what we are as women: a headless, nameless joy-hole for a man.

She follows my gaze. 'Interesting, isn't it?'

It's disgusting and it *definitely* shouldn't be out there on display for everyone to see: clothes ripped off, body exposed. I want to take it down, put it away.

She looks at me closely and her expression changes. 'What is it that you came here for, Tara?'

What was I thinking? I can't tell her. What if she tells Margo? What if she tells someone else? I get up and go to the door. There's no such thing as confidentiality in this town. Someone will find out. Someone will whisper and someone will spread it around. I'm not going to be that girl everyone looks at with pity in their eyes. If people are victims, it's because they choose to be. Whoever those guys were last night, they're nothing to me. It didn't happen and my life *will* go on like it didn't happen.

'Stop. Wait,' Jessie says, as I'm halfway to the door. 'I'll take your obs.' She reaches for the trolley and wheels it to my side. 'Sit,' she orders, pushing lightly on my shoulders so I sink into the chair.

She rests her backside against the desk and rolls up my sleeve. There's a frozen moment when she doesn't move and I don't pull away. Part of me needs the scratches and the bruises to speak for me. Without comment, she slips the cuff up my arm and presses two fingers into my wrist. She pumps the little black balloon until the cuff tightens. Counting seconds on her watch. Counting. *Counting*. She releases the pressure, the machine gives a morose hiss. She scribbles on her notepad.

'What happened?' she asks, not looking at me.

I hear him. *Don't say a word . . .*

'Tara?'

Don't say a word . . .

'Do you have cuts elsewhere?'

Don't say a word . . .

'Do you need them treated?'

Don't say a word . . .

I focus on her shoes – her soft, white shoes. She wears beige stockings and I wonder if her feet sweat. I barely hear her when she asks me what happened.

Here's my answer: I got drunk. I got so far off my face I let a whole swag of guys stand around ogling my naked body, taking pictures. And that's not the worst of it. I got so paralytic I couldn't stop a guy and his mate from . . .

Jessie rests her hand on my knee. 'Sweetheart?'

I shrink in my seat. 'Sweetheart' is wrong – *all* wrong. Try: *Drunken slag. Slut. Whore. Bitch.*

Jessie takes my hand in hers. Her touch is gentle. I wonder what it must be like to be Margo. To be loved and cared for, to have a mother who's part of your life. Does Jessie kiss Margo goodbye when she leaves for school? Does she cook her family dinner, wash their clothes, pack school lunches and cut the crusts off Margo's sandwiches? Does she let

Margo know she's the most important person in the world, that everything and everyone comes second best?

Jessie waits for me to speak, but I don't. I sit there, my mouth welded shut. On the inside, I'm burning, choking with fury and frustration. This wasn't my plan, to play the mute. I was supposed to act normal. I was supposed to come across as a responsible teen sorting out an irresponsible problem. I was supposed to *fix* this.

She strokes my hair away from my face. 'Did someone hurt you.' It's not a question. Her voice filters through the fog in my brain. 'You were at the party last night? The same party as Margo?'

I bite the inside of my cheek and taste the salty tang of blood. I remember my teeth smashing into Justin's as we kissed.

'This,' she says, pointing at my arms, 'this happened at the party?'

Say it! Say it for me because I can't!

'It was a guy who did this to you, wasn't it, Tara?'

'I need the morning-after pill.' There. Said it. Plan back on track.

Jessie grips the lip of the desk and squeezes so tight her knuckles turn from brown to yellowish-white. One of her sneakers pushes down on top of the other as if she's crushing a cigarette.

She looks angry. I panic. I give her my rehearsed spiel, the one I practised on my way here. It spews out of me like the vomit I spewed last night. 'There was this guy at the party. We got a bit heavy. What we used, um, well, it didn't work . . . and he, um, he wanted to keep going and I'd been drinking and I didn't really think too much about it and I let him –'

'The doctor may want to do an examination. Do you give your consent?'

An examination?

She clicks her pen. 'Do you want to talk about it?'

I shake my head.

'Are you sure?'

I nod.

'I'll get the doctor.'

That's it? She's not going to insist I say the words out loud and tell her the truth?

With a hand resting on the doorhandle, Jessie stops. 'Don't let him know,' she says. 'Don't let him *ever* have the satisfaction of knowing he hurt you.'

I catch my breath. Minutes go by. A volume of unsaid pain passes between us. And instead of feeling shame or fear or anything like what I thought I'd feel, relief washes over me.

Something happened to her too. She understands.

Her hand still on the doorknob, she doesn't move. And then she hangs her head and starts shaking it, over and over. 'I'm sorry. I shouldn't have said that.'

'It's okay –'

'No, it was inappropriate.' She turns to look at me. 'I get what you're trying to do here, Tara. How you're trying to handle this ... and I respect your strength, I do. But, sweetheart, it would be remiss of me not to follow protocol in a situation like this. We need to do a rape kit.'

I stiffen. *Rape.* Used in association with me. 'But I haven't –'

She holds up a hand. 'Your health is my priority. It's also imperative we collect evidence. The doctor will –'

'Can't it be you?'

'I won't leave you, Tara. I swear. I'll be with you the whole time. I'll hold your hand and I won't let go.' She comes close and cups my chin, making me look her in the eye. 'I know this is hard. But you're a strong girl. You've proven that already by coming here and seeking help. Somewhere, deep down, I know you can find the strength to do this too.'

And as much as I want to argue – as much as I want to get up and run – I ask, 'Did you have to do one?'

She pauses before shaking her head. 'You *can* trust me, Tara. I wouldn't put you through this unless there was a damn good reason for it.'

She takes my hand in hers. I squeeze it and nod.

'I'm proud of you,' she says. 'Remember: I will *not* leave your side. Not for one second. That's a promise.'

And she's true to her word – she doesn't leave me. Not even afterwards, when the counsellor the hospital has called in suggests that maybe we could talk alone. I tell her I want Jessie there. Jessie says that's fine; she has all the time in the world. The counsellor asks a bunch of questions. I don't say anything. I can tell she's trying to be nice and she's good at her job, but I'm not ready. I don't think I'll ever be ready.

Finally giving up, she makes an appointment and asks me to come back tomorrow.

Later, I'm walking home, morning-after pills in hand, appointment card in my pocket, job done, event over. Jessie Bonney's words play on my mind; the ones she let slip. *Don't let him ever have the satisfaction of knowing he hurt you.*

What would she say if she knew there were two of them?

At home, there's a message on the answering machine from Mum. She and Trevor have stopped off at a caravan park for the night. The police told her the car has been impounded pending further investigation. There's no need to hurry home.

I grab the water jug from the fridge, but then I see the bottle of champagne Mum is saving to toast her birthday. It's on the second shelf, basking in an almost holy glow.

The cork pops and I swallow the tablet with a mouthful of sweet fizz. Half a bottle later, I'm me again – the girl *before* last night – the girl who goes out and hooks up with whoever she wants, parties and has fun. The girl who doesn't take shit from anyone.

And the champagne tastes exactly how a lie should: *unbelievable.*

Justin

Tiny Johnson and I beat a path to Margo's door. We've got to stop my old man and Keita's dad from taking on Ralph. There's one saving grace: I know my old man won't be capable of inflicting much damage. The last time I saw him take a swing at someone, he did a big airy and kept on spinning. But from what Tiny's told me, this Daryl Sanders bloke is a bloodthirsty pit bull. Last year, apparently, he smacked the absolute hell out of a guy at the footy. He had the bloke in traction, eating through a straw. Word is, he has links to bikies.

Geez, the old man can pick them.

As we round the end of the street, it's as we feared – the show is in full swing.

'Aw, hell,' Tiny breathes, winding down the car window. We've pulled up two houses back from the Bonney place. 'I'm not sure if we can do this on our own.'

We hear Ralph, bailed up inside, yelling through the security door. 'For the last time, Daryl, get off my property! I'll call the coppers, you 'ear! You wanna 'nother run-in with the law, mate? 'Cos yer sure as heck going the right way about it!'

Daryl wields a tyre lever, taunting Ralph to come outside and face him like a man. He's wearing stubbies, thongs, a blue singlet and more tattoos than Angry Anderson. My old man staggers about in the middle of the road, neck of a Bundy bottle clutched between his knuckles. Halfway up the street, neighbours pour onto their front porches, sneaking a peek at the commotion. Some of them watch with one hand rested on the doorknob, ready to turn back if things get ugly.

'We need the cops,' Tiny says.

'But I just came from the station . . .' I stop mid-sentence because Corey and Margo plough past our car, running towards the house. Moments later, so does Hamish. 'What the . . .?'

'What's Hamish doing here?' Tiny grumbles.

'Come out 'ere, ya black bastard!' Daryl shouts. 'I shoulda fucked you up a long time ago!' He grabs a river stone from the garden bed and hurls it at the Bonneys' security door. It ricochets as the next one hits. He keeps them coming like an automatic paintball gun. *Bang! Bang! Bang!*

'Sticks and stones!' The old man sings, zigzagging up the driveway. 'Sticks and stones!' Then, as if he's had an epiphany, he trumpets, 'Sticks and stones! Bones! Bones! They took her bones!'

'Crap,' Tiny sighs, his head in his hands. 'What was Daryl thinking, bringing your old man here?'

With one hulking arm, Daryl pushes my father away. 'Shut up, Sparksy! I said I'll take care of it! Keep watch for the coppers, mate, that's yer job!' He turns his attention back to the house and hurls another rock. And it hits me – not the rock, but the fact that my old man is talking about Mum's remains – he knows what happened to her grave. *He cares.*

Up the other end of the street, a ute slides sideways as it rounds the bend, clipping the gravel, sending dust billowing into the air. Wheels squeal as the driver performs the mother of all burnouts and pulls up in the centre of the road. When the plume settles, I see a girl. She's running kind of awkwardly, one arm nursing the other. *Keita.* She's yelling something I can't make out.

Tiny reaches behind the bench seat and finds a cricket bat. He jumps out, swinging, beer gut bobbing, an unanchored buoy in choppy water. 'Daryl! Doing this won't fix nuthin'! It'll only land ya in the clink.'

'You stay out of it, Tiny!' Daryl roars. 'I'm not going nowhere till I'm done takin' this bugger down.'

It's then I know I've got no choice – I have to get out of the car.

Armed with a pair of hospital-issue crutches and a bad case of five o'clock shadow, I climb from the vehicle, locking eyes with Keita. 'Hey! Keita! Tell your old man to settle down before someone gets hurt!'

She looks at her father. He's indiscriminately redecorating the yard. The water meter takes a beating. A metal mailbox is converted to a pancake. The white picket fence cops a flogging, posts unstuck and airborne like giant toothpicks. Ralph's ute, parked in the driveway, is also on Daryl's extensive to-do list. He climbs onto the bonnet and brings the tyre lever down hard, shattering the windshield.

'Stop it!' Margo screams, running at Daryl. 'Stop!'

Corey is behind her. 'Daryl! Settle down! You've got it all wrong!' He glances back at Hamish like it's time to take down the opposition, except Hamish's legs are like the concrete pylons of Ralph's front porch. Corey is on his own.

'Stop!' Margo screams.

Daryl holds the tyre lever midair, staring at Margo. Something flickers across his face – satisfaction? He jumps down from the bonnet and rears up, an animal gone from all fours to standing on two. He puffs out his chest, every muscle flexed. 'Well, well, well. She finally shows her face! Now ya gunna cop what's coming to ya, aren't ya?'

'Can't you do something?' Hamish yells at Keita.

But Keita looks like she's *enjoying* this.

Daryl throws his arms out wide, an invitation: *Come and get it.* Margo takes a step, but Ralph thrusts open the security door and bolts across the lawn.

'Don't you lay a finger on her, Daryl! Don't you touch her!'

Daryl's dark eyes flit between Margo and Ralph, spoilt for choice. The old man laughs and slaps his moleskins, crying, 'Place yer bets, people! Place yer bets!'

I don't think – I just *do.*

'Margo!' I'm on my white horse, galloping in to save the fucking day. Except I'm not galloping, exactly. I'm limping as fast as my injured leg will carry me. I plant myself smack between Margo and Daryl, and it's a stroke of brilliance, really, because the unwritten rule of male-on-male combat forbids taking out an injured man.

'Get outta the way, young Sparksy!' Daryl warns, creeping towards me, tyre lever itching his hand. 'Yer oughta know better than to protect this good-for-nothin' brat. She put you and me daughter in hospital.' He adds, with a snarl directed purely at Margo, 'I reckon an arm for an arm is fair, don't you?'

Ralph comes at him from behind. Next thing I know, he's on Daryl's back, climbing up there like the great Gavin Wanganeen, taking a hanger destined for the record books. Knees buried in Daryl's shoulderblades, he reaches for the tyre lever. Daryl drops it, rotating one way then the other, trying to peel Ralph from his back. Ralph slips down and now he's got his arms around Daryl's neck, his legs swinging. Tiny grabs for the tyre lever, but Daryl shoots out his foot, delivering a swift kick to Tiny's jaw. Tiny's head springs back like a flip-top rubbish bin. He takes a single sideways step and plummets to the ground.

Something inside me snaps. I go for Daryl's legs, tunnelling into him, scooping him up from underneath. I'd like to think it's my brute force that brings him down, but Ralph's weight on Daryl's upper back is what tips the big man over.

Daryl's flat out, face first on the grass. Me and Ralph sit on him, holding him down. Corey dives in and adds his weight.

'Get off, ya mongrels!' Daryl grunts, writhing around. 'Get off!'

I look at Hamish. He kneels with his old man's head in his lap. Tiny isn't moving.

Before I can do anything, someone's shoving me off Daryl, beating my shoulders. 'Leave him alone!' Keita screams. 'Get off him! Leave him alone!'

I'm caught off guard. She hip and shoulders me so hard I tumble. She belts me with her uninjured hand, crazy burning in her eyes.

Daryl breaks free, bucking like a just-been-branded bull. He rolls onto his back, enraged and refuelled, swinging from the ground up. He buries a fist in Ralph's guts, winding the poor bugger with such a force he's choking on his tongue. Ralph is jostled to one side, and seconds later, Corey gives a howling cry as Daryl delivers a knee fair into his happy sac. With both men rolling in pain, Daryl crawls to his feet and stands tall, his eyes surveying the yard for Margo.

I can't let it happen. I swing one of my crutches at Daryl's face. He's too quick and he grabs the crutch, turning it on me. It happens fast. He smacks me across the jaw. The pain is blinding. Blood and spit go flying slow-mo into the air, my face a sunken airbed, blood flowing freely from my nose.

I don't see it, but I hear it: the fractured crack of a bottle.

Daryl kisses the ground, coated in brown syrupy liquid. His black eyes roll and he moans a sickening moan. Keita gives an ear-piercing scream.

My old man stands over Daryl, jagged neck of a Bundy bottle dangling. 'Gotcha!' he burps.

So much for my old man causing limited harm. He's taken down the opposition with one slick move. The sozzled idiot forgot which team he was on.

Hamish's cries rise above the fog in my brain. 'He's not breathing! Someone help me! Dad's not breathing!'

Margo goes to Hamish. 'Lay him on his back,' she instructs. She pinches Tiny's nose between her forefinger and thumb and pulls back his chin so his mouth gapes. 'Call an ambulance,' she says, then takes Tiny's lips in hers.

Ralph crawls to Margo's side and together they give Tiny CPR. Ralph comes down hard on Tiny's chest time and again, and Margo's cheeks fill and expel repeatedly. I sit there, watching, witness to a man's life hanging in the balance and nothing about it seems real.

I hear someone moaning, crying, pleading with God, *Let him live! Let him live!* It's Hamish.

Corey goes to him. 'Easy, mate. Easy. Help's on the way.'

But help arrives too late.

Tiny Johnson is dead.

Margo

You're going to Tiny Johnson's funeral whether you like it or not – the first words Ralph had spoken to me since two weeks ago, when he told me to get out of the house. *It could've been you in that casket.* I wonder if he wishes it was.

The church is still – *dead* – despite the open windows and the hum of a white plastic fan whirring in the corner behind the pulpit. People make their way to available seats, hushed voices murmur. Bums shuffle, memorial books flap. I take a seat up the front, determined not to hide. I have nothing to hide. Mum and Ralph squeeze in beside me. Perhaps they, too, want to make a statement.

I can feel people watching me. I feel their eyes drilling the back of my head. *There's that Bonney girl. She was in the car with Corey. Did you hear that's what caused Daryl to go off the rails? How can she show her face? And what about the copper's daughter? Word is the poor kid might never walk again.*

I take it in as punishment. Why not? I deserve it. I couldn't save Tiny. I couldn't breathe life back into his slack, breathless mouth. The ambos said he was dead before he hit the ground. How do they even know that? Maybe Tiny suffered. Maybe he suffered because of me.

Like Amy is suffering because of me.

Amy.

My text messages have gone unanswered. I wanted to take her some flowers, but I didn't think I'd be welcome. Sergeant McGovern knows I wasn't the driver, but that doesn't mean he isn't angry. I *did* drive from the servo to Jaycee Park. Really, I'd been just as reckless as Corey. And Amy. We were all reckless – not that Sergeant McGovern is ready to acknowledge that. Fate has judged his daughter.

I close my eyes and imagine Tiny thundering up the aisle, telling everyone, 'Show's over! Time to go! Big mistake!' I see him hurdle church pews to shake Ralph's hand, thanking him for saving his life. I feel him kiss my cheeks and tell me everything will be okay. He flings open the casket, searches the lining and demands, 'Where's the bloody beer?'

I look around for the others. Corey isn't here – at least, I didn't see him when I walked in. I haven't spoken to him since the day Tiny died. Sergeant McGovern charged him with three counts of causing serious injury by dangerous driving. Corey was also charged with leaving the scene of an accident, failure to render assistance *and* supplying alcohol to minors. He was stripped of his licence. I lost my learner's for driving to Jaycee Park. His court hearing is two months from now.

I search for Keita. She isn't here. I can't imagine she'd be welcome, anyway. Daryl is facing jail time. The police

184

interviewed Sparksy and let him go; they could have charged him as an accessory, but they decided not to. Mental incompetence or some such. Too-hard basket. I wonder what Justin thinks of that. I can't see him here either. Is it because he's ashamed of his father? Truth is, Sparksy may have come to our house baying for blood, but he saved me and Ralph.

I spot Tara. She's seated alone at the back of the church, wearing a white, long-sleeved shirt buttoned to her neck. I've never seen her dress like that – like she's a primary school teacher or something. I catch her eye, but she doesn't see me, or she pretends she doesn't. I guess some things never change.

The music starts and Hamish and his mother appear in the doorway, ready to walk to their seats. Hamish has his mother by her arm, supporting her with each slow step. As he approaches the front pew, he looks my way, but it's as if he doesn't register who I am. I see it in his eyes. He's lost in the same strange world I woke up in after Kylie's eighteenth. Something's shifted. The Earth's axis has tilted. Nothing will ever been the same again.

Hamish takes a seat and stares at his father's casket, as if he's trying to understand what it is. His mother puts a hand on his back, but he shakes her away. 'Don't touch me,' he slurs.

The service begins. Reverend Thompson invites a friend of Tiny's to speak. A stumpy, bald man with a beer gut to rival the best of them takes the stand. His name is Strapper and he talks about Tiny's early life while photos of Tiny flash from the overhead projector. Tiny is beamed onto the wall, larger than life. *Real* life. A life no more.

When Strapper finishes, he places a hand on Tiny's coffin. 'There'll be one glass missing at the bar this arvo, mate.'

Next, Reverend Thompson asks if Hamish would like to come up and say a few words.

Hamish stands. Fumbling a Bible, he turns and places it on his seat. He looks at the pulpit and at the crowd, wringing his hands.

'Son?' Reverend Thompson prompts.

The congregation is silent, waiting. Someone stifles a cough.

Hamish nods at the Reverend like he understands what he has to do.

Then he turns and walks out of the church.

Corey

Four days.

That's how long it takes for the shiner the old man gave me to start healing.

He delivered his in-house justice after Tiny's wake. Belly full of do-as-I-say-not-as-I-do. Felicity screamed the roof down. The old girl tried to get between us, but, like usual, I made sure they didn't see the brunt of it. Besides, I deserved it this time. There's only so much you can get away with before you have to start copping it sweet. My number's up. Well and truly. The old man knows it. *I* know it. He enjoyed the excuse.

And who was I to argue?

There's a story about my old man. On his twenty-first birthday he got blind drunk and took his car for a midnight joy ride to the end of an Adelaide jetty. In his confusion, he stopped the car just shy of the precipice, got out and staggered over to a bench seat, where he fell asleep. In the morning, he woke up and saw he'd almost become shark feed; the front wheels were hanging off the end of the jetty. How the car didn't topple into the drink is anyone's guess.

The State Emergency Service had to tow the car and the incident made the front-page news.

I'd grown up hearing that story at parties, at dinners, at barbecues with friends, new and old. Until now – until *right now* – I'd thought it was the funniest story ever. The old girl always said he had the luxury of laughing because he lived to tell the tale. That was the part that was lost on me. But now it sinks in. Like a rogue wave rolling over that jetty. I *am* the old man. *I* had survived the accident. *I* had lived to tell the tale. And yet, still, here I was, hanging off the end of the proverbial jetty about to drown if I didn't do something. This morning when I woke up, I realised what that something was.

I have to take back the bones.

That day down by the river, Margo made me promise. For whatever reason, neither she nor Amy had said anything about the bones to the cops. It means I still have a chance to make things right. And maybe the universe *wants* me to.

I'm eating my Vegemite crumpets when a friend of the old girl's rings up.

'You don't say,' the old girl breathes into the receiver. 'Well, I never ...' It goes on like this for a while. 'Yes, okay ... Well, thanks for filling me in, Jackie. Yes, you too.' She hangs up and stares at her coffee mug.

I nod at the phone. 'What was that about?'

She refills the kettle and hits the switch. 'Nothing.'

'Didn't sound like nothing.'

She tips cold coffee down the drain and spoons fresh granules into her mug. 'If you must know, it was about those bones that went missing from the cemetery.'

188

My gut clenches. 'What about them?'

'Word around town is that they belong to Sparksy's missus. Her name was Martha.'

I choke on my crumpet. *Holy shit! Justin's mother!*

The old girl gives me a look. 'Your Vegemite got bones in it or something?'

I get up and scrape my leftovers into the bin. Felicity's schoolbag is on the kitchen chair. I grab it and empty it out.

'What are you doing with that?'

I pile textbooks on the dinner table. 'I'm borrowing it.'

'Why? What for? Where are you going?'

'Out.'

'Corey . . .'

'Back off, will ya?' I snap.

She recoils, stung. The kettle whistles, but she doesn't take it off the heat.

Feeling shitty, I kiss her forehead. 'I'm sorry, Mum. I love you. I won't be long. Okay?'

She reaches up to trace my black eye. 'Your father will be back at five.'

'Yeah, righto.'

Heart thumping, I press Hamish's doorbell. The neighbour's shih tzu barks. It jumps at the gate, rattling hinges. Ever since the neighbours got that dog, Tiny has wanted to deposit a lump of lead between its eyeballs. *Shih tzu is a darn good name for it. Shits you, shits me.*

I guess the dog had the last laugh.

I adjust Felicity's backpack, shifting it on my shoulder. I hope it's big enough. I can't remember how many bones there were. What happened that night at the cemetery is hazy, and worse now, after everything else that's happened. I hope Hamish hands them over and doesn't try to flatten me in the process. I don't think I can take another beating.

I press the doorbell again.

Mrs Johnson appears, a shadowy outline behind the screen. 'Corey?'

The shih tzu barks. I swear I can hear Tiny bashing his fist on the fence. *Shut that yappy trap or I'll tear ya limb from limb!*

Mrs Johnson opens the door. 'Come in.'

She pulls the belt of her dowdy pink dressing-gown, drawing the garment tighter. I follow her to the kitchen, transfixed by the back of her head. She's cut her hair – no, hacked it off. Her head is a prickly landscape of stiff grey tufts. She sits at a green vinyl-covered dining table littered with sympathy cards. 'You've got a hide coming here.' She lights a smoke, draws back. A puffy grey cloud wafts in my face. 'Hamish says it was you driving that car.'

I don't deny it.

She clutches a tissue and dabs red-raw eyes. 'I got a steak out of the freezer for him this morning. Can you believe that? A steak.' Hand trembling, she takes another drag. 'Ah! You can't change nothin' now, you stupid kid. It's done. Done like a roast turkey. That's what Tiny would have said.'

'I'm sorry for your loss, Mrs Johnson.'

190

She thumbs a china teacup. 'We're all sorry about something.'

I shift the backpack and move my weight to the other foot. 'Can I see Hamish?'

She shrugs. 'He's in his room, hasn't come out today. Maybe you'll have better luck.'

I nod and go to the hallway door.

'Corey?'

'Yeah?'

'Go easy on him.'

I feel my way past Hamish's parents' room – the door is open, blinds drawn, double bed piled with pillows on one side, blankets pulled back on the other. I push on, past the study, past a wooden desk stacked high with books and papers spread haphazardly like they were sorted through in a hurry. At the end of the hallway is Hamish's door, a foot-sized hole at the bottom of it. A poster of a blonde bikini babe greets me.

I knock, but he doesn't answer. I push on the door.

The stench hits me – the way a locker room smells after a match. My eyes take a second to adjust. I see him curled in the foetal position, his back to me. 'Hamish?'

He turns, stretching.

I negotiate an obstacle course of magazines, clothing and empty beer bottles. 'Hamish, we need to talk.'

Forearm covering his face, he reaches up and pulls back the vertical blinds hanging by his bed. He lets the plastic strips flop into position, leaving a gap – a single strip of daylight invading the dark. 'What are you doing here?'

At first I think it's grief and exhaustion slurring his words, but then I see an uncapped bottle of Bundy rested on his stomach, two-thirds gone. I try to take it, but he moves it out of my reach.

'You know . . . he cracked his skull,' Hamish says. 'From his eye socket all the way to the back of his head.' He makes a whooshing sound, demonstrating the moment his father's head shattered. 'Popped like a corn kernel. Doc says a king hit. A coward's punch.'

I reach for the bottle. This time I get it. He wrestles me but lets go without much of a fight.

'His brain swelled with fluid. Too much pressure . . .'

'Hamish . . .'

He rolls onto his front and brings himself up on all fours. Standing on the mattress, he wobbles and grabs at the blinds, ripping them from their tracks. One by one, the darkness is stripped and plastic ribbons float across the room. Dust particles dance, lit up like tiny stars. Hamish is enveloped in a sparkly, ethereal back-glow. He jumps from the bed, falls to his knees and lifts the bed-skirt. He dumps them on the mattress – my reason for coming here.

'It's payback,' he says, spreading out the bones. 'Whoever this is, they got real mad at me for disturbing them. And now Dad is . . . Dad is . . .'

'I know who it is. Who we dug up,' I say, unzipping the backpack. 'Martha Sparks.'

His bloodshot eyes stare. 'Justin's mother?'

I pick up her skull. It's small, generic-looking; it could be anyone's. Call me crazy, but in the harsh light of day,

I expected it to be more feminine, a skull that indicated *kind and loving mother* or *long-suffering hard-done-by wife*. But it's just a skull.

Hamish removes a small white box from beneath his bed. 'We dug this up too,' he says, passing it to me.

I take the box from him. 'You sure?'

'Yeah.'

Little white flakes of paint flutter from the box. Faded pictures of Uluru are revealed beneath. There's a groove in the top as though something was once stuck to it. I lift the rusted latch and peer inside. Blue velvet provides a soft nest for a string of brown beads.

I look at Hamish as though he might explain – a stupid notion. I close it and put it in the bag. 'I'll handle it,' I tell him, gently placing the bones on top.

'But –'

'Leave it with me.' I zip the bag. 'Get some sleep.'

I head for home, body in a backpack – a school backpack, no less. If only Mr Vermont could see this. Hey, Vermont! Here's a History project for ya. Wanna fail me for this too, cockhead?

I'll say one thing for Martha: she isn't remotely judgemental. She goes along for the ride without giving me any grief. And she's happy enough to listen. She's a good listener.

'I'll have you back soon enough, Martha. This is just a short excursion, okay? You need to understand, I'm real sorry about all this. We didn't know it was you we were digging up. Not that it makes it right to dig up anyone, but you've gotta know, it was nothing personal.'

A car zooms past, horn honking. It must be one of the lads, maybe Cammo. I pull my cap low and pick up the pace.

'So . . . I'm guessing being hitched to Sparksy wasn't all beer and skittles, eh? Silly ol' bloke doesn't know what side of Sunday it is. He can't have always been *that* bad. I mean, you married him, right? You thought enough of him to have his kid. And Justin seems a decent enough bloke. Good-looking too. I'm convinced he takes after you in that department.'

A guy dressed in speedos and thongs is watering his front lawn, hairy white chest glowing in the sun. He gives me a strange look, which is fair. I *am* talking to myself.

I decide Martha can hear me even if I don't say the words out loud. The dead can do that. They can walk through walls, so they sure as eggs know the stuff going on inside your head. You can communicate with that mental telepathy shit. Send them secret messages. Confess all your sins.

'So, Martha, I'm guessing you didn't think you'd take the town tour again. Did Sparksy let you out much? Maybe he kept you chained to the kitchen sink? Wouldn't surprise me if that was his caper. He seems the sort.'

I turn the corner, a few blocks from home.

'Do you want to tell me *why* you did it? You had a kid, so it must've been pretty bad if you didn't want to stick around for him.' I adjust the backpack. Something slips and changes position. A chill runs up my spine. Forget Hamish and his vengeance theories – now *my* imagination is getting the better of me. 'Don't you go getting impatient on me, Martha. Don't go throwing your weight around, you hear?' Something sharp digs my backbone – it must be the jewellery box. 'Hey, what's with the beads? Did you go to Uluru? Is that what the box is about? Uluru would be awesome, I reckon. I've never been outside of Mildura. Well, except for the odd footy trip, but we never go anywhere *that* exciting. And on a footy trip, nine times out of ten my head's stuck in the toilet, anyway. I'd love to see the big red rock. I'd love to see lots of things. But you've gotta have money, don't you? Money helps. I've got bugger all.'

I make my way across the intersection. I'm just a few houses from home now. We're on the home straight, me and Martha.

'I bet you think I'm a royal tosser because of what I did. I know I could've killed your kid. I could've driven that car into a tree. Killed *me*. Trust me, Martha, as long as I live, I'll *never* do something that stupid again. I've learnt my lesson good and bloody proper. Even if the whole town thinks I'm a loser.'

Martha doesn't argue. It gives me some comfort.

'I'm going to change. You'll see. I'm really going to knuckle down. Live right. Get a job. Do all the stuff that makes you respectable.'

At home, the front door is unlocked. I find Felicity at the kitchen table, books spread everywhere, doing her homework. A half-eaten bowl of cornflakes rests on top of papers and textbooks. When she sees her schoolbag slung over my shoulder, her blue eyes grow wide. 'Corey, why do you have my –'

'Back in a tick. Gotta go strangle one.'

She pulls a face and leaves me to it. She's not gunna chase me to the dunny.

In my room, I pull back my doona and tip Martha's bones onto the mattress. Empty eye sockets glare at me.

'Don't you go giving me the evil eye, Miss Martha. This is just a pit stop.'

I lift out the jewellery box, sit it on my bed and open it.

'Would you like to wear your beads for old time's sake?' I loop the string around her skull. Her jaw gapes a breath of relief. 'Wow. Suits you. Wanna see?' I pull out my shaving mirror. It's cracked and smudged-as, but it doesn't matter to Martha. 'What do you think?' She seems unimpressed. 'Yeah, you're a little underdressed.' I put the mirror back in the drawer. I'm about to put the beads in the box when I notice something poking out from beneath the blue velvet lining. I wiggle it out, gently sliding it free.

It's a tiny newspaper cutting. The words are small but easy to read.

BIRTH NOTICE

BONNEY (nee Rankin):—Jessie is proud to announce the birth of Margo Justine. Born 28 February 1997, 9lbs 1oz. Mildura Base Hospital. Mother and daughter are doing well.

I look at Martha's skull and I swear she winks at me.

Tara

When my mum broke up with the boyfriend she had before Trevor, she lay on the couch and got plastered. She was seething that not one of her friends had bothered to ask if she was okay. She said something to me I'll never forget: *Here's a cold, hard truth for you, Tara. People don't care.* She'd swished her glass, punctuating the gravity of her words. *When they ask if you're all right, they don't really want an honest answer. They're going through the motions. Believe me, Tara, when I tell you: you're on your own in this life. The only person you can rely on is yourself.*

Despite all my mother's failings, I'm beginning to think she knew what she was talking about. No one has asked me about the photos from the party. No one has asked me if I'm okay, if I'm embarrassed, if I'm good with it, angry, humiliated – nothing. There are plenty of appreciative comments online, though. Heaps of bitchy, trolling commentary.

The photos must be easy to believe. *Tara Ramsey would do that. She'd lay back and let any guy have her. She's the hugest slut in town. The biggest slut in this state. She's the most massive slut in the whole entire universe.*

197

And if everyone's thinking it, there must be truth in it. It's simple math. Majority rules.

———————

I wake to someone knocking on the front door. I mute the TV, peel myself off the couch and peer through the window. Jessie Bonney. What's she doing here?

She knocks again. 'Tara? I know you're in there.'

I consider staying silent, but something tells me she won't give up easily. Besides, she's already heard the TV. I hide the vodka bottle under the couch, then open the door.

She beams a toothy smile. 'There you are!'

Her voice is too loud for my thumping head. She's wearing her work uniform, the same soft shoes and beige stockings. Maybe her visit has something to do with the hospital, some kind of follow-up.

'This isn't official or anything,' she says, as if reading my mind. I start to say I'm not feeling well, but she bustles past me into the living room. 'Good grief, it's dark in here! Are you in training for the Vampire Academy?' She goes to the window and opens the shades. Sun streams inside. Dust bunnies skip and roll across the tiled floor. 'There, that's better.'

It comes on fast. My mouth goes dry and I feel myself tip sideways. Before I know it, Jessie is holding back my hair as I vomit onto the floor. There's not much to it – it's mostly fluid – but my stomach spasms again and again, wringing me out. I think of Amy throwing up in my toilet. *Amy. The accident.* I double over again.

Jessie strokes my back. 'That's the girl . . .'

Spent, I stand there shivering.

Jessie leads me to the couch. I sit, hunched, head between my knees. Moments later, she's handing me a glass of water. 'Small sips. Just enough to wet your tongue.'

I do as she says, then sink back into the couch, empty, *cleansed*. The cool glass pressed against my cheek, I watch her use newspaper, toilet paper, whatever she can find to mop up the floor. She doesn't even flinch or pull a face. Mess dealt with, Jessie sits down and takes my hand in hers. We don't speak. She's just *here*, and it feels good.

I'm not sure how much time passes. Eventually, I tell her I'm feeling better. She pats my knee and hoists herself up. 'Now, where's your kettle?' She makes off for the kitchen. 'I'm not a tea person, myself. Tea is for librarians. And hippies.' She spies the tin of International Roast on top of the microwave. 'Cups?'

'I'm not really –'

But Jessie's not listening – she's singing. Busily, she opens cupboard doors one after the other until she finds the cups. She selects two and fills the kettle from the sink. 'Now, Tara, I bet you're asking yourself, *What's she doing here?* Well, I'll save you the trouble. I'm here because you've been skipping school.' She flips the tin lid and peers inside. 'Good Lord, did this go solid back in the Ice Age?'

'Mum scrapes it with a fork.'

She puts out her hand. I get up and fetch her a fork.

She digs the coffee tin with vigour. 'A jackhammer might have been more useful.' She scoops the granules into mugs. 'Andrea Houghton is your Maths teacher, right?' She flicks the kettle switch and it gurgles to life. 'We catch up for coffee on Tuesday afternoons.' She looks around. 'Where's your mother? Still camping?'

I hand her the sugar pot.

'One or two?' she asks.

'Three.'

She measures three. 'Being on your own can't be easy.'

'I'm used to it.'

'But that doesn't mean you *like* it.'

I go to the fridge. Yellow light blinks, the glass shelves bare.

'No milk?' Jessie guesses. 'Never mind. We'll have it nice and strong.' She digs a thumb into her chest. 'Like me!' She pulls a packet of Tim Tams from her handbag and offers me the tray. 'Go on. I fully encourage Tim Tam slams.'

I take one and bite it. It's the first thing I've eaten today and it sits on my tongue, sickly sweet.

The kettle whistles and Jessie pours hot water. 'Counselling services are there for a reason, Tara. I know you cancelled your last appointment.' She passes me a steaming mug. I take it, my hand shaking. 'You don't have to go through this alone. I can make you another appointment, if you want?' She sips her coffee. 'Whatever you need.'

My stomach contracts, an uneasy heat rising up. 'I don't *need* anything.'

Jessie lets out a raucous laugh. 'And I got these hips and arse from doing squats and eating salad.' She pinches a sizable chunk of flab and gives it a good jiggle. 'The truth now, girly, and don't bother with the BS. Trust me, I'm fully

200

immunised. Dealing with hospital administration took care of that.'

Open and as generous as she is, I can't talk to her. The idea of discussing that night with anyone makes me nauseated. I suddenly want her out of here. I want her to leave me alone. I want to go back to bed, pull the covers over my head and forget the world exists.

'Not a day goes by that I don't think about what happened to me.' Saying this, she watches me closely, waiting. 'It's the little things. The smell of eucalyptus leaves. It happened beneath a eucalyptus tree.'

I watch her fingers curl around the lip of her coffee mug. She heads for the living room. I stand in the kitchen doorway, a spare part in my own house.

'Sit,' Jessie insists, waving me over. 'You're making the place look untidy.'

Reluctantly, I sit in front of her, on the coffee table.

Jessie laughs. 'You're determined not to get too comfortable, aren't you?'

'Honestly, I'm fine.'

'I said no BS! You got that, missy?' She waves a finger. 'I'll be honest with you if you're honest with me. Them's the rules and there ain't no breakin' 'em!' She dunks her Tim Tam and bites it. Half of it falls into her mug. 'No good ever came from bottling stuff up. Bottling stuff is for sauce-makers. People gotta learn to talk. Gotta let stuff out. All there is to it.'

Let it out? But he's in my mouth, in my throat. *Inside me.* The more I run, the more he pulses through my veins. Year Eight biology: the parasite takes up residence, feeding on the host, sucking lifeblood, killing it slowly. I'm the host, and day by day I'm dying just that little bit more. 'I can't.'

'Then you can listen.' Jessie gets up and stretches, leaning back, her hands massaging the small of her back. She takes her mug and goes to the fireplace, where she rests it on the mantle. 'Here's the thing, Tara. Nowadays, I only think of the details very occasionally.' She waits, as if she expects me to say something. I sip my coffee. 'Of course, there's one thing I can't escape . . .' Her hand hovers at the nape of her neck, fingers tracing an invisible necklace. She takes a deep breath. 'Margo. She's his.'

The coffee swamps my mouth, heavy and bitter. I'm unable to swallow.

She picks up a ceramic jar from the mantle and twirls it between her fingers. 'There's no good can come from telling her. I mean, if that were you – if *you* were Margo – would you want to know that's how you came to be in the world?'

If I were Margo.

I think of the day we locked Margo in the boys' toilets. It comes flooding back, crisp and clear. It was lunchtime in primary school. Mum was on canteen duty. They'd given her a master key because they couldn't find the spare. When Mum wasn't looking, I nicked it from her handbag. A group of us lured Margo into the toilets and shoved her into a cubicle. A few of us held the door shut. Keita was singing, 'Gotcha! Gotcha! Gotcha!' as Margo cried and screamed. None of us cared. It only made it all the more funny. We tipped orange juice on her head, then we locked the main

202

door and left. Hours later, one of the teachers heard her cries and freed her. She told them it was me, but Keita and the others backed me up and said she was lying. In the end, we blamed this kid from Year Five who was a known troublemaker and he copped the blame. I never stopped to think about how Margo must have felt.

I've never stopped to think about how Margo feels, period.

'If I told Margo,' Jessie explains, 'there'd be no taking it back. Besides, I already told her that her father is dead to me. And there ain't no coming back from the dead, is there?'

'She believes you?'

Something flickers in her eyes. 'Yes,' she says. 'I understand that when people ask her about him, she tells them that her father is dead.'

'But you know who he is? He's alive?'

Jessie moves along the mantle to an elephant figurine. She runs her finger along its tiny trunk. 'It's hard to forget when we live in the same town.'

'He still lives here?'

'Yes.'

'Why didn't you report him?'

'Why didn't *you*?'

The question hangs between us.

'I thought about it, but I was pregnant and I guess I had other priorities . . .'

'Did you think of . . .?' I can't finish the sentence. How can I suggest getting rid of her baby? I'm talking about Margo.

'It crossed my mind,' Jessie admits. 'But then I met Ralph and he was the most caring soul in the world. He asked me to marry him and he promised to support me. We could have pretended Ralph was Margo's father, but Margo's father is a white man.' She pauses and then adds, 'He was my best friend's husband.'

The words jar me. I'm not sure I heard her right. 'Sorry?'

'He was drunk when it happened,' Jessie says, her fingers skimming the elephant figurine. 'It's not an excuse – far from it.' She flips the small creature, swinging it by its trunk. 'But he was . . . a *changed* man.'

Drunk. I'm back in that room. I smell his stinking breath, hear his slurred words, feel him crawling all over me. 'Did you tell your friend?'

'Out of everything, strangely, keeping it from her was the hardest part. When I finally told her . . .' She stops, her teary eyes fixated on the tiny Uluru figurine. She picks it up and turns it over.

I remember Justin playing with the same ornament. 'My mum bought that thing at a garage sale,' I tell her. 'I have no idea why she likes it so much.'

'I gave my friend something like this,' Jessie whispers. 'Only, the one I gave her was attached to a jewellery box. It was a birthday present. She was always talking about going to Uluru. Her mother once worked at a nearby Aboriginal mission and she'd wanted to go there on a holiday, to retrace her mother's footsteps. They never had enough money to go.' She puts the Uluru figurine back into position and comes over to the couch.

'What did your friend say when you told her? About Margo, I mean.'

She sighs. 'It was complicated. They already had a child. He was older than Margo and I guess she had to think about him.'

'Did she leave her husband?'

Jessie bites her bottom lip. Her eyes fill with tears. 'Eventually, yes.'

'But how do you . . .?'

'Live in the same town as him?'

I nod.

'Answer me first,' she says, her brown eyes searching mine. 'How will *you*?'

A door slams inside my heart. I turn away.

'I thought as much.' Gently, Jessie asks, 'Do you want to try talking to me?'

But I can't talk about it the way she just did – so open, so calm. Jessie might have been able to share her story, but I can't offer her the same. I can't even make the sounds when I'm alone. I've tried – I've sat in front of the mirror and I can't even meet my own eyes. How am I going to meet anyone else's? Until that night, I'd never done anything with a boy I didn't want to. *Never.* Nothing can describe what happened. And even if words were enough, what then? It can't be taken back. What's done is done.

'Tara?'

I shake my head.

'Do you know who it was?'

I twist my blue-jay ring, sliding it up and down my

finger. The skin is raw, but I do it anyway – the pain distracts me.

Jessie leans forward and cups my head in her hands. 'Tara, look at me. Do you remember anything? His voice? Did you recognise it? What about something he was wearing? A belt, perhaps? Jewellery?'

I close my eyes and see his glinting silver watch.

'What about at the party? Was there someone who . . . I don't know . . . made unwanted advances?'

Cammo. In the toilet. But he wouldn't, would he? Was it *his* voice I heard?

And what about the others – the ones who stood around taking my photo? It could have been *any* guy in that room. They all saw me. They all thought I was fair game. How could I tell Jessie about that? What would she think if she knew? She'd think I deserved everything I got, that's what – exactly like the people commenting online.

'It's okay if you can't remember, Tara. It's not your fault – none of this is. Trust me. I spent years second-guessing myself. Did I flirt with him? Did I wear something that turned him on? Did I say something he may have interpreted as an invitation? Did I have one too many drinks and let myself go? Then one day I woke up and realised that what I did or could have done has absolutely nothing to do with it. *Not a thing*. It's as simple as this: I said no. He heard me say no – over and over – and he did what he wanted to do anyway.'

I'd said no . . .

'Any excuses men use are just that: excuses. Rape is

about power. It's about one person asserting their will over another. There's no situation where a woman deserves it. Not one.'

I swallow hard, trying to understand, trying to make her words ring true. But I hear him: *Now she's gunna get what's coming to her.* He was telling me I'd asked for it. Had I?

Jessie reaches out to smooth my hair, brushing it from my face. 'Tara, soon people will start asking questions. Are you prepared for that? Because there will be questions. *Why are you looking so sad? Why weren't you at school? Why did you act weird around that guy? Why won't you come to the party?* People ask things and you can't stop them. You can't hide from them either. You really should see a counsellor. It's important to set up boundaries.'

I dare to look at her.

'Trust me,' she adds. 'I'm a mum. Mothers know best.'

'Not my mother.' It comes out like that – like some sort of reflex. 'My mum wouldn't know what to do.'

Her voice is soothing. 'Darling, are you sure that, if you told your mum, she wouldn't come rushing to your side?'

I can't remember the last time my mother came rushing to my side for anything.

'I think you're underestimating her,' Jessie says, squeezing my hand. 'And I think she's overestimating you by leaving you on your own for so long. Anyway, one hurdle at a time. If you're not comfortable talking to your mother, that's okay by me. She isn't my priority. *You are.* I need to get you some help.'

'But –'

'Uh-uh-uh.' She holds up a hand. 'Enough BS. It's getting tired. Time to try a new routine.'

There's no winning with her. I feel a smile playing on my lips. 'Margo's lucky to have you.'

She pats my knee. 'And I'm lucky to have her. How she came to be in this world is irrelevant. She's mine and that's all that matters.'

Justin

I wrap a towel around me and hunt for my jeans. The stitches came out yesterday and I'm patched up, ready to go. Where to, though, is a bloody good question.

I ransack the old man's two-bedroom dog box, stacked high with moving crates he never unpacked after he sold the family home. He unearthed the essentials – bed linen, dinner plates, kettle, a pot for heating tinned spaghetti – and forgot about the rest. There's a dead pot plant on the TV. A TAB guide stuck to the arm of a cracked-leather La-Z-Boy. A fridge with an ice dispenser. All a man needs, apparently.

I search for my jeans, then realise I'm looking for the pair I wore the night of the accident. The hospital gave them back to me, bunched inside a white plastic bag. *Your personal effects.* Bloodied, hacked-up jeans and a soiled shirt – awesome. At the time, all I bothered to rescue was my wallet before throwing the rest in the closet and forgetting it. I know the jeans are cactus, but there might be money in the pockets.

I find the bag and deposit the contents on my bed. It's a confronting sight: shredded denim stiffened by dried blood. I sink a hand into the back pocket and come up empty. One of the front pockets produces a roadhouse receipt for a pie and Coke, a guitar plectrum belonging to the bloke I scored my last hit from and a two-dollar coin. The other pocket holds something unexpected, something soft. Tara's underwear.

My phone buzzes, ringing muffled. I fish it out from under the doona. 'Yeah?'

'Justin? This is Dominic Carbone, Mildura Police. I'm calling to update you on your mother's grave situation.' There's a *clunk*, as if he dropped the phone. 'Sorry, I mean, I'm updating you on your mother's *grave*.'

Did they know something? Had they found her?

'This is a courtesy call to advise there have been no further developments.' I wait, expecting him to tell me more, but he follows this up with, 'Righto. I'll keep you posted,' and hangs up.

I stare at my phone. The update is, there is no update?

Outside, around the back of the house, I dispose of my bloodied clothes in the red-lidded wheelie bin. I'm about to turf Tara's undies when I think better of it. They're a reason to see her. I've messaged her dozens of times, but she hasn't responded. I look at my watch. It's after four. She'd be home by now.

Back inside, I ditch the towel and find some jocks. The counsellor I saw when I was coming off ice said, if you're going to make a positive change, you have to start by

210

being honest. I came back to Mildura to sort out my life. I can't keep going on like this. I can't keep drifting without a plan. Something tells me that, if I don't start by being honest with Tara – *really honest* – bad shit will keep happening.

Then there's Margo. I haven't spoken to her since that afternoon in the cemetery. Chances are she doesn't even know how I feel. What with the accident and Tiny's death, there hasn't been a right moment to talk. But there's something between us – I can feel it.

I pull on a T-shirt and trackies and shove Tara's undies in my pocket. I'm about to leave, when I hear keys rattling in the front door.

The old man grunts, shoving past me, reeking of beer and smokes. His tweed jacket has remnants of whatever he had for lunch stuck to it.

'You're back early.'

'Mongrel doggies.'

'No good?'

He shrugs. 'Pay day's tomorrow.'

'Got some spare?'

He sinks the tip of a worn Blundstone into the rug. 'Fresh out.'

Expected. I bypass him, headed for the door.

'What's for grub?' he asks.

'Meatballs.'

He shuffles off to the kitchen and opens the fridge. Glass clinks against glass, ice cubes jingle. Meatballs are the last thing on his mind.

———

Tara's doorbell must be faulty. I'm about to give up and leave her undies in the mailbox, when I catch sight of her stomping up the street, schoolbag wrenched over her shoulder like she's carrying the weight of the world. She's fuming about something.

Maybe that something is me.

I consider doing the bolt, but then I man up and sit my sorry backside on the porch and practise my speech: *I'm sorry for leaving you at the party, Tara. There's this thing I've been meaning to say. I can't work out how I feel about us. Maybe it's best if we cool it. Is that all right with you?*

Head down, earphones in, she doesn't see me until she enters the front gate.

'Tara?'

She pulls the buds from her ears. 'Justin?'

I thumb at the front door. 'I gave breaking and entering a miss today.'

She doesn't even crack a smile. Storm clouds gather across her face and I brace myself, ready for the cyclone.

'What do you want?' She unzips her bag with unnecessary vigour and extracts a lanyard dangling a key.

'I haven't seen you since the party.'

Her back to me, she puts the key in the lock. 'So?'

'Can I come in?'

She stands there, considering her options. She leaves the door open and I follow her inside.

You know how people say a place looks like a bomb has hit it? Well, the whole fucking artillery has been used on Tara's place. Dirty plates, half-eaten mould-green

212

sandwiches, empty soft-drink cans, chip packets, mugs, clothing, blankets, fluffy toys, DVD cases, magazines . . . I almost blurt out, *How do you live like this?*

Dumping her schoolbag on the floor, Tara picks over the mess and opens the blinds. Everything lights up in my face, as if magnified.

'Well?' she asks.

'I owe you an apology.'

She crosses her arms. 'For which part?'

And she's right. There are several apologies to be made. I'm not sure where to start, so I pull her undies from my pocket, hanging them from my finger.

It's like I've shot her. She stumbles back, her expression somewhere between horror and confusion.

I put the undies on the coffee table and step away with my hands in the air. 'I'm sorry. I helped you to a bedroom. You . . . you took them off. I was coming back for you. I went to get you some water. Do you remember?'

She nods, barely.

'I found them in my pocket. I must have put them there, thinking I didn't want for you to lose them.'

In one swift move, she grabs her undies and shoves them down the side of the couch, as if I don't know they're hers, as if I haven't already seen so much more than that. 'I've got homework to do,' she says stiffly. 'I've fallen behind.'

I can't work out what it is but something about her is different. Maybe this is about the photos. 'You know, Tara, I reckon it was a low act what those blokes did to you. Taking your photo like that was unforgivable.' I wait, gauging her

213

reaction. Her expression doesn't change. 'I tried to stop them. Actually, I *did* stop them.'

She looks away.

'Tara, is everything –'

'You didn't stop them fast enough, did you?'

'You're right. I got there too late.'

She presses her lips. 'Like I said, I have homework to do.'

I get the feeling I'm barking up the wrong tree; this isn't about the photos. 'Tara, about the accident –'

'Don't bother. Keita filled me in.'

It wasn't my plan to come here and stir up trouble, but I say it anyway. 'And did Keita tell you that *she* caused the accident?'

Tara stares at me.

'I'm guessing that's a no.'

Gingerly, she seats herself on the edge of the couch. 'Why didn't you tell the police?'

'Because it wouldn't change anything.'

She rests her head in her hands. I expect her to explode, to demand I go to the cops and tell them what *really* happened, but instead, her shoulders dip and her body shrinks before my eyes.

I look around at the mess and she follows my gaze. 'It can't have been easy to wake up to those photos,' I say, taking a seat next to her. Tears spring into her eyes. She worries a blue-jay ring on her pinkie finger, twisting it, wincing. 'Don't give those arseholes a second thought, Tara. They're bottom feeders, pure and simple. They don't have a single brain cell between them.'

She fidgets with the hem of her school dress, pulling it down over her knees. *What's with her?* Gone is the flirty, fun girl I met a few weeks ago. Someone guarded is in her place.

'Why are you looking at me like that?' she asks.

'Like what?'

'Like *that*.'

I shrug. 'You seem different.'

She shoots me an annoyed look. 'I really do have homework to do.'

Call me selfish, but I don't want to leave. I thought she was the needy one, but maybe I am. I came here to set things straight, and I plan to – I do. 'You know that day we ...' The day we slept together, I think, too much of a pussy to say it out loud. 'I didn't tell you about what happened.'

She looks at me, waiting.

'My mother's grave was vandalised.'

'That was *your* mother?' she says, her mouth agape.

'You heard about it, huh?'

She nods. 'The whole town has.'

'I was fourteen when she killed herself. That's why I ran away from home.'

She smooths her school dress, ironing out the creases. 'That must have been horrible.'

'Horrible. Yes. Horrible. That's one way to describe it.'

We sit there, staring at the wall. Eventually, she asks the million-dollar question: the key in the lock that never turns; the reason I lie awake at night, playing back every childhood memory, every moment in time, trying to piece together my jigsaw life. 'Do you know why she did it?'

215

I shake my head. She reaches for my hand, but I pull back. 'Tara . . . I think we should chill for a while.'

She cups her hands in her lap and nods like some office-desk bobble-head figurine.

'So you're good with that?' I'm not sure if I should be relieved or cut. Something tells me I should be neither.

'A lot has happened,' she whispers.

We stare at the mess. I feel it pressing in, suffocating me. 'Are you sure you're okay?'

She forces a smile. 'I'm fine.'

I get up and head for the door.

'Justin?'

'Yeah?'

'Do you think the police will find her?'

'I hope so.' The conversation feels surreal. I can barely believe we're talking about *my* mother: dug up, skeleton dismembered, scattered fuck knows where. 'It wouldn't be right if they didn't.'

'What will you do if they don't?'

'Patch up her grave, I suppose.' But the thought of doing that without all of her buried makes me queasy.

'Have you been there?'

'To the cemetery? Yeah, I've been.' I neglect to mention Margo. 'They did a real job on it.'

'Can I see it?'

Her request catches me off guard. 'See her grave?'

She fiddles with her ring. 'I don't know anyone who's dead.'

It's such a strange thing to say. I have no idea what it means.

'How about Saturday?' she suggests. 'People play sport or go to the pub on Saturdays. There won't be anyone there.'

She's smiling now. It's the first time she's smiled since I stepped foot inside her house – smiling about visiting the grave of a dead woman she never knew.

'Okay,' I agree, not wanting to steal that smile away. 'Sure. Why not.'

'I'll meet you there at, say, five? I'll bring flowers.'

I get up and go to the door. 'Saturday it is.'

'Saturday,' she says, like she's clinging to it.

I leave her house, wondering what the hell I've just agreed to.

Margo

Justin pushes back on his blue plastic chair, slurping a raspberry milkshake. It's late afternoon. The service station is empty except for us and the attendant, Mrs Perkins. She comes and goes from the storeroom, restocking the cigarette cabinet, keeping one eye trained our way, as if we might steal something.

'Thanks for coming. When I called, I wasn't sure you'd be up for it.' Justin plucks a newspaper from the nearby stand and spreads it on the table between us. 'Nothing reported today. Maybe they've lost interest?'

The thought is optimistic. When Corey goes to court, the accident will be splashed across town again. And *again* when Daryl Sanders' number comes up. There's no escaping my role in it. I'm part of this whether I like it or not.

'Is Ralph okay?' he asks. 'After the fight?'

'Doc thought he had a broken rib. Turned out to be bad bruising. His diabetes played up, but it's under control now.'

He runs a finger over the death notices. Tiny's name no longer appears. 'Did you go to the funeral?'

'Yes.'

'Did my dad?'

I raise an eyebrow. 'What do you think?'

'Figures. His best mate is dead and he can't tear himself away from the bar for one day. What a surprise.'

'Why didn't *you* go?'

He raps his hands on the table, playing that non-existent drum set that follows him everywhere. 'I couldn't ...' He stops and looks at me as though I'd understand.

'Justin ... about that day at the cemetery –'

'I spoke to the cops about Mum's grave.' He shakes his head. 'You'd think someone would know *something* by now.'

'I ...' My cheeks fill with heat and I look away.

'You know something, don't you?' His fingers tighten around his milkshake, crushing the cardboard walls. 'I'm gunna get the bastards. Jesus Christ! I'm gunna get them! Tell me, Margo. Tell me who it was.'

'You can't.'

'What do you mean *I can't*?'

'You can't *get* them. You can't have a go at them.'

He laughs bitterly. 'You're joking, right? You think whoever did this doesn't deserve to cop it sweet?'

'It was Hamish Johnson and Corey Williams.'

He stares at me like I'm joking, then realises I'm not. 'Fuck.'

'I'm sorry ...'

'Fuck!'

He lifts the lid on his milkshake and stirs the soupy froth with the straw. One glance at the counter, then he hurls it at the wall. Pink cream sprays everywhere. I look for Mrs Perkins, but I can't see her – she must be out the back.

'Corey told me.'

He scrunches the newspaper, squeezing hard, trying to contain every molecule of his rage. He knows as well as I do that he can't do anything. Hamish is untouchable. And Corey? Well, the law is already making a meal of him. The only person he can be angry with is me for keeping it from him for so long.

He looks at me, questioning. 'Why did Corey tell you?'

'He said something about it the night of the accident.'

'You've known since then?'

He's right. It *does* sound bad. 'I was going to tell you, but then the accident happened . . . and Hamish's dad, and I . . .'

He buries his face in his hands, silent.

'Look, if it makes any difference, the night they did it, they were ripped off their nuts. They had no idea whose grave they'd broken into. It wasn't intentional or anything. Well, it was, but not towards you or your mother.'

Justin considers this. A glint of worry appears in his eyes. 'What have they done with her?'

'She's safe.'

'Safe?'

'Corey plans to take her bones to the police station.'

'He *plans* to?'

'He told me he would.'

'And you believe him?'

I reach for his hand. 'It's over, Justin.' I stop short of telling him to let it go. He's held on to his mother's death

220

for ten years. Digging her up has dug up the past. The earth has been churned, the dirt scattered, life breathed into an old wound.

He holds my hands almost desperately. Like he *needs* to cling to something. 'Before all this happened, Margo . . . On that day I first met you . . . The truth is, I liked you. I like you a lot.' His fingers stroke my skin and I feel a smile rising up, warming my lips. Mum was wrong about a guy from out of town being the only guy good enough for me. She hasn't met Justin. If she did, if she just gave him five minutes of her time, she'd be sold like I am.

And then it happens: he leans in to kiss me.

I lean forward, but as his lips brush mine, I knock over my orange juice. It pours across the table, running into his lap.

'Damn,' he says, looking down at his jeans. I scout for something to wipe up the mess but there's nothing. 'Where are the restrooms?'

I point the way.

'Back in a minute.' He stops and smiles. 'Then maybe we can try that again?'

He heads out the door.

I mop up the orange juice, cursing the whole time. It could only happen to me – first kiss equals major embarrassment.

'Margo?'

I look up. Tara is standing by the table.

'Had an accident?' Quickly rethinking her words, she stutters, 'I–I mean, you had a bit of a spill?' Her blue eyes flit from me to the cashier's desk and back to me again.

She twists each of her fingers, as if she's trying to unscrew them. 'How are you, Margo?'

I don't know what to say. Tara's never spoken to me this way. Like she *cares*. We haven't even looked at each other without vying for a fight. A one-role actor, I find it difficult to step out of character. 'How are you?' I ask, redirecting the conversation.

A red wash climbs her neck. I can't help but feel bad for her. Those boys snapped a pic and walked away, leaving her snap-frozen in a living hell.

'I'm not sure who has and hasn't seen them, you know?' She slides a silver blue-jay ring up and down. There's blood under her nails.

'Have you heard any more about Amy? How is she?'

She appears uncomfortable. 'I tried ringing her. Her dad isn't letting her take calls.'

I get it. If it were me, I imagine Ralph would do the same.

Tara nods at the empty chair. 'Can I join you?'

'Oh. Actually, I'm here with someone.'

She looks crushed. Just as quickly, though, a playful smile lights her lips. 'Margo's on a date,' she teases.

I smile. 'He'll be back in a minute.'

She gives my shoulder a friendly punch. 'Anyone I know?'

Justin pushes through the door. Tara's smile vanishes.

Justin may as well have 'GUILTY' painted all over him. One look at Tara and I know they've had something going on – something that lasted longer than that first night he spent with her.

I feel sick. I want to crawl under the table. But I'm like Tara's sordid image, suspended in time.

Justin goes to speak, but Tara doesn't wait. Through the cloudy window, I watch her run past pumps and hoses and honking cars. She collides with someone getting out of their vehicle. I can't see who it is; they're obscured from view by a petrol pump. She waves her hands animatedly, pointing at the servo window, then steamrolls off, not turning back.

I look at Justin. 'Haven't been able to get me out of your head, hey?'

'Margo . . . let me explain . . .'

And then my mother is standing in the doorway behind him. Her stunned face swings from me to Justin. She marches over and grabs my arm. 'You're coming with me!'

'Mum!'

'Outside! *Now!*' She shoves me through the door but doesn't follow – she yanks it shut between us.

I cringe as I watch her wave a finger in Justin's face, saying something I can't make out. He appears confused, hands spread wide. Mum isn't buying it. She picks up a salt shaker and slams it on the table. Moments later, she opens the door and grabs me again, steering me to the car. When we reach the passenger side, she barks, 'Get in!' then strides around to the driver's side.

I stand by the open door, staring at her.

'I said, get in!'

People are watching. This is no place to argue. I get in the car. I see Justin standing at the window, looking at us.

'Put your seatbelt on.' She starts the engine. 'Now, listen to me and listen carefully. You stay away from that boy, Margo. Do you understand?'

'Why?'

'*Because I said so!*' Mum puts her foot down and we launch out of the servo into oncoming traffic she barely misses.

'Is it because you heard he took drugs? Because he doesn't do it any more. He gave it up. I swear.'

She shoots me a look as we round the corner. 'That's got nothing to do with it!'

'Then what?'

'After all the trouble, Margo ... with everything – the accident, what happened to Tiny. You can't associate with these people. You just can't. Ralph's already on tenterhooks and I've got enough on my plate what with work being understaffed and all the extra shifts I'm doing. I'm tired, Margo – I'm *so tired.*'

It's not what she says, but the way she says it; an unrehearsed story, spat out on the spot without time for it to ruminate and gel. Something's not right.

'Did you know that while all this stuff was going on with you, Bradley has been hanging around that idiot Jackson? He thinks you got away with poor behaviour and he'll do the same. I can't keep doing this, Margo. I just can't. I'm at my wit's end.'

I'm about to question if there's more to it, when she bursts into tears. It stuns me. Mum *never* cries. She's as resilient as they come. I feel horrible. I reach across to touch her shoulder. 'It's okay. I get it.'

She blinks at me, her eyes hopeful. 'You do?'

'I won't talk to him, I promise.'

'Really?'

'I won't talk to Justin or to anyone involved in the accident, okay?' I don't say it to pacify her. I say it because there's no point arguing. Five minutes ago, I thought I had something with a boy. Now I know that something was nothing more than a lie.

Mum takes her hand off the gearstick and reaches for mine. 'You lost your way for a moment, Margo, that's all. What happened – for want of a better term – was a bump in the road. We're over it now. It's back on the straight and narrow. Understand? We'll get past this. We'll do it as a family.' She says it like she's begging, like her life depends on it.

'Okay,' I reassure her. 'Straight and narrow. Got it.'

She nods and wipes away tears.

'I love you, Mum.'

'You too, button. Don't you ever forget it.'

Corey

I've had my share of camping in bushes and stormwater drains, but hiding behind the chook shed in Margo's backyard takes the cake. I've *got* to speak to her and this is the only way. Martha was giving me a hint. That birth notice means something. I have to tell her.

When I scaled Margo's fence, it occurred to me I could be waiting a while. I know Ralph won't allow me through the front door; he won't allow me within three feet of her. And calling her is a dead-end deal – she'll likely hang up. It's now or never. I just have to wait until she shows.

It'd help if I knew which window was hers. I could take a gamble, but the thought crosses my mind that I could pick the wrong one. What if I bust Ralph going at it with Jessie? That happened with my olds once. I walked into their room with perfect twenty-twenty vision, and after seeing my father's pimply white arse driving it home, I came out practically blind.

I shift my weight. It's a bit cramped behind the chook shed. The pain in my feet is worse than a cork thigh. One thing's for certain: these damn chooks stink. I don't understand why people keep them. All they do is attract snakes.

And here I am, with Martha in a bag at my feet – proof of that theory.

This time Martha's travelling in style. I have her inside the old girl's blue-and-white striped beach bag. It isn't exactly a guy accessory, but it's clean and it has a zip. If anyone asks, I'll tell them it's the old girl's groceries.

The screen door swings open and I hold my breath. Bradley struts onto the grass, footy tucked under his arm.

'And he's off!' he cries, running around the Hills hoist, dodging several basket loads of drying laundry. 'Bradley Bonney, AFL superstar, has the ball!'

Watching him, it's hard not to acknowledge he's a handy little athlete. I get the feeling I'm in the company of future greatness, like I'm getting a sneak preview of the next Adam Goodes or Buddy Franklin. Too bad he's not old enough to play Colts. We could really use a player like him.

'Bonney goes out wide . . .'

I wonder if I can trust the runt to speak to Margo. Chances are, if I call out, I'll scare the crap out of him and he'll run off and rag to his parents. Next thing I know, I'll be busted for trespassing – something else for my rap sheet. Then they'll find Martha: two crimes for the price of one. Coppers will have a field day.

'And he takes the mark!' Bradley commentates, tossing the ball. He tumbles onto the grass, wrestling an imaginary player. 'It's a free to Bradley Bonney! The crowd goes wild!' He stands, gearing up for a kick. He talks out of the side of his mouth. 'This will be Bonney's twentieth goal. Geez, I reckon he's topped Buddy Franklin, hasn't he? Well, Bob, Bonney *is* a three-time Brownlow medallist. What do you expect?'

He lines up the shot, aiming between the veggie patch and the chook shed.

Shit!

He delivers the kick straight as an arrow. It flies up the guts and right into my face.

I get to my feet, holding my nose. 'Nice shot, kid!' Blood trickles down my chin.

'Corey? What the . . .?'

I put out my hand, unable to see him; there's something wrong with my eyes. 'Don't yell, okay, mate? I don't mean any trouble. I'm here for Margo. I need to speak to her. Your olds can't know I'm here, okay?'

He shoves something soft into my hand. 'Use this.'

I pinch my nostrils and tip back my head. With my free hand, I wipe away blood from my chin and chest.

'How long have you been here?' he asks.

'Long enough to hear you've racked up three Brownlows.'

'Aw, man. Don't tell anyone, will ya?'

I'm the one hiding in his backyard and he's asking *me* to keep secrets? 'Can you get your sister for me?'

'Why?'

'Can you get her or not?'

He digs my ribs. 'Do you have the hots for her?'

Two of him slowly merge into one. 'What makes you think that?'

''Cos you're hiding in our backyard, you perv.'

'I'm hiding because your olds will string me up if I try to come through the front door.'

'Mum's at work. Dad's at the shops.'

That figures.

'Give me a minute,' he says. 'I'll go get her.'

It's the longest minute of my life. When Margo finally appears, the first thing she asks is, 'Corey, why do you have your nose buried in my mother's underpants?'

I look at the bloodied mess in my hand – white elasticated nylon undies. The little brat must've got them off the clothesline! 'Your brother sure has a sense of humour,' I say, dabbing my nose. Jessie won't be wanting her undies back. 'Cheeky rabbit.'

'Why are you playing footy with my brother?'

'I came here to talk to you, Margo.'

She crosses her arms. 'We haven't got a whole lot to say to each other.'

'But that day by the river . . . you offered to come to the cops with me.'

'So you think we're friends? Is that what you think?'

Her words sting worse than my nose.

'What do you want from me, Corey?'

I consider walking away, birth notice or no birth notice. 'Just give me a sec to explain, will ya?'

'Go on, then.'

I take a deep breath. 'It's about the bones . . . I chickened out.' I glance at the chook shed. 'No offence, girls.'

Margo blinks, wide-eyed. *'You still have them?'*

'Yeah.' I point to the grass corridor between the veggie patch and chook shed. She looks at me like I'm kidding, then gasps when she realises I'm not. 'Well, I couldn't exactly leave her at home, could I?'

She paces in circles. 'After everything that's happened ... after the accident ... you brought another crime to my doorstep? What is wrong with you, Corey?'

'I have to take them back.'

'So take them back!'

'I need your help.'

She stares at me. 'My help? Why not one of your drinking buddies? Why not Cammo Gibson?'

'You're the only one I can trust. You did right by me after the accident, Margo. You knew about the bones and you didn't say anything. The police would've been knocking on my door by now if you did.'

She looks at the sky, shaking her head.

'I don't know why you haven't told the police, Margo, but I'm thankful you haven't.'

'Corey, do you know *who* those bones belong to?'

'Martha Sparks.'

She blinks. 'How do you –'

'You know how news travels in this place.'

She twists a strand of hair, not looking at me.

My gut clenches. 'You *knew* it was Martha? Why didn't you say something that night at the park?'

She sighs. 'It's complicated.'

I turn and head back to the chook shed. 'No one trusts me. No one tells me squat.'

'Corey . . . stop.'

I stop but don't turn around. 'What?'

'What happened to your eye?'

I touch the spot where the old man clopped me. I'd almost forgotten it was there. 'It's nothing. It happened when your brother's ball hit me.'

I feel her behind me now, hands on my shoulders. She turns me to face her. Her fingers gently skim my skin, running a half-circle under my eye. 'No, it didn't,' she whispers.

There's no lying to this girl. It's as if she'll see right through me, no matter what.

'Tell me the truth.'

'The old man gave me a hiding, okay? It's no big deal.'

'No big deal? Oh, Corey . . .'

'I deserved it this time.'

'No one deserves that.'

'I do.' Her brown eyes swim. Curiosity gets the better of me. 'What?'

'That happens to you a lot, doesn't it?'

'If "a lot" means on a weekly basis, then yeah.'

'But you always seem so . . . so . . .'

'Like I couldn't give a fuck?'

She nods.

'Good cover, eh?'

A shadow of a smile plays on her lips.

'Look, Margo, I don't care about my old man. I don't even care about me. I need to fix things. I have to take back the bones. Will you help me or not?'

She glances at her house. 'I'm not sure.'

I think about telling her about the birth notice and the jewellery box like I'd planned to, but for some reason, instead I say, 'I need someone to help keep a lookout. It's a two-person job. And Hamish ... well, you know about Hamish.'

She rolls her eyes. 'Oh God, how did I get dragged into this?'

And that's how I know she's onside. 'Good. I want to go tonight. It's Saturday. The cemetery should be quiet. We can do it quickly.'

'How do you know her grave is even accessible? When I last saw it, it was a mess.'

'We broke into it, so I figure we can ...' Hang on a minute – what did she say? 'You saw Martha's grave?'

Margo fiddles with the gold chain swinging from her neck. 'I went there with Justin.'

I don't get it. Are they old family friends or something? Maybe there was a perfectly reasonable explanation for Margo's birth notice being inside the jewellery box, after all. 'How do you know Justin Sparks?'

She turns away.

'Margo?'

When she looks at me again, her eyes burn. I get it – it practically smacks me in the face. Geez, I'm slow on the uptake sometimes. 'You're kidding. *You* and Justin?'

'There is no *me* and Justin. It's over. Honestly? It never really happened.'

'But I thought he and Tara ...?'

Her mouth draws a thin line. 'You thought right. I was

the last person to know.' She looks rotten about it too. 'Tell me, Corey, is there *any* guy in town Tara Ramsey hasn't slept with?'

'Aw, c'mon, that's a bit harsh, don't you think?'

She shrugs. 'You're the one who showed me proof.'

It comes back to me: sitting at the servo, I'd showed her the photo of Tara on my phone. 'Hey. People are thinking the worst of Tara right now. I get it. But I *know* her, okay? It's obvious she was passed out. Those idiots took her photo without her permission.'

Margo's eyes narrow. 'Passed out or *acting* passed out?'

'Passed out,' I say firmly, and she pulls a face like she doesn't believe it. 'What's your problem with her, anyway?'

'Don't tell me you're in love with her too!'

'In love with her? No, I'm not in love with her. She's a hot chick, but she's not my bag.'

Margo's face softens. 'Really?'

'Really.'

'But I thought every guy in town was falling over themselves to be with her.'

'Not this guy.' I swallow a blood clot running down the back of my throat. It must have legs because it threatens to run straight back up. 'Now it's your turn to be honest. What's *your* problem with Tara?'

She fidgets with her neck chain and doesn't answer.

'Girls,' I say. 'You don't like sharing the limelight, do you?'

'What is that supposed to mean?'

'Aren't you the smartest girl in school or something?' I say, watching her prickle. 'And Tara's the prettiest, right?'

Margo shrugs.

'Well, it's like on the footy field. The brightest stars always butt heads. There can only be one best on ground. One best and fairest.' I think of Bradley, kicking his footy. 'One Brownlow medallist.'

Slowly, a weird, appreciative smile spreads across her face. Just as quickly, it disappears. 'I like that you're trying to understand this, Corey, but it's not that simple ... It's messy.'

'Yeah? Messy and me, we're old friends.'

She clucks her tongue, searching for the right words. 'Tara and I ... we do things differently. I have this skill called empathy. She doesn't.'

I might not get a lot of stuff, but I get this. 'And how do you *obtain* skills?'

'Huh?'

'You don't just magically wake up with them. You weren't born with them. You have to learn, right? Like footy. You have to practise. Where do you get *your* skills from, Margo?'

She bites her lip.

'I'd reckon your mum would be pretty good in that department, being a nurse and all. Yeah?'

She nods. 'I s'pose.'

'And from what I know about Ralph, he's a slick negotiator too.'

'I guess.'

'Well then. Have you ever met Caroline Ramsey?'

There's a long silence – proof she has. She cracks a smile. 'You're not as stupid as you look.'

I feel myself buzzing. No other girl has ever made me feel like Margo does. Like respected or whatever. It's weird. It's different. It's kind of awesome.

'Right,' I say, changing the subject. 'Now, what did you tell lover boy about the bones?'

She looks uncomfortable again.

I can't believe it – she told him. 'You didn't! Oh, fantastic! That's just brilliant. When he catches up with me, I'll be sucking my meals through a straw. Wow. I'm screwed, aren't I?'

'Corey . . . it wasn't like that.'

'Yeah? How was it?'

'He has a right to know.'

And she's right, he does. But it cuts me nonetheless. 'When did you tell him?'

She looks at the back fence, but it's as if she's looking somewhere a million miles away. 'Earlier today,' she says.

'What did he say?'

'What do you think he said?'

'I'm imagining the word "castration" came up once or twice. Is he going to the cops?'

'I don't think so.'

My nosebleed has stopped. I hand over the underpants. She takes them, staring at the blood.

'You said the bones are here?'

I point to the bag. 'Wanna see?'

After a moment's consideration, she shakes her head.

'I promise it's not gross or anything. Martha's not crusty. She's really nice.'

Margo's face may as well be a question mark.

'What I mean is, I hope I'm buried next to someone like her – someone I can talk to. You're a long time underground is all I'm saying.'

'You really are left of field, aren't you?'

I take my chances and give her a wink. 'If you really want to know, I'm good on *and* off the field.'

She suppresses a smile. 'Look, Corey. If we're going to do this, the bones are your problem, okay? Like you said, I'm there to keep watch. I don't want to know any more about it than that. Is that clear?'

'Crystal meth.'

'Beg yours?'

'Clear as glass.'

'And do you promise you'll make an anonymous phone call to the police after you've put them back?'

I grab the bag. 'I promise.'

She gawks at it. 'A beach bag? Seriously?'

'What? It's my mum's good one.'

She rolls her eyes for what seems like the twentieth time. 'Have you got a torch? A hand shovel?'

Good point. I didn't think of that. 'Can I borrow yours?'

Sighing, she heads inside. 'Wait there. I'll get the keys to the tool shed.'

I cradle the bag, feeling pumped. This is going to happen. I'm finally going to do it. 'What did I tell you, Martha? I promised I'd sort it out. Did you ever doubt me?'

Inside the bag, her bones jostle for position, restless as ever.

Tara

I stand by the entrance to Nichols Point Cemetery. It's almost five o'clock. I thought it would be quiet on a Saturday afternoon and I was right. There are no cars parked outside. Any visitors have been and gone. And after the other day at the servo, there's no way Justin would come here. The place is mine.

Sort of.

I make my way up the gravel footpath. The evening air is warm, breathy on my shoulders. Birds caw. The dying sun casts fragments of orange light through the blackening tree branches, the sky a stained-glass window.

Seeing Justin with Margo underlined what I'd suspected all along. He's the same as every other guy. He took what he wanted and walked out the door.

Like my dad walked out the door.

I find his mother's grave easily; the police tape flaps, demanding my attention. Up close, I see broken cement piled into a neat mound beside a desecrated headstone. Sheets of MDF cover the grave. There's a notice that says a crime is under investigation and a directive not to go beyond the tape.

I read the names on the neighbouring graves. *Albert Fairfield. Cornelia Hunterfield. Gillian Maxwell.* Weathered and mostly uncared for, it's hard to tell if anyone visits. Maybe their relatives are long since dead too.

Beyond Martha's grave, there are hundreds of headstones. Countless plaques and mini monuments. How can you condense a life into a few sentences carved in stone? It doesn't seem enough.

I duck under the police tape and sit cross-legged among the rubble and weeds, positioning myself close to where Martha's head would've lain. There's no visible writing on what remains of her headstone, so I imagine her name and the date she died. I wonder if it also had a prayer or a verse. Maybe it mentioned Justin or Old Man Sparks. I envisage curvy old-fashioned letters framed by chiselled stone roses. I bet it was pretty.

I collect little grey pebbles, piling them on the edge of Martha's boarded-up grave, building a tiny fortress.

'Hello, Martha. Justin told me about you. I'm a friend of his. Actually, no, I'm not his friend. I'm not his anything, really.'

Rustling leaves stir the trees. I shake off the feeling someone is watching me. There's maybe a few hundred listening, but no one watching.

'My mum tried to kill herself.' The words sound strange; I've never said them out loud. 'It happened the day after Dad left. I was seven and I found her on the bathroom floor.' I close my eyes and see a jumble of pink towels, chequered floor tiles, Mum lying there in her nightdress with thick, white foam on her lips. At first I thought it was toothpaste; I thought she'd slipped over. But then I tried to wake her and she wouldn't open her eyes.

I pick up a pebble and roll it between my fingers. Chalky dust stains my hands. I use it to draw a crude bunch of flowers on the MDF: daisies, thin blades of grass, a butterfly landing on a drooping stem.

'I ran to the neighbour's house. Mrs Detloff called for an ambulance and they took Mum to hospital. Dad had gone overseas, so they called Grandma – my mum's mum. I'd never met her. Mum hadn't spoken to her in years. When she arrived, the first thing Grandma said was, *Your mother's attention-seeking behaviour has reached new heights.*'

I draw a thorny rose with falling petals, smudging the edges, softening the lines.

'Grandma stayed for two days before she said Grandpa and her horde of cats needed her at home. She asked if Mr and Mrs Detloff could keep an eye on me. I guess they didn't have much of a choice.'

The sky is murky now, grey clouds closing in. The sun pokes its thin fingers, clutching at one last minute of the day.

'Four weeks. That's how long Mum was in hospital. Four whole weeks. I stayed with the Detloffs during that time. Mrs Detloff didn't like me being there, I could tell. She was all ... I don't know ... jittery or something. But Mr Detloff ...'

I draw fat raindrops and colour them, full and heavy. Tears slide down my throat, tiny jagged ice cubes. My artwork grows, flower after flower, chalk shimmering as it catches the last rays of sun.

'That's the first time I knew men liked me. It was wrong what he did. So wrong.'

The wind sighs. It's Martha – I'm sure of it. I run my hand over her boarded-up grave, hoping to feel her warmth, her presence. Tingles surge through me.

Darkness descends, the sun dipping below the horizon. Shadows of headstones stretch – ghoulish arms, reaching for me. I draw vines intertwining with vines; a brutal, unforgiving forest of thorns.

'I spoke to a rape counsellor. Jessie arranged it. I told her about those guys at the party and how they . . . how they . . .' I cry now – the kind of crying that sucks your insides and makes it difficult to breathe. 'So many things are my fault, Martha. The accident was my fault. After what happened at the party, I was walking home . . . I was on the road. I don't even know how I got there. It's like I woke up from this horrible dream and found myself there and all I remember is seeing these lights coming at me and –'

'Jesus, it was you.'

I turn around, hot prickles washing over me.

'On the road,' he says. 'It was *you*.'

Justin

I ditch the flowers. Rose petals scatter. 'Tara! Wait!'

She legs it, hurdling graves, but then trips and stumbles, landing awkwardly on a wire grid covering a dirt mound. There are flowers tied to it – it's a freshly filled grave. Her face is an avalanche of horror. She scrambles away, fighting to get up. I put out my hand to help, but she whirls around and kicks me, her foot connecting with my injured leg.

'Christ!' I collapse on the grass, grabbing at my wound. The pain is beyond savage.

'Justin! I didn't mean to . . . Are you okay?'

I reach out and pull her to me, drawing her head to my chest. She struggles at first but then lets go, clawing her way up my T-shirt, climbing me like a branch to safety. Her hot tears soak the crook of my neck. 'It's okay,' I say. 'It's okay.'

But it's not okay. It never will be okay. The words she spoke by my mother's grave bounce around inside my head like a pinball machine. I don't even know where to start. If I'm overwhelmed, she must be drowning. Here I was thinking she was acting weird because of the photos. Or because of her mother's trashed car. I wasn't even close. I was nowhere *near* close. Those bastards! Those fucking bastards. I should have known. I should have joined the dots. *Why didn't I join the dots?* I left her alone. *I* put her in that room.

I cup her chin and try to get her to look at me. She wiggles away, burying her face in my chest, and I hear the words I said to her at the party: *You're a polished act, I'll give you that.* I feel sick. Even sicker when I realise how I've used her too.

'Tara?'

'Don't,' she pleads, and draws her knees to her chest.

We sprawl on the grass, a tangle of limbs.

'Lie to me?' she whispers. 'Tell me I mean something to you.'

'You did, Tara. You *do.*'

She shudders, breaking down in my arms. 'Liar.'

And that's when it starts. The beast is off its leash – the beast I worked so hard to hold at bay with drugs and booze and sleepless nights and wasted days and pointless arguments and thumping music and cigarettes and sex and running – always running. I let go and howl. Tara holds me and I hold her, both of us crying, wrapped up in blue.

I stroke her head, brushing her silky hair, breathing her in. She twines her fingers through mine and turns to face me. I melt into her, desire giving way to something more meaningful. I kiss her cheek gently, lovingly, the way I should have kissed her from the very beginning.

As my lips brush hers, she pulls away. 'I can't…' She rolls onto her back, gazing up at the stars. Then she covers her face, crying.

I lie next to her and wait, determined I won't be one of *them*; I won't pressure her. I won't ask questions she doesn't have the answers to. I won't tell her to stop crying. How to act. What to say. How to feel. I won't do a single thing she doesn't want me to do.

'I'm not sure I'll ever be ready,' she says, wiping her eyes. 'After . . .' But she chokes on the words. 'Why can't I say it out loud? Why can't I?'

'Because it makes it real.'

'Oh God . . .'

'One day at a time, Tara. One hour. One *minute*, if that's what it takes. The counsellors told me that when I was trying to get clean.'

'Did it help? Did *any* of it help?'

'Honestly? I dunno. Counsellors say stuff and some of it makes sense and some of it's bullshit. But I can tell you one thing: if you're not ready to hear it – to *believe* it – it won't mean anything to you.'

She hugs herself, shaking her head. 'How could they possibly know what it's like?'

'They don't. They haven't got the first idea what it's like to be you. Not even I know that. Only you do.' I turn on my side, facing her. 'Somehow, I had to find the fight within me. I had to reach down, grab it, hold on to it. Then I had to climb back up. I made mistakes, but that's part of it. I'm going to keep making mistakes. Just have a look at me. I *am* a fucking mistake!'

A sudden peal of laughter. It's the first time I've seen her relax. 'You're not a mistake, Justin. You're *you*. I like you.'

'As a friend?'

'A friend,' she confirms. We lie there, nightfall pressing in on us.

'I'm leaving. I'm going back to Melbourne. I need to make something of my life.'

'Take me with you.'

I look at her, surprised. 'Running won't change anything. Of all people, Tara, I should know.'

She reaches for my hand. I see her eyes, hope gleaming. 'Please? Take me.'

I hoist myself up and help her to her feet. 'We should get going.'

She pulls me back. 'But you came here for your mum.'

'I can come back another day.'

'For me?' she whispers.

She knows I can't argue with that. Reluctantly, I follow her. We tread carefully, picking our way back to my mother's grave.

'Are you sorry you came home?' she asks.

'No.'

'Even after what's happened?'

'I met you, didn't I?'

A smile. 'What about Margo?'

'When I first met Margo ... it's hard to explain. It's like we had some kind of connection. A weird chemistry. I couldn't figure it out. I *still* can't figure it out. But that day at the servo, when I saw her mum, Jessie, it made me realise –'

She stops. 'Wait a minute. You know Jessie?'

'Yeah. I mean, I haven't seen her since I was a little kid, but she was close friends with my mum. Jessie was my mum's best friend.'

'*Best* friend?'

'Yeah. Jessie used to visit our house. She and Mum would sit in the kitchen, drinking coffee, nattering about this and that. I was a kid, so I was usually in the sandpit or in the lounge room, playing with toys. But I remember it well.'

She's looking at me more intensely now, as if she's trying to work something out. 'Jessie talked to you that day at the servo, didn't she? What did she say?'

'I wouldn't call it talking. She was screaming that I should get out of town. I guess she's dark with me because of Ralph and the fight. I'm the first to admit my old man went there looking for trouble, even if it was him who finished things. I can understand how Jessie would be sore about that.'

'Justin,' Tara says with a sudden urgency, 'I think . . .' She looks around. 'Did you hear that?'

At first I think she's hearing things, but then I see it – a small, bobbing light.

We stand perfectly still, listening.

Margo's voice wafts through the air. 'Corey! I said, be careful! Do it *slowly*.'

'Well, hold the light straight, damn it! I can hardly see what I'm doing!'

Margo

Corey is on his hands and knees, trying to get leverage on the wooden boards that cover Martha's grave. He huffs, wrenching hard. 'They must have nailed this thing down or something.'

'Hurry up!'

'Shit!' he curses, losing his grip. He stumbles back, almost falling over. 'Shut up for a minute, okay? Let me concentrate.'

'This is a bad idea, Corey. A *really* bad idea. We should take the bones to the police. We could go now and leave them outside the station. No one has to know.'

'The station has cameras, Margo.' He rears up, legs wide apart, straddling Martha's grave, puffing like he's just come off the footy field. 'I should've thought to bring a crowbar. Do you think you could you give me a hand?'

The torchlight is weakening. I belt it against my thigh. 'Forget it, Corey. I said I'd hold the torch – that's it. And surely it can't be *that* hard. How did you break into it in the first place? How did you even see what you were doing?'

'Beer goggles,' he says, wiping his brow. 'Same ones you

use to see through a girl's dress.' He grasps the edge of a board and jerks it with extra grunt. 'Hamish must have used the torch on his phone. He probably took photos for all I know.'

I search my pocket. In my hurry to leave, I must have left my phone at home. 'Do you have yours?'

'Nah. I haven't got any credit.'

A strange noise comes from over by the trees. I swing the torch in that direction but can't see anything.

Corey laughs. 'You've watched one too many scary movies, haven't you?'

'I don't watch scary movies.'

'Maybe that's because you need someone to cuddle up to.'

I point the light at him. 'I haven't got all night, Corey.'

He shields his eyes. 'Yeah, all right. No need to flap your petticoat.' But there's a smile in his voice. 'So is Ralph still sore with you or what?'

'Sorry?'

'That day, down by the river, you said he laid into you about the accident.' He tries another angle, yanking at the boards. 'How often does he get stuck into you? Does he hit you?'

I'm about to ask him why he'd think that when I realise he's asking because of his own experience. 'No, he doesn't hit me.' And saying the words out loud makes me understand how lucky I am. Ralph's a good father – the only father I've ever known.

Corey hitches his jeans. He reaches for the hand shovel and chips at the dirt beside the boards. 'My old man reckons his dad was the same. Reckons Gramps almost killed him a few times.'

'And he thinks that makes it okay? Because his father did it to him?'

'Guess so. I can't see myself treating *my* kids that way, though.'

'You want kids?'

'You offering?'

I laugh.

Corey looks at me, his face serious and true. 'I don't want much, Margo. I just want for someone to give me a fair go. A job, maybe. A chance to prove I'm not stupid. That's it.'

'I don't think you're stupid.'

Head down, he kicks at the boards. 'Yeah? How do you figure that?'

'I've seen you do things – *good* things.'

With a cynical laugh, he turns his back. I wonder if anyone has ever bothered to tell him he's worthwhile. 'My gramps is buried here,' he says, lumbering away. 'Maybe that's who I was after that night.'

'You'd want to dig up your grandfather?'

He shrugs. 'The bastard doesn't deserve eternal peace.' He pulls at one of the boards with extra effort, wrenching it up. 'There!' he says, triumphantly casting aside the piece of board. 'Got it!'

'It's open?'

'Well, if I could see anything, I'd tell ya.' He waves me over. 'Give me the torch.'

Heart pounding, I don't move. 'What about her coffin? Can you see it? What about the rest of her bones?'

He puts out his hand. 'Give the torch to me.'

I shake my head.

'Margo! Like you said, we haven't got all night. Give me the flamin' torch!'

'Come and get it if you want it.'

He strides over and picks up the beach bag. Breath on my face, lips inches from mine, he whispers, 'Now there's an offer.' He pecks my cheek and goes back to the graveside.

Oh my God! Corey Williams just kissed me?

He unzips the bag and sinks an arm inside. He positions himself over Martha's grave, pulling the bag wide open like a yawning mouth.

'Corey, stop! You're not going to tip her in, are you?'

'You know a better way to do it?'

'She's not a bag of popcorn.'

'Oh! I'll defer to the expert then, shall I? Go on, tell me. How should I do it?'

'You have to put her back the way you found her. You have to *lay* her to rest.'

'She's a bloody jigsaw puzzle!' He holds the bag out to me. 'Be my guest.'

'I said I'd hold the torch.'

He puts the bag down. 'Well, if you're gunna hold it, pointing it straight would be a good start.'

Reluctantly, I shine the light on the bag. I peek at him through one eye. He extracts something I wasn't expecting – a little white box. 'What's that?'

He places it on the ground by his feet. 'Her jewellery box.'

I don't get it. Her jewellery box?

'Hamish reckons it was in her grave. He says we dug it up, not that I can remember.'

Something about that makes me feel even more uneasy. Not only had Corey and Hamish taken bones, but they'd stolen from a dead person. 'Is there anything in it?'

'A string of beads.' But the look on his face is suspect.

'Corey, you didn't keep them, did you?'

He shoots me an angry glare. 'You think I flogged them? Is that what you think of me, Margo? Geez, give me some credit!' He opens the box and shows me. The beads are there, nestled in velvet. He closes it and puts it back by his feet.

'Sorry.'

'Don't sweat it.' But I can tell he's wounded. He reaches into the bag, this time retrieving Martha's skull. I knew it was coming and yet I'm not prepared for it. My heart beats wildly. He holds it up, one-handed, gleaming golden-yellow in the torchlight. 'To be or *not* to be buried, Martha, that is the question.'

'*You arsehole!*' A figure lurches from the darkness, knocking Corey to the ground. Martha's skull goes rolling – *bouncing* – landing at my feet. I scream. Someone seizes my shoulders and I spin around, my heart wedged in my mouth.

'Margo?'

'Tara?'

She points over my shoulder. 'Oh no . . .'

I turn around to see Corey and Justin on either side of Martha's grave, circling it, fists clenched.

'You're dead, Corey!' Justin shouts. 'Do you hear me? *Dead!*'

Corey's voice wavers. 'Look, I admit it, I screwed up. I know that. Trust me, this was the mother of all mistakes.' He pauses and scratches his head. 'Well, technically it was *your* mother and *my* mistake.'

'Wow,' Justin growls. 'You really are a piece of work.'

'I really am sorry.'

'You will be.'

'Can't you see I'm trying to fix it?'

'You think you can *fix* this?'

Justin makes a sidestep, closing in on Corey. Corey leaps back in equal measure. 'Just hear me out, okay?' he begs, hands in the air. 'We never meant to pick on your mum.'

'I don't give a fat rat's what you meant to do!'

Corey drops his hands by his sides. 'Fine, have it your way.' He puffs out his chest, jaw stiff and ready. 'One free punch. That's all you get. Then it's anyone's game, got it?'

Justin doesn't need a second offer. He hurdles his mother's grave and slams a fist into Corey's jaw. The scream I hear is my own. Corey topples back, hitting the dirt in a cloud of dust.

'Justin!' Tara yells. 'Stop!'

But Justin grabs Corey by his T-shirt and drags him over to Martha's grave, where he forces his head down the gaping hole. 'You see that? See what you've done? I've got half a mind to bury you right here, right now!'

'Justin! Please!' I choke.

He turns to glare at me, torchlight burning a fire in his eyes. 'Stay out of it, Margo. You're not who I thought you were.'

'Listen to me,' I plead. 'Corey was trying to do the right thing. He was trying to put your mother back. He cares about her. He cares about *you*.'

Justin forces Corey further into the hole until his muffled cries are barely audible. 'You think he shouldn't pay for what he's done?'

'No . . . I think –'

'Justin?' Tara says shakily. 'This isn't what she would have wanted.'

She's holding Martha's skull.

Exasperation gives way to despair. Justin pulls Corey up, heaving him onto the gravel. Corey rolls onto his back, mucus streaking his face, wiping his bleeding mouth. Justin walks towards Tara, each step weak and unsure.

'It's all right,' Tara whispers.

Justin stares at her and then at the skull. Carefully, he cradles it in the crook of his arm and walks back to the grave.

Things are quiet now – a strange calm fills the air. Corey watches on, reverent, as Justin kneels before his mother's grave. He leans in, delicately placing her skull inside. He puts a hand out to Corey. 'The rest?'

Corey brings him the bag. Together, they return Martha's bones to her grave.

Justin steps back and bows his head. 'I'm sorry, Mum. I'm sorry for everything you went through – now and back then.' He looks at Corey. 'Can you help me with the boards?'

Only then do I see it – the jewellery box, lying in the dirt on its side. 'Wait, you forgot something.' I pick it up. The lid is open and a string of beads are jumbled inside.

The boys must have kicked it over when they were fighting. 'Tara, can you hold the torch?'

She takes the torch and shines it on the box. 'Oh my God ...' she gasps. She covers her mouth, making small, unintelligible sounds, looking at me, then at Justin, eyes wide.

Justin comes to her side. 'Mum's jewellery box,' he murmurs. 'I put it in her casket on the day of her funeral.'

I turn the box so the open lid faces him. Beneath the peeling white paint are little pictures of Uluru. Justin picks up the beads and loops them around his fingers. He takes something from the box and holds it up – a piece of paper. He shines the torch on it. 'What the hell is this?' he demands, turning to Corey.

Corey backs away. 'I'm sorry. I'm so sorry ...' But he's not saying it to Justin – he's saying it to me. 'I was going to tell you, Margo. I was, I swear. I just didn't know how.'

Corey

Justin holds the paper clipping out to me. 'Is this some kind of joke?'

Margo grabs it and reads. She blinks, questioning. 'Corey?'

Why hadn't I said something before now? I'd had plenty of opportunities. But something held me back. Something told me it was a secret – one to be careful of.

Justin looks at Margo, as if she might explain, but all she does is shake her head at him. He turns to Tara.

'Don't,' she pleads. 'It isn't my place.'

'You *knew* about this?' he says.

I can't work it out – what could Tara possibly know about it? She looks at each of us in turn, fear shining in her eyes.

Justin takes her by the shoulders. 'Say it, Tara. Whatever it is you know, *say it*.' Frustration gets the better of him. He shakes her, trying to rattle the answer out of her. 'Tell me!' She cries out and he reacts as though he's been burnt. 'God,' he breathes, letting go. 'I'm sorry. I'm sorry . . .'

Torchlight flickers. Trembling, Tara turns to Margo. 'There's no good way to tell you this . . . Old Man Sparks . . .'

Margo backs away, shaking her head.

'Jessie told me he's your father.'

The torchlight dies. There's a moment where nothing happens and then Margo launches herself at Tara, pummelling her with her fists. 'Why are you talking to my mum? Why would she tell you? Why would she tell *you*?' I restrain her, pulling her away. She struggles in my arms. 'Let me go, Corey! Let me go!'

'Listen, Margo,' Tara pleads. 'Your mum's been helping me.' She glances at Justin, as if trying to find the right words. 'You need to trust me.'

'Why would I trust *you*?' Margo spits.

Tara stops and stares at her. Then she says, resigned, 'I admit it, okay? I've done things to you, terrible things that I'm not proud of. If I could take them back, Margo, I would. I swear to God I'd go back and erase all of it – every unkind word, every horrible look, every bitchy thing I did or made other people do to you. When I think about how I've treated you, I feel sick. Truly, I do. I'm so very, *very* sorry.'

'Yeah, well, it's a bit late for that,' Margo says stiffly.

'You're right, it probably is. But where does that leave us?'

It leaves us nowhere, I think. Unable to go back, unable to go forward. Something – *someone* – has to give.

Tara sighs. 'I could stand here and beg you to forgive me, Margo, but this isn't about me. It's about you. It's about what that means.' She points at the piece of paper in Margo's hand.

Margo cries, 'What *does* it mean?'

'Your mum was best friends with Martha Sparks.'

It's like I can hear all the broken pieces in Margo's mind clattering into place. 'And Sparksy? He . . . he . . .?'

Tara gently nods. 'That's how Jessie became pregnant with you. He forced himself on her.'

Margo goes limp in my arms. 'No . . . no . . . no!'

Justin sinks to his knees, the box tumbling from his hands. 'That's why she did it,' he whispers. 'That's *why* she killed herself.'

Tara

When I was little, I liked to draw. Mum would stick my artworks to the fridge. Crayon creations. Kindy craft. Dry pasta tubes, pop sticks, sparkles set fast with generous dollops of PVA glue. My favourite subject to draw was a house. I always drew a pitched roof with a brick chimney coughing out a curly puff of smoke, a smiley-face door and two big yellow windows for eyes. Yellow meant the lights were on. Yellow meant someone was home.

I stand by my front gate, looking at the windows.

Yellow.

Something is wrong with this picture.

Justin nestles his head on my shoulder. 'You want me to wait?' He draws my hair into a loose ponytail. 'Did you know your mum was coming home?'

'No.'

His hand trails down my arm, catching my fingers. 'The bus leaves at eleven. Meet you at the stop?'

I look at him. 'You'll wait?'

He nods. Then he disappears into the dark.

When I open the front door, a cocktail of detergents greets me: air-freshener, bleach, spray-and-wipe. Our tiled floor gleams, a portal to another world. Magazines are stacked, cushions plumped. A brand-new throw hugs the couch. It's as if I've stepped into a show home. This isn't where I live.

Mum is seated at the kitchen bench, drinking coffee. Just like that. Like she never left. Her bottle-brown hair is tucked under her chin in a short bob. Heavily made-up eyes peer at me from behind red spectacles. I didn't even know she wore glasses. They're thin and square with little diamantes in the corners; they must be new. Her white cheeks are sunken, tired. She's aged. How long has she been gone?

She throws her hands in the air. 'Finally!' She taps the seat next to her. 'Come. Sit. Do you want coffee? I bought a plunger.'

I glance around the room. 'Where's Trevor?'

'I've sent him home for a few days.' She pours me a coffee and adds milk. *We have milk.* 'I needed some space, you know?'

But I don't know. All I've had is space.

She hands me the mug. The heat radiates, warming my hands. She makes fish lips, blowing on her coffee. 'Where've you been? Another party?'

I close my eyes and see the shadowy outline of Justin on his knees by his mother's grave. The reflective gleam of Margo's sneakers as she took off into the dark. Corey chasing after her, pleading for her to stop.

I open my eyes.

Mum's pencilled eyebrows climb her forehead. 'If you don't mind me saying so, Tara, you look like hell.' Blunt as always. She shrugs. 'You expect me to lie?'

We stare into our mugs, fortune tellers looking for answers.

'Where were you?' she presses.

'Where were *you*?'

'I'm your mother, Tara.' Like that explains everything. And in a weird way, perhaps it does.

'Thanks for doing the cleaning.'

She surveys the room, proud of herself.

I point to the drying rack in the corner – undies, socks, wrinkled T-shirts spread out scatter-gun approach. 'How long have you been home?'

'A few hours. I didn't have anything else to do.'

'You couldn't plan another holiday?'

'Don't, Tara.'

But I'm a dog on a leash, barking at someone I have no way of reaching. 'Don't what?'

'Can't we just pick up where we left off?'

'Where was that?'

'Can't you tell I'm trying here?'

'You've been gone for weeks.'

'You could have called me anytime. I called *you*. I left messages. You didn't answer. You're the one who didn't call *me*.'

I sip my coffee. Technically, she's right. And I hate her for it.

'When I am here, you're not here, so what's the difference? You're always out with your friends. Or you've got those damned earphones stuck in your ears. Or you're bailed up in your room, doing who knows what. You act like you don't need me, Tara, so what's the point?'

'What's the point?'

'Yes. What's the point?'

I'm your daughter! You're supposed to care for me! You're supposed to fight for me! You're supposed to mother me! Love me! I head for my room.

'Jessie Bonney rang.' Her words sting my back like bullets. I stop where I'm hit. 'She said she saw you at the service station. You were upset. Something about a boy?'

Blood thumps in my ears. *Did Jessie tell her?* I turn and look at Mum.

She peers over her thin-framed spectacles, waiting. 'Well?'

'It's old news, Mum.'

'Do you want to talk about it?'

'Have I ever wanted to talk about it?'

She strokes the side of her mug. 'It's just that Jessie was insistent. She sounded panicked.'

'I guess it's good that someone is.'

She bangs a hand on the kitchen counter: a full stop, a directive. This conversation ends *here*. She reaches for the *Sunraysia Daily* and unrolls it, spreading it out. 'You don't have to be so dramatic, Tara,' she says, sounding chirpy again. 'Come here and finish your coffee. Let's catch up. I hear things around town have been a bit out of the ordinary.' She points to the paper. 'Did you read this? Everyone's talking about these bones. The article says the grave belonged to Martha Sparks. I knew her, you know.'

I can't hide my shock. Everything I'm made of becomes wired. 'You *knew* Martha Sparks?'

She gives me this weird look like she can't work out why I'm suddenly interested. 'Yeah. She was in hospital with me, years ago, after I . . .' But she can't finish the sentence. She's talking about when she tried to kill herself. 'She was in the room next to mine. It was only for a few nights, but trust me, it was long enough.' She fidgets with her silver hoop earring, turning it the way she does when something troubles her. 'Martha had these episodes. "Turns", the doctors called them. She'd take out these brown beads, put them on and spin around, making a lot of noise. She did it until she was dizzy and couldn't stand up.' She points to our living-room mantle. 'See that over there? That Uluru thing? I took it from her.'

'I thought you said you bought it at a garage sale?'

'Well, that's probably what I told you. The truth is, I snapped it off the top of Martha's jewellery box.'

Her voice sounds like it's coming from somewhere else – like I'm floating outside of my body and none of this conversation is real. 'Her jewellery box?'

'The one she kept the beads in.'

'Why?'

Mum shrugs. 'The woman got up my nose. I was sick of her stupid spinning. Sick of that bloody box.' She flips the paper over, shuffling the pages. 'Anyway, Martha never knew I took it. She thought it was one of the hospital staff.'

'Why did you keep it?'

'Because it reminds me that I'm the sane one.' She pushes back her hair and breathes long and deep. 'We were there for the same reason, her and I. I survived. She didn't.'

I turn and head for my room, grabbing the walls – *anything* – to hold me up.

'Tara,' she calls. 'I'll be out first thing in the morning. I need to get groceries and pay some bills. I thought maybe you and I could do something afterwards? We could drive up to the national park? Go for a walk?'

'Sure.' By then, I'll be an hour outside of Mildura, on a bus with Justin, headed for Melbourne.

'Night, sweetheart!'

'Night.'

Old Man Sparks

Bloody Graham kicked me out again. Pub's a church, yer understand? You're supposed to sit quiet and reflect. But he's dead determined to interrupt the serenity. Thinks he's a priest after a confession. Wanted to know the story between me and Ralph Bonney. Reckons our feud is legendary. The hell I'm telling him.

I take a slash against the bottle shop wall. My one-eyed snake stops and starts.

Go see me girlfriend, Graham reckons. I tried talkin' to Jessie. Fat lotta good it did. Mistakes have gotta be forgiven, don't they? It's the way it was back then. I drank the hard stuff. Didn't know what I was doing. I thought she wanted it – she was the one being friendly and all. After that, I learnt that the hard stuff is no good. Gotta stick to beer or wine, if I can manage it. Jessie changed me like that. I tried to tell her once, but she didn't understand.

A white sedan towing a caravan pulls in. It's got out-of-towners written all over it. I flag it down and the window whirrs into the door cavity. I chuck in a fifty. 'Get me a flagon, will ya? Can't go in on foot.'

'Can't stand up, by the look of you,' says the mouthy missus sitting in the passenger seat.

Driver tells her to put a cork in it. Good man. A little slap wouldn't go astray either.

'Meet ya on the other side, mate?' I ask.

I watch them drive their shiny white beast inside. I make my way round the other side to watch it be reborn.

Across the road, a pretty blonde leans against a brush fence near a bus stop. There's a suitcase by her feet. She has a sour look on her mug like someone nicked her doll collection, twisted the heads off and gave it back.

'Oi!' I yell. 'What's ya name, girly?'

'Tara.'

'Cheer up, Tara! When I was ya age, I was in the army. Now *that's* somethin' to be a misery guts about.'

The sedan's engine finally fires and I move in to collect my prize. But the bastard floors it, clipping me hip on his way past. 'Thanks for the tip, ol' man!' he shouts, caravan bouncing behind.

The pain in my chest comes on sudden, like someone is stabbing me with a screwdriver, twisting it for good measure. I go down fast.

The blonde girl. I call out to her. She appears, standing over me, long hair hanging like a sick-bed curtain.

'Call the ambos, love . . . It's me heart.' But she doesn't move. She couldn't have heard me proper. 'The ambos, love. I need the ambos. *Please* . . .'

Her slim fingers slide over my mouth, pressing down. She leans in and whispers, 'Don't say a word.'

Pain rips me apart. Needles stab. My ears burst. Daylight flickers.

Don't say a word. Don't say a word. Don't say a word.

The servo attendant's voice comes thick and fuzzy. 'You need help there, young Tara?'

She lets go. Blonde hair floats away.

'Holy hell! Have you called an ambulance?' He hovers over me. 'Sparksy? Can you hear me? Sparksy? Try to stay calm, mate. Help's on its way . . .'

But help doesn't come.

My heart reverberates, an empty drum.

Margo

Mum passes me a tea towel. She sinks her hands into the soapy dishwater and scrubs. I pick up a plate and dry it.

My head goes round and round. The party. Amy's limp body lying in the grass by the roadside. Daryl Sanders wielding a tyre lever. Tiny's coffin. Corey holding the stripey beach bag. Justin on his knees by his mother's grave.

My birth notice.

Sparksy's death notice.

Tara.

On my doorstep.

Handing me a letter.

Her perfect handwritten words dance in my mind. *They held me down. Afterwards, he told me, 'Don't say a word.'*

'People placed a skull on their living-room table as decoration . . .'

I look at Mum. 'Huh? What are you talking about?'

Mum dumps a clattering bunch of cutlery on the draining rack. 'I said, I was watching a documentary this afternoon. In the Middle Ages, people kept a skull in their living room. It was to remind them of their mortality – that death is ever present and they should enjoy life while they can.'

She's thinking about Martha again – we've been talking about it for days. 'Do you miss her?' I ask.

She smiles a weary smile. 'Every day.'

Corey did as he promised. He anonymously phoned the police station to say Martha's bones had been returned. At first, when I told Mum, she was angry and she threatened to call the police, but then I told her about how sorry Corey was, how he was angry at his grandfather and it was him he had meant to dig up. I told her how his father beat him and how his grandfather beat his father. She knew I wouldn't lie about such a thing.

She threads her wet fingers through mine. 'I love you, Margo.'

'I love you too, Mum.'

She turns back to the sink and fusses over the plates, reshuffling where they sit in the pile. Then she grasps the bench, as if it's holding her up, and lets out a deep, deep gasp. 'I should have told you, Margo. I should have trusted you'd be able to handle the truth.'

I felt numb when Ralph told me Sparksy was dead. I didn't even go to the funeral. None of us did. 'Mum, it's okay . . .'

She busies herself, dunking plates into the sink until the water overflows and soap suds run down the cupboard door. As she bends to mop it up, her shoulders cave and she crumbles, slumping to the floor. Tears streak her cheeks. 'You and Justin. You could have . . . you could have . . .'

I squat on the tiles next to her. 'I told you, Mum. Nothing happened between us.'

'But it *could* have. And I would have been to blame. He's your brother!'

We hold each other for ages, until the water in the sink goes cold. I feel close to her, more so than I ever have. There are no secrets standing in the way.

She brushes back my hair, her thick fingers tracing my fringe. 'Are you going to keep in contact with him?'

'He left for Melbourne yesterday.'

I know it's not an answer; the truth is, I haven't decided yet. In years to come, when there is enough distance between Justin and me and what happened, maybe things might be different. I might want to get to know the brother I never knew I had. But for now there are other things. Like being here for my mum. Like finishing school.

Like helping Tara.

I know Tara's truth. How my mum helped her and how Tara had planned to go to Melbourne with Justin, but something held her back. She went to the police instead. She told them about the party. Some of the boys who'd texted her photo have already been charged. Her assault is under investigation.

Mum kisses my cheek. 'Maybe it's for the best.'

We sit, our backs against the cupboard, my head on her shoulder. She holds my hand, stroking it.

'Mum?'

'Yeah?'

'Was Martha a good person?'

Mum chuckles. 'I thought she was. The police might tell you different, though.'

'Really? Why?'

'Oh, Martha was a bit of hellraiser, that's all. She'd had a tough childhood. I think that's why she hit it off with Sparksy – he came from a similar background.'

I think of Corey and his black eye. 'Was she beaten?'

'No, but something awful happened to her when she was young.'

I tense, Tara's pained face swimming in my mind. 'What?'

Mum takes a deep breath. 'Her mother was an outback missionary and Martha idolised her. She wanted to grow up to *be* her. But her mother died. And Martha saw it happen.'

'She *saw* her mother die?'

'It was one of our own who caused it. They called him Gungi. He was a strong, proud leader of our mob. That was, until he got a taste for the white man's poison. Anyway, one day, the authorities got wind of the fact Gungi was up at Red Cliffs, getting drunk and dancing dangerously close to the cliff's edge.'

I've been to Red Cliffs, to the lookout on Pumps Road near the pumping station. Those cliffs are spectacular, but they're also deadly. A big drop with no soft landing.

'Gungi wasn't threatening to jump – he just had no concept of how close he was to the edge. The police called in Martha's mother for assistance. She had a good rapport with Gungi; they thought she could talk some sense into him.

'Martha's mother drove to Red Cliffs with Martha in the back seat. When they got there, Martha was told to stay in the car. She watched as her mother tried to talk to him. Unfortunately, Gungi wasn't having a bar of it. He was more interested in having a good time. He grabbed her and started dancing.'

My stomach clenches at the idea of what happened next. 'Did he throw her off?'

Mum shakes her head. 'He spun her. Around and around and around. Finally, he let her go. Dizzy, she took a step back to steady herself and that's when the earth gave way.'

I imagine the little girl watching this through the car window.

'I guess you could say Martha never really recovered from witnessing that. She battled depression on and off throughout her life, a long time before meeting Sparksy – a long time before what happened to me.'

'But if that was how her mother was killed – if Gungi was drunk – what did she see in Sparksy?'

'Sparksy wasn't always a heavy drinker, Margo. In the beginning, he liked a tipple as much as the next bloke. He was older than Martha. He'd been to Vietnam. You must understand, Vietnam was a war the Australian people didn't want. Veterans weren't welcomed home as heroes like they were in World War Two. Some soldiers were ridiculed, even spat on when they returned, such was the sentiment of the day. There was little – if any – support for men like Sparksy. He was made out to be a villain – a role he didn't bother to fight.'

'But he was violent, Mum. What he did to you was unforgivable. There's no excuse.'

'I know that, Margo. I'm not suggesting otherwise. But life isn't always black and white. I'm not prepared to say that, if Sparksy hadn't suffered as he did, things would have been different. We don't know. We will never know. Maybe if Sparksy had been treated better . . . Maybe if someone had had faith in him early on, he wouldn't have turned out as he did.'

I can't get past the anger I feel for what he did to her – for what he did to *me*. 'Some people are bad eggs, Mum. They just are.'

'Are they, Margo? Are you sure? You thought that about Tara until recently, right?'

It was true – I did.

'We are born innocent, Margo. I believe that. Once, we were all a babe in our mother's arms.'

My phone buzzes on the kitchen bench. I get up and grab it.

Mum looks up at me. 'Margo?'

'Yes?'

'Anger only makes you tired, my darling girl. Don't be angry, okay?'

I can't bring myself to tell her okay. Maybe one day but not yet.

'And don't forget,' Mum adds, 'I have a good husband. That's why I've been able to keep my shit together. He's got my back and I've got his.'

As if she summoned him, Ralph comes through the door. When he sees Mum, he laughs. 'Sitting down on the job, I see.'

Mum doesn't bother to get up. 'What are you doing back? Did footy training get cancelled?'

'Nah, forgot my sunnies.' Ralph heads off to the bedroom to find them. 'The glare makes it hard to see if Bradley's kicking straight!' he yells out.

Bradley pokes his head around the door. 'I *always* kick straight!' He scoots over to the biscuit tin and grabs a stack of choc-chip cookies. 'Guess what?' he says through a shower of crumbs. 'Jackson Swinburg's mum shaved his head.'

'Is that so?' Mum says.

Bradley nods. 'S'pose he was sick of getting teased about his hair. He *did* look like a bit of a knob.'

'*Language . . .*' Mum cautions.

'Now he looks like an even bigger one!'

I laugh and Bradley winks at me, pleased.

Ralph returns to the kitchen and snatches the biscuits from Bradley. 'I thought I told you to stay in the car?' He shoves a whole biscuit in his mouth.

'Ralph!' Mum says, waving her finger. 'No biscuits! Remember your sugar levels!'

'Yeah, yeah.' He pinches Bradley by the scruff of the neck, steering him to the door. 'We'd best leave these women to their floor picnic or whatever it is they're doing.'

And with that they're out the door.

Ralph and I may have come to blows, but we figured it out in the end. He apologised for telling me I was like my real father. He said that was a cheap shot and I was nothing like Sparksy and never would be. He said he was angry with himself more than anything. I believe him. He's a good father. The best father I could hope for, really.

My phone buzzes again. It's a text from Corey: *Got a fruit-picking gig. Start Monday.*

'That wouldn't be a boy you're grinning about, now, would it?' Mum hoists herself up. She pulls the sink plug and water gurgles. She flips a tea towel over her shoulder. 'Remember what your old ma says.'

'No boy round here is good enough for my girl,' I say, mimicking her, and we both laugh.

A boy. From round here. Corey Williams.

Was Mum right about putting faith in people? If I gave Corey a chance, would he reward me? Or would he fall back into that role he knows so well and do something stupid?

Corey texts again. *Celebrate?*

How?

Get smashed. Lay tracks. Dig up a grave.

Boring.

Horror movie? You can cuddle me.

I smile.

Have you checked your mailbox?

'Back in a sec, Mum.' I head out the door and across the lawn to our new mailbox. It was replaced after the fight with Daryl Sanders. It's shiny blue and has a little red flag, which is up, indicating mail has arrived.

I lift the lid. There's a large red envelope with my name on it. My heartbeat quickens. I open it and carefully remove a package wrapped in pink paper. Onto my hand rolls something brassy-gold. Initially, I think its jewellery – a brooch or a pendant – but it's neither. It's a footy medallion threaded through a ribbon, the kind they hand out to players

273

at the end-of-year awards night. Bradley has several of them in his room. In the centre of the medallion is the letter 'M'.

On the paper, inside a pencilled love heart, are neatly written words that leave me breathless.

> You're *my* best on ground, Margo.
> You're *my* Brownlow medallist.
> Like Uluru,
> you're the centre of my everything.

'You like it?'

I look up. He's standing in the flowerbed beneath my bedroom window, the flyscreen off and leaning against the wall, my green paisley curtains flapping in the breeze.

He slips his phone into his pocket. 'I've always wanted to do the whole Romeo thing, but I think I need a ladder.'

'I could have sworn you were into *Hamlet*.'

'Who goes around talking to a skull? I mean, that's just seriously messed up.'

'You really are left of field, aren't you, Corey Williams?'

He grins. 'I'm good on and –'

'Off the field. I know, I know.'

'So you like it?'

I turn the medallion over. 'I do.'

'Put it on.' He takes it and loops it around my neck. I think of Martha and her beads. I do a little twirl. 'Looks good. Be careful your brother doesn't nick it.'

I touch the medallion. 'M' for Margo. 'M' for Martha. 'Thank you. It's really nice, Corey.'

He shrugs.

'You're going to have to learn to accept a compliment at some point.'

He rolls his eyes. 'It's hard when all you've done is beat yourself up your whole life.'

'*You* didn't beat *you* up.'

He kisses my cheek. 'You make me buzz, Margo Bonney.'

And *you* steal my oxygen.

'So . . .' He raps his fingers on the mailbox. 'My hearing date got shifted.'

'And?'

'Three weeks away.'

I hesitate. 'How does that make you feel?'

He looks me in the eye. 'I'm kinda crappin' myself, but there's not much I can do, is there? I did what I did. Gotta cop it sweet.'

'Maybe they'll go easy?'

'I think you're forgetting Amy.'

He's right: a policeman's daughter.

'Have you heard how she's getting on?' he asks.

'Yeah. Tara said something.'

'Tara? You two speaking now?'

'Let's just say the war is over. She's agreed to drop "Racist Cow" from her résumé.'

''Bout time.' He laughs. 'It's pretty big of you to forgive her.'

'I wouldn't call it *that*. I'd call it reconciling our differences.'

He grins. I can tell he gets it. 'What'd she say about Amy?'

'Amy's up and moving around. It's not going to be easy. She's got months of rehab ahead of her.'

'Which is *why* I shouldn't expect them to go easy on me,' Corey says stoically. He changes the subject. 'How should we celebrate my new job?'

'Can we do what normal people do?'

'What's that?'

'Go to the milk bar, get a milkshake or something?'

'A milkshake?'

'Yeah.'

'I guess I could try one . . .'

I laugh. 'A bit different to beer, I suppose.'

'Haven't touched it in weeks,' he says proudly.

'Really?'

'Not a drop.'

'How long will that last?'

'Dunno. But for now, it's working.'

'Wait there. I'll get some money.'

'Nah, my shout.' He digs his pockets and pulls out a wad of twenties. 'I'm fully cashed now I'm not spending all my Centrelink dosh on booze and ciggies. Plus, I'm walking everywhere. I might as well turn bloody vegan too, be a full-on health nut.'

'I'm proud of you, Corey.'

He touches my medallion and grins. 'Let's go get that milkshake.'

We walk up the road together, hand in hand.

Me and a boy. From round here.

Acknowledgements

Daryl and Dillon, I couldn't do what I do without your love and support. You come first. *Always.*

This novel is dedicated to my stepdad, Peter, a Ngarrindjeri man living on Meintangk/Thangal land, SA. Thank you, Peter, for reading the many drafts and for your sensitivity advice. This is my love letter to you; my special thanks for raising me. This work is also for your children, Amanda and Andrew, my much-loved sister and brother, and for our extended family. To Michael and Brenton, I'm glad we share such a wonderful stepfather. And to *our* father, Dad: thank you for building a harmonious partnership with this beautiful man. Nice job, Mum, for snagging such a tremendous bloke!

In 2009, I applied for an arts grant, won it (thanks, Arts SA) and wrote the first draft in 2010. Long after the funding ran out, and after countless incarnations, I found a home for this work thanks to Zoe Walton. To you, I am forever grateful.

Enormous thanks to arts supporters and Aboriginal elders: Uncle Moogy (Major Sumner), Ronni O'Donnell,

Gloria Clark, Troy Bond, Rev. Ken Sumner and Dennis Mitchell. For some of you, that support extended beyond the grant, to sensitivity advice *and* to calming my nerves/ reminding me of what I set out to do. (I'm just so bloody relieved I have an opportunity to publicly thank you. Your efforts were not wasted!) An extra-special thank you to Ronni and Gloria for allowing me to portray their heritage as Margo's. Meeting you has been one of the most treasured aspects of this work. There will be many more coffee dates/ lunches to come, I'm sure of it.

To Vikki Wakefield, Rebecca Burton and Andrea Altamura – how do I quantify what you do for me? When it comes to my reader dream team (*and* friendship), I'm truly blessed. Special thanks to Sue Lawson for our many chats (and for reading the final version), and mega thanks to editor-with-da-mostest Catriona Murdie. *You* make me look a gazillion times cleverer than I actually am. Thanks also to proofreader Jess Owen for her eagle eye. To Nicole Hayes and Dianne Touchell, thank you for taking the time to read my work. I can't believe I keep such company – someone pinch me!

To Emma Walmsley, thanks for being my go-to gal for setting issues, and special thanks to recording artist Bec Willis for allowing me to publish her lyrics. Brian Webster – you've been an unexpected source of Aussie quips/inspiration, and Christine Webster, your support is dependable as always. To Kristin Weidenbach, Lia Weston and Katrina Germein: you're an ongoing source of comfort and sanity. Being with you feels like home.

Thank you to early readers Anna Solding and Lynette Washington. (We have one under our belts. There will be more!) Thanks to my agent, Jane Novak, and appearances agent, Becky Lucas – it's a blessing to have you on my team. To the writing community, particularly SCBWI and eKIDs: you guys rock. And to the readers: without you I'd be in some other miserable occupation – a terrifying thought.

Finally, I want to relay that, in 2015, I almost died, spending weeks in Intensive Care followed by many months of recovery/drug therapy. By way of accepting this novel, Penguin Random House Australia gave me something positive on which to focus. You, PRH team, have been my shining beacon guiding me to safe shores. My heartfelt thanks to you all.